KU-415-191

AFRICA

A Natural History

AFRICA

A Natural History

CHRIS AND TILDE STUART

SWAN HILL
PRESS

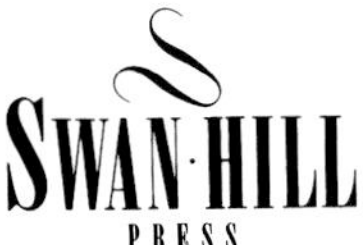

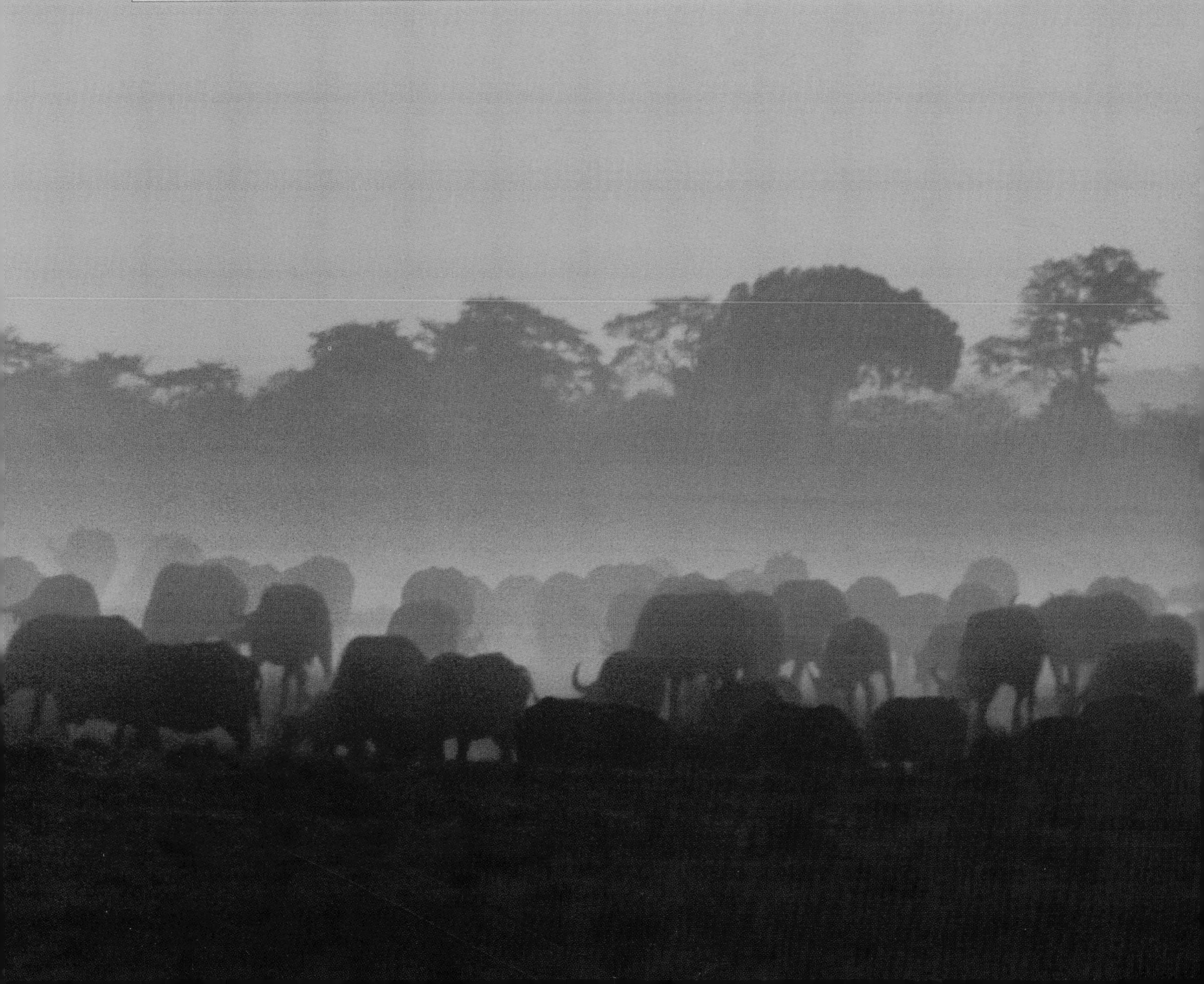

Halftitle page: *The armadillo lizard,* Cordylus cataphractus, *in defensive posture.*
Title page: *A herd of buffalo,* Syncerus caffer. **Contents page:** *A frog of the genus* Hyperolius.
Imprint page: *Troops of banded mongoose,* Mungos mungo, *are a common sight in open woodland.*
Acknowledgements: *Hymphaea* sp., Bushmanland, Kalahari. Photo: Anthony Bannister, ABPL

Originally published by Southern Book Publishers, South Africa
First edition, first impression 1995

Cover design by: Alix Gracie
Cover photograph by: Anthony Bannister, ABPL
Maps by: CartoCom, Pretoria
Designed by: Alix Gracie, t/a Design Dynamix, Cape Town
Set in: Garamond 9/12
Reproduction: Hirt & Carter Repro, Cape Town
Printed and bound by: Singapore National Printers Ltd, Singapore

First published in the UK in 1995 by Swan Hill Press, an imprint of Airlife Publishing Ltd

British Library Cataloguing in Publication Data
A catalogue record for this book is available from the British Library

ISBN 1 85310 737 9

Swan Hill Press
an imprint of Airlife Publishing Ltd
101 Longden Road, Shrewsbury SY3 9EB

Contents

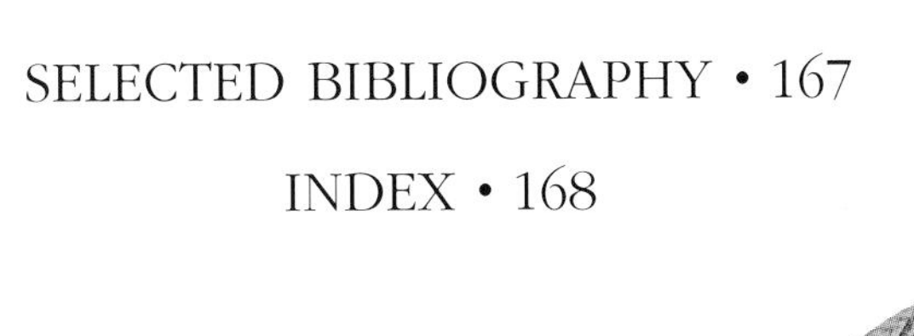

Acknowledgements

We would like to offer special words of thanks to Louise Grantham of Southern, firstly for her stoic patience and understanding, and not least for her friendship. The other Southern staff members are thanked for the various ways in which they have made this book possible. A number of friends helped us fill in our photographic gaps and we offer our thanks; they are: John Carlyon, Pat J Frere, Ian Manning, Penny Meakin, Harry van Rompaey, Peter Wyss, Roland van Bocxstaele (slides from Antwerp Zoo). Ms Heydoorn is thanked for supplying African coastline lengths. The Schaffer family allowed us to spend three months in their forest home in Schallenberg, Austria, whilst writing this book. It was a special time for us and we offer them our grateful thanks. *Ein Hoch den Mühlviertlern!*

INTRODUCTION

The African continent covers 30 million square kilometres, making it second only to Eurasia in size, and it is graced by vast desert lands and savannas, forests and lakes, rivers, swamps and inland deltas, mountains of volcanic origin and those resulting from folding. Parts of the eastern coastline are fringed by coral reefs and there are mangrove swamps lapped by the waters of both the Atlantic and Indian oceans. With such a broad range of habitats available it is not surprising that the vegetation and animal life is amazingly diverse. The tropical forests are home to a primate fauna that includes the gorilla, chimpanzee and bonobo, as well as many smaller species. The savanna provides stretches of grassland that sustain the world's largest herds of hoofed mammals. There are species such as the elephant that range through virtually all vegetation zones but others are restricted to a single mountain, or a tiny fragment of heathland. A great many plants and animals are endemic, which means they occur only in Africa. How did it all begin?

GEOLOGICAL HISTORY AND LANDSCAPES

Up until some 270 million years ago Africa formed part of the ancient super-continent of Gondwanaland, a land mass that incorporated all of the southern continents that we know today. Between 270 and 200 million years ago powerful disturbances took place deep under the earth's surface, causing the sub-oceanic basaltic rock plates upon which Gondwanaland lay to split apart. The separated land masses began to

Top: *Lake Bogoria is just one place in East Africa where water is super-heated deep within the earth's crust and emerges as steam or piping hot water. At some locations, such as Hell's Gate to the north of Nairobi, this energy is harnessed in geothermal power stations for the production of electricity.*
Below: *Open, sandy beaches are typical of many stretches of Africa's coastline, many being unspoiled.*

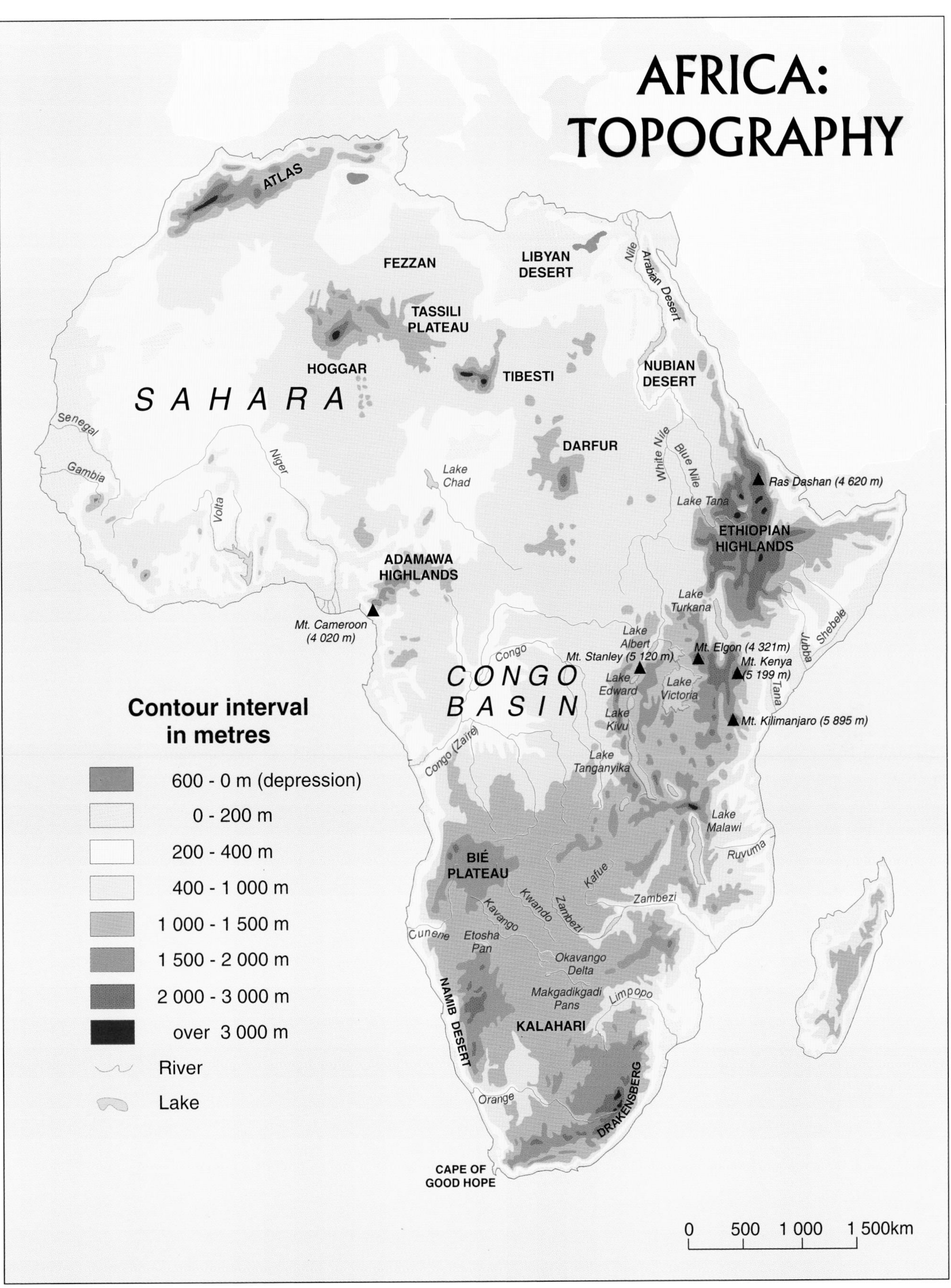
AFRICA:
TOPOGRAPHY
ATLAS
FEZZAN
LIBYAN
DESERT
Nile
Arabian Desert
TASSILI
PLATEAU
HOGGAR
TIBESTI
NUBIAN
DESERT
SAHARA
Senegal
Gambia
Niger
Volta
DARFUR
Lake
Chad
White Nile
Blue Nile
Ras Dashan (4 620 m)
Lake Tana
ETHIOPIAN
HIGHLANDS
ADAMAWA
HIGHLANDS
Mt. Cameroon
(4 020 m)
Lake
Turkana
Lake
Albert
Mt. Stanley (5 120 m)
Mt. Elgon (4 321m)
Mt. Kenya
(5 199 m)
Jubba
Shebele
Tana
Congo
CONGO
BASIN
Lake
Edward
Lake
Victoria
Lake
Kivu
Mt. Kilimanjaro (5 895 m)
Contour interval
in metres
600 - 0 m (depression)
0 - 200 m
200 - 400 m
400 - 1 000 m
1 000 - 1 500 m
1 500 - 2 000 m
2 000 - 3 000 m
over 3 000 m
River
Lake
Congo (Zaire)
Lake
Tanganyika
Lake
Malawi
Ruvuma
BIÉ
PLATEAU
Kafue
Kwando
Zambezi
Kavango
Zambezi
Cunene
Etosha
Pan
Okavango
Delta
Makgadikgadi
Pans
Limpopo
NAMIB DESERT
KALAHARI
DRAKENSBERG
Orange
CAPE OF
GOOD HOPE
0 500 1 000 1 500km

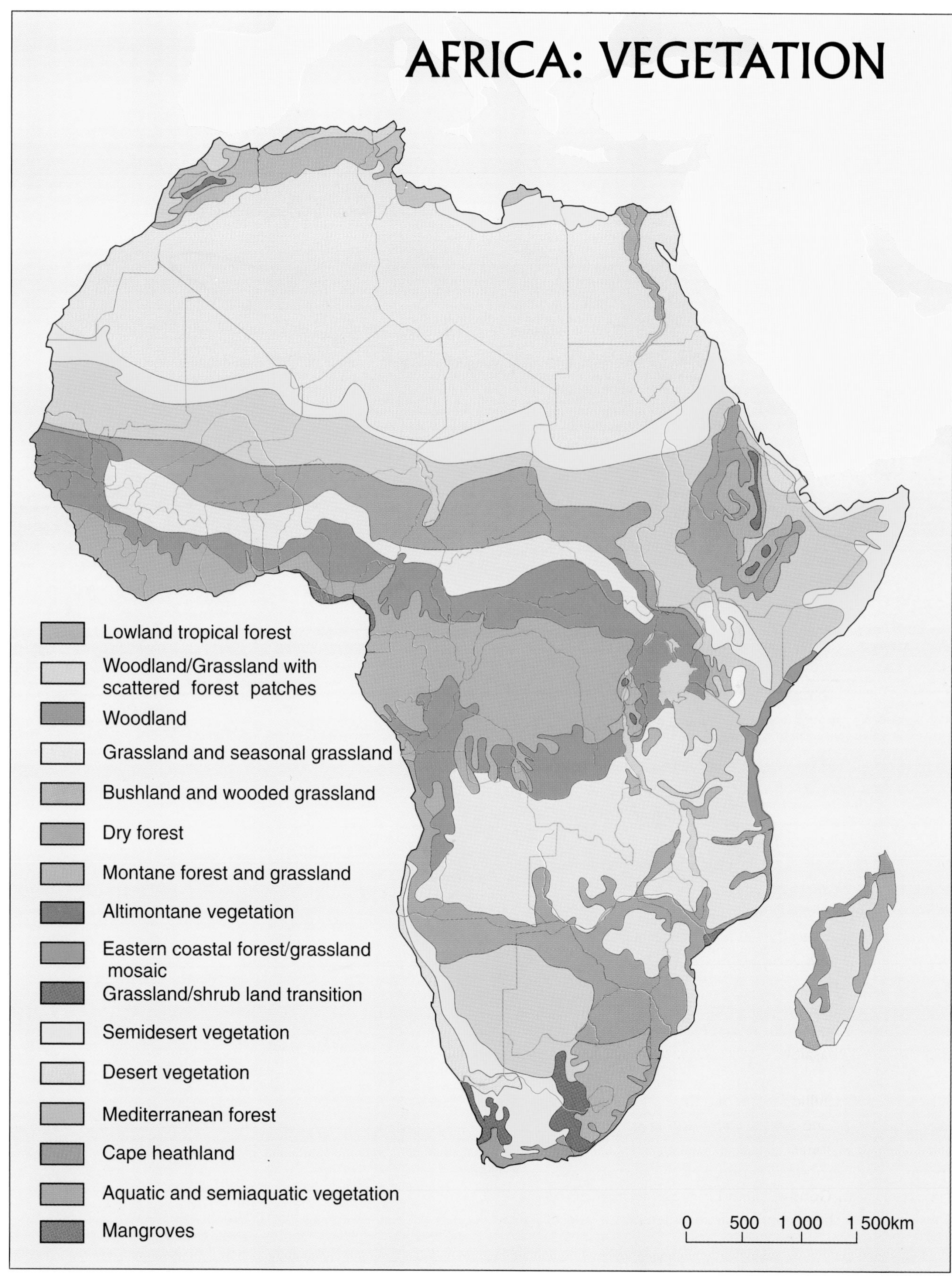
AFRICA: VEGETATION
Lowland tropical forest
Woodland/Grassland with scattered forest patches
Woodland
Grassland and seasonal grassland
Bushland and wooded grassland
Dry forest
Montane forest and grassland
Altimontane vegetation
Eastern coastal forest/grassland mosaic
Grassland/shrub land transition
Semidesert vegetation
Desert vegetation
Mediterranean forest
Cape heathland
Aquatic and semiaquatic vegetation
Mangroves
0 500 1 000 1 500km

Above: *A typical scene in the mountainous Algerian Sahara. Photo: Peter Wyss.* **Right:** *Ammonite fossils, part of Africa's extremely rich fossil record.* **Overleaf:** *Rain clouds gathering at the beginning of the wet season. The rain raises the levels of rivers and lakes, as well as filling temporary pans and waterholes that allow many game and bird species to disperse over wider areas.*

move slowly apart. This movement was made possible because the rigid basaltic plates floated on the more malleable mantle below.

By about 100 million years ago the new continents had all separated from one another and Africa continued its eastward drift, until some 30 million years ago when it came into contact with the northern continent of Eurasia. Evidence for the existence of Gondwanaland is presented by the very outlines of the southern continents and matching strata of rocks that are more than 570 million years old and were clearly joined originally.

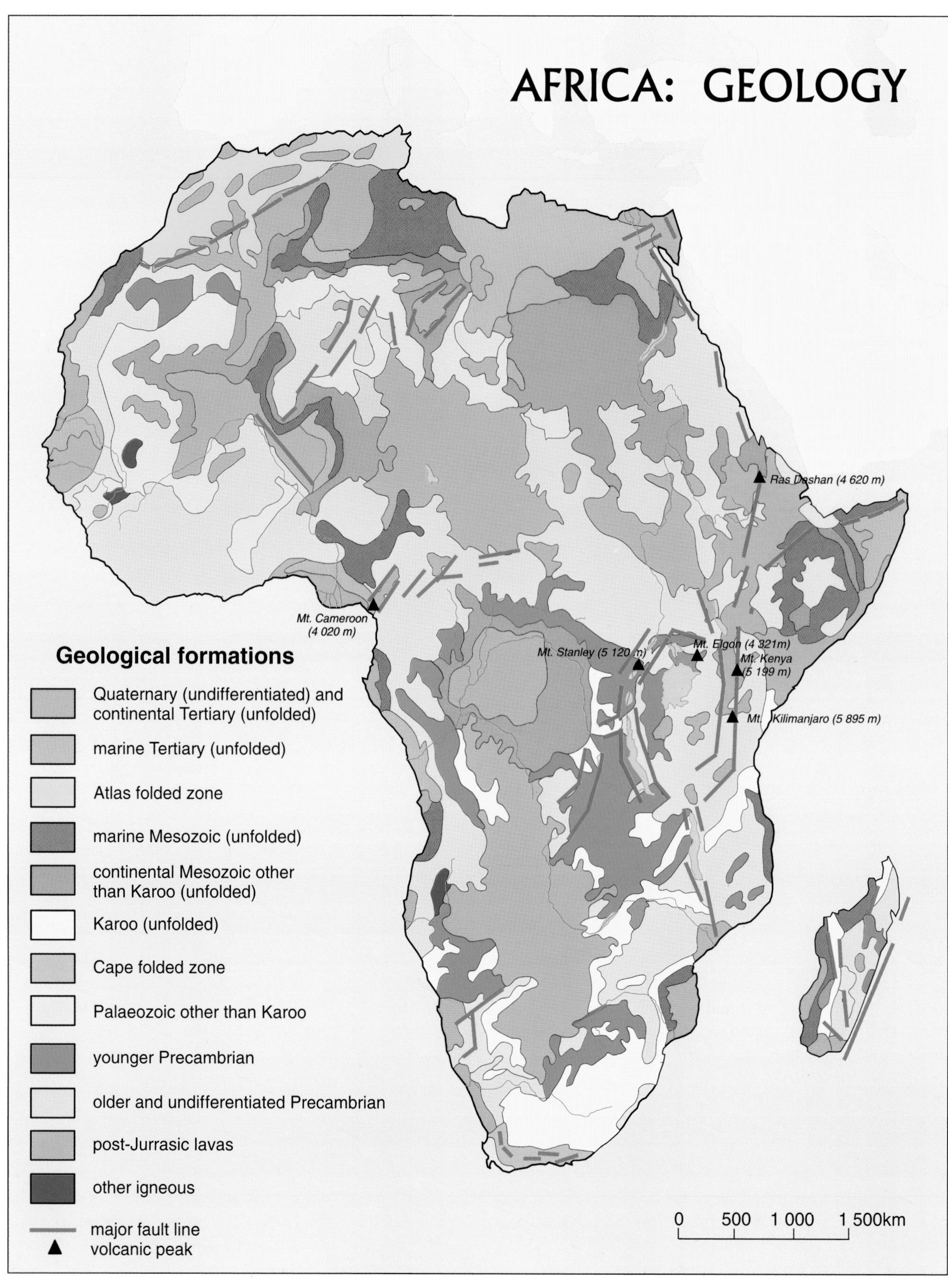
AFRICA: GEOLOGY
Ras Dashan (4 620 m)
Mt. Cameroon
(4 020 m)
Mt. Stanley (5 120 m)
Mt. Elgon (4 321m)
Mt. Kenya
(5 199 m)
Mt. Kilimanjaro (5 895 m)
Geological formations
Quaternary (undifferentiated) and continental Tertiary (unfolded)
marine Tertiary (unfolded)
Atlas folded zone
marine Mesozoic (unfolded)
continental Mesozoic other than Karoo (unfolded)
Karoo (unfolded)
Cape folded zone
Palaeozoic other than Karoo
younger Precambrian
older and undifferentiated Precambrian
post-Jurrasic lavas
other igneous
major fault line
volcanic peak
0 500 1 000 1 500km

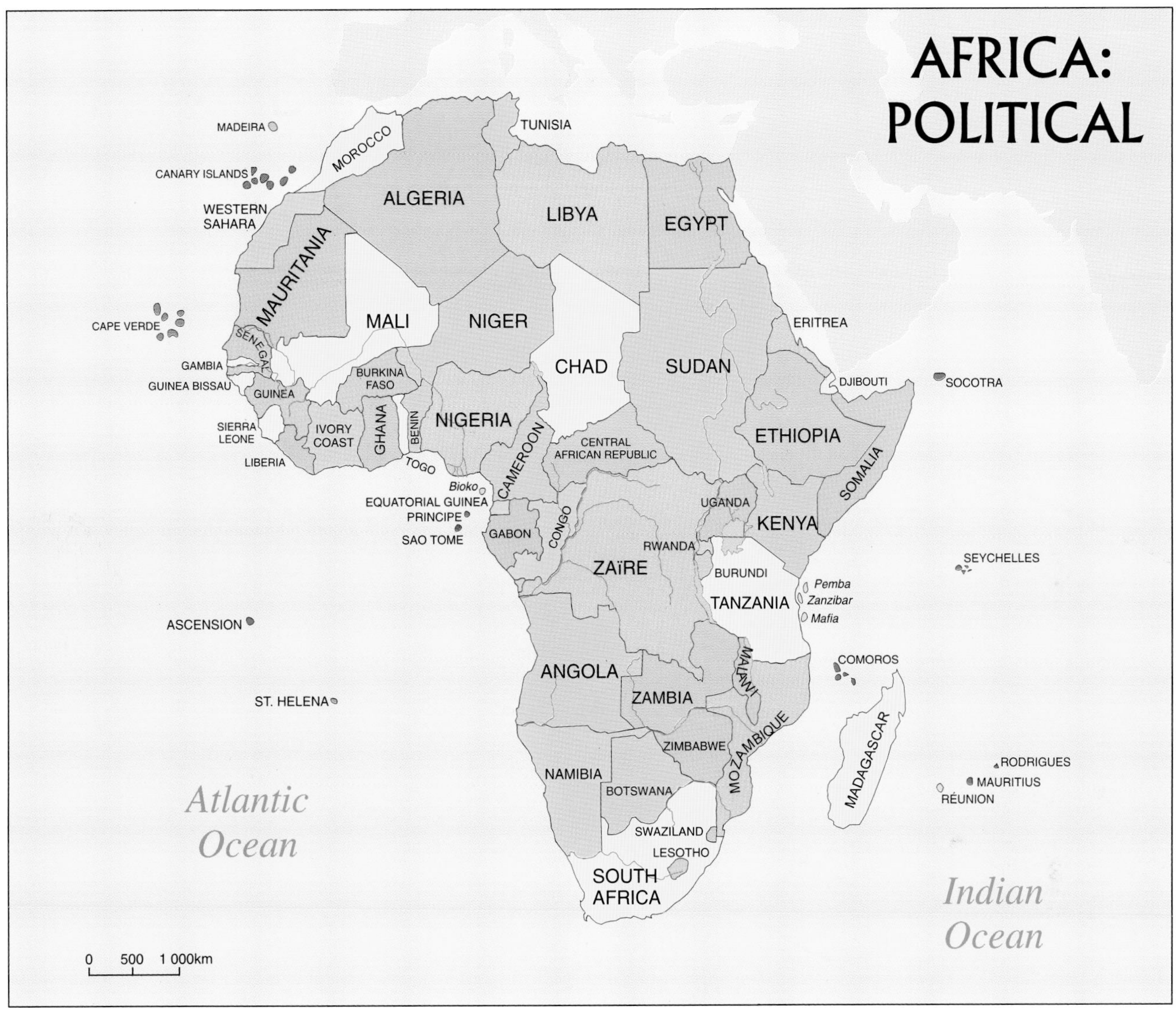

One of Africa's most impressive and geologically influential features is the 5 600 km-long Great Rift Valley. This great rift, or scar, developed as the layers underneath the earth's crust moved, causing the earth's surface to crack. The two plateaus thus formed moved apart, so forming a deep gully. This took place along parallel fault planes, with the different layers of rock sliding past each other and leaving the step-like formations that can be seen on the walls of the rift. The Rift Valley extends from the Red Sea southwards, cleaving its way through the great lava dome that we know as the Ethiopian Highlands and then splitting to form two roughly parallel arms. The western rift gave rise to the legendary Mountains of the Moon, the Ruwenzoris, and the volcanoes of the Virunga Range. A great chain of lakes, including the almost 1.5 km-deep Tanganyika, nestle in the bottom of the rift. The eastern branch is characterised by shallow alkaline lakes and volcanoes such as 5 896 m-high Mount Kilimanjaro, Mount Kenya and Mount Meru. Africa's largest body of open fresh water, Lake Victoria, was formed by downwarping of the earth's crust between the two arms of the Great Rift, causing the Kagera and other rivers to reverse their flow and feed the lake basin.

Despite the dry nature of large tracts of Africa, it is drained by some mighty rivers, including the world's longest, the Nile. This 6 695 km-long watercourse draws its waters mainly from the Great Rift and the Ethiopian Highlands. The Zaïre, or Congo, River is second only to the Amazon of South America in the size of its drainage area and the volume of fresh water that it pours into the ocean.

Apart from the mountains, ranges and highlands of eastern Africa, only a few elevations elsewhere on the continent can be considered significant: the two Saharan massifs of Tibesti and the Hoggar, the Atlas Mountains in the extreme northwest and the Cape Folded Belt at the south-western tip. Much of Africa to the west of the Great Rift Valley is relatively flat and large expanses lie at altitudes of 1 000 m and below.

Above: *A storm brewing over African mountains. Summer storms are common in many parts of the continent.*
Left: *Lichens thrive in cloud and rain forest.*

CLIMATE AND VEGETATION

Africa has experienced numerous wet and dry phases that have moulded and modified its vegetation. The dry periods lasted longer than the wet ones and the once extensive equatorial forest belt was forced into retreat. At times the drylands of the south-west and the north-east were linked, allowing certain animal and plant species to disperse. However, later wet periods changed the vegetation of the central area making it unsuitable for animals adapted to life in arid conditions and they became isolated. For example, the oryx (*Oryx gazella*), Kirk's dik-dik (*Madoqua kirkii*) and the bat-eared fox (*Otocyon megalotis*) today survive in widely separated populations in the two dry regions. The Sahara Desert has also experienced periods of higher rainfall, even in the past few thousand years, that allowed such species as elephant, hippopotamus and many others to survive in an area which today would be totally hostile to them.

Despite these climatic changes some regions of the continent have been able to maintain their ecological integrity

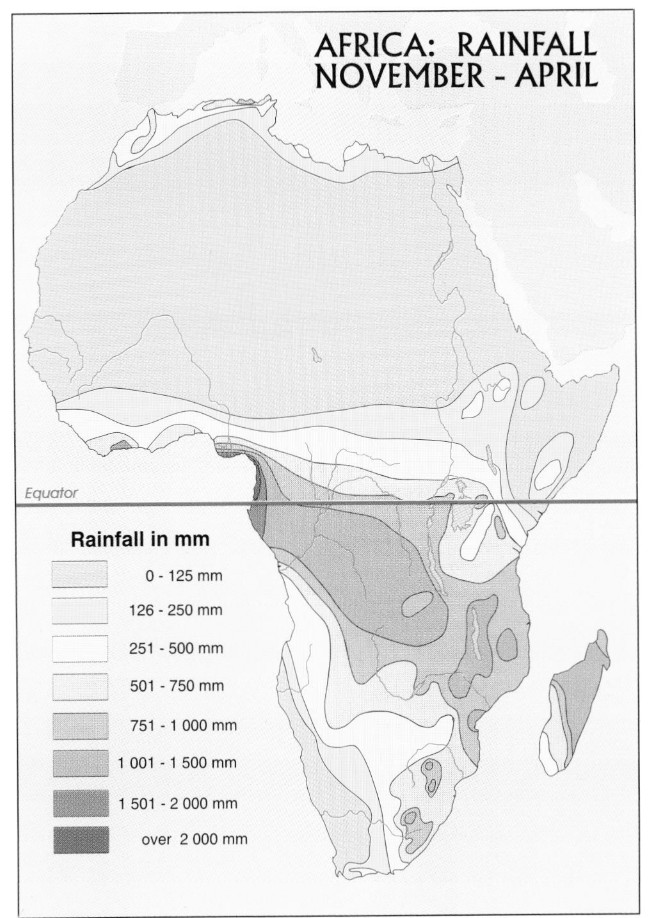

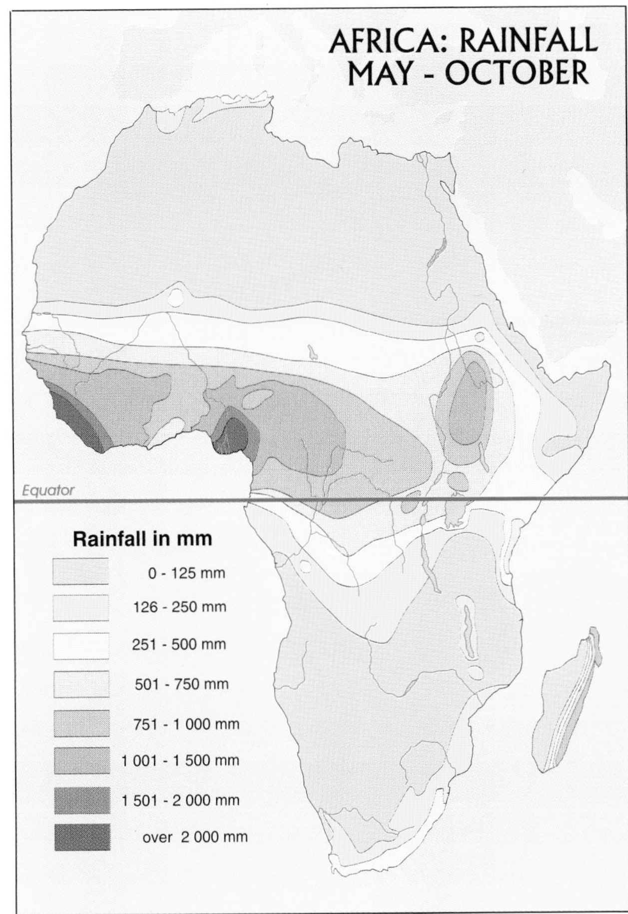

over many millions of years. Africa's climate today can be briefly summarised as follows: Along the equatorial belt in association with the tropical rain forests temperatures are generally high and rain falls throughout the year. To the north and south of this zone rain falls during the hot summer months, that is around June in the northern hemisphere and December to the south of the equator. To the east of the Great Rift Valley there are two distinct rainy seasons: the "little rains" from mid-October to December and the "big rains" from March to May. Within the south-western area of South Africa and along the coast of the Mediterranean Sea the main rainy season falls within the winter months. Annual rainfall ranges from a few millimetres in the deserts to more than 3 000 mm in some mountainous areas and in parts of the tropical forest belt. Temperatures are influenced by such factors as distance from the equator, proximity to the oceans and altitude. The low-altitude areas of the equatorial belt have the smallest daily and yearly temperature fluctuations; variation is greater as one moves to the south and north.

To match its great differences in rainfall, temperature, soils and altitude Africa has a wide range of vegetation types and an impressive array of plant species. The tropical forests of the Congo Basin are the second most extensive in the world after those of the Amazon Basin. The forests of West Africa have been severely fragmented. The savanna areas to the north, south and east of the tropical forests include huge tracts of grassland, grass/tree savanna and open and closed woodlands. By far the richest floristic area is the Cape Floral Kingdom which lies at the south-western tip of Africa. Much of the plant cover of Africa has suffered dramatic modification and destruction and although many of these changes have taken place in the past 100 years, continuous settlement in areas such as those along the Mediterranean seaboard had already altered those regions as much as 2 000 years ago. However, the acceleration in human population growth in recent decades has speeded up plant and ecosystem destruction.

THE FILLING OF THE AFRICAN ARK

Despite the relative geological stability of Africa, the animals that occupy its great diversity of habitats have very different zoogeographic backgrounds. Ancestral stocks arrived at different times and from different locations and evolution has progressed at different rates. Some species are survivors of the Age of Gondwanaland, a few have remained relatively unchanged, others have evolved and diversified. Africa has maintained contact with the northern continent of Eurasia for

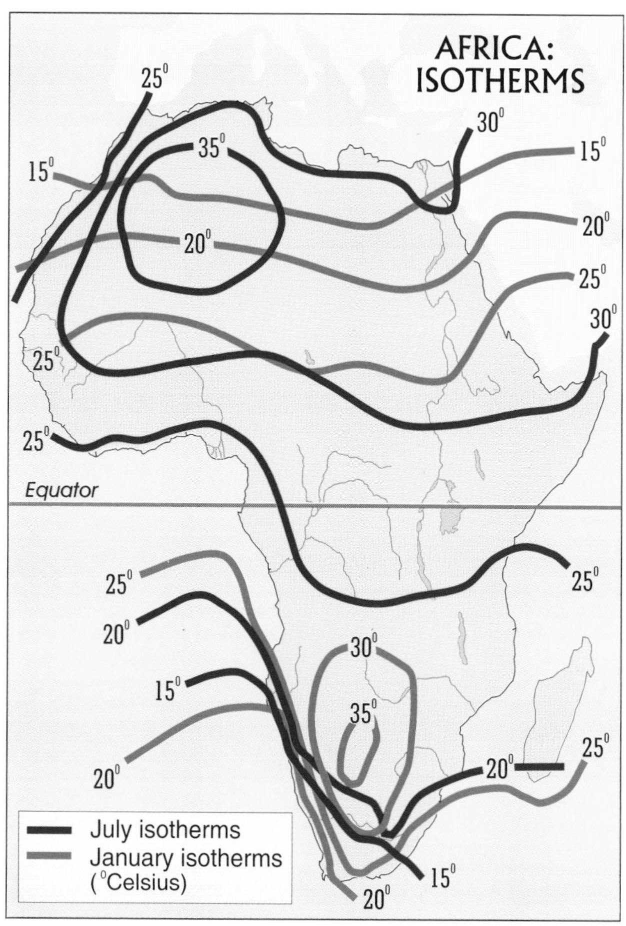

Right: *Many species of squirrels occupy the different types of African forests; this, the bush squirrel, is one of the most adaptable and is absent from gallery and riparian forest.*

some 30 million years, with a geologically brief break in contact during this time of about six million years. It was during this period of contact with the "outside world" that the dispersal of most vertebrate groups took place. Anthropoid apes and ancestors of the elephant, for example, migrated out of Africa for the first time and horses, bovids, carnivores and the "modern" rodents moved in only at this time to occupy vacant niches, or usurp the niches already occupied by other species. New species are constantly evolving in order to adapt to changing conditions, or to exploit another niche. An individual of a particular species that has a set of genes giving it features well suited for its specific environment has a better chance of surviving to reproduce, and thus pass on these genetic "benefits" to its offspring. But another individual within the same species that has less well adapted genetic material is less likely to survive to pass on its genes to future populations. In other words only the fittest and most adaptable individuals survive. A fine example of rapid, and "explosive" evolution is found in the hundreds of species of cichlid fishes that occupy the great lakes of the Rift Valley.

Above: *The elephant* Loxodonta africana *is found in most African habitats but today large populations are restricted to the major savanna reserves and national parks.* **Below:** *One of the best fossil records of man's evolution in Africa is preserved in the rocks of the Olduvai Gorge in north-western Tanzania.*

One cannot cover the natural history of Africa without briefly reviewing the evolution of the continent's most destructive mammal, man (*Homo sapiens*). Archaeologists have found a cornucopia of hominid fossils, dating from as far back as four million years, at such sites as Olduvai Gorge, Laetoli, Hadar, Koobi Fora, Sterkfontein and Rusinga Island. Many sites are located in the silts and volcanic ashes of the Great Rift Valley. It is still a puzzle as to why our early, tree-dwelling ancestors descended to the ground and then developed into so many different lineages some five million years ago. Climatic changes are believed to have been the catalyst between five and six million years ago. At this time there was a considerable drop in temperature following aeons of high temperatures. This caused a massive accumulation of ice in the Antarctic, drawing so much water from the oceans that their levels dropped by as much as 60 m. The African tropics were colder and drier and the extensive forests gave way to savanna vegetation. This probably forced some of our ancestors to move onto the plains and learn to utilise new food sources. The first hominids appear in the archaeological calendar some two million years ago but these australopithecines were later supplanted by the larger brained *Homo habilis* and *Homo erectus*. By the time *H. erectus* disappeared from the fossil record some 300 000 years ago, modern man – *Homo sapiens* – had arrived!

BIODIVERSITY

The biodiversity of Africa at the present time is massive; biodiversity simply indicates the total variety of all living organisms that exist on earth. For example, Zaïre is known to harbour at least 409 different mammal and 1 086 bird species, the highest recorded for any country in Africa. South Africa, thanks to the rich Cape Floral Kingdom, has by far the largest number of plant species (at least 20 300), almost twice as many as recorded for any other country. But the lower vertebrate groups have been poorly surveyed in most countries and the invertebrates remain a largely hidden treasure-chest.

This book offers you a brief glimpse of Africa's natural history, its richness and diversity, the problems and the hopes.

Right: *The blackcrowned night heron* Nycticorax nycticorax *is a common and widespread African species.*

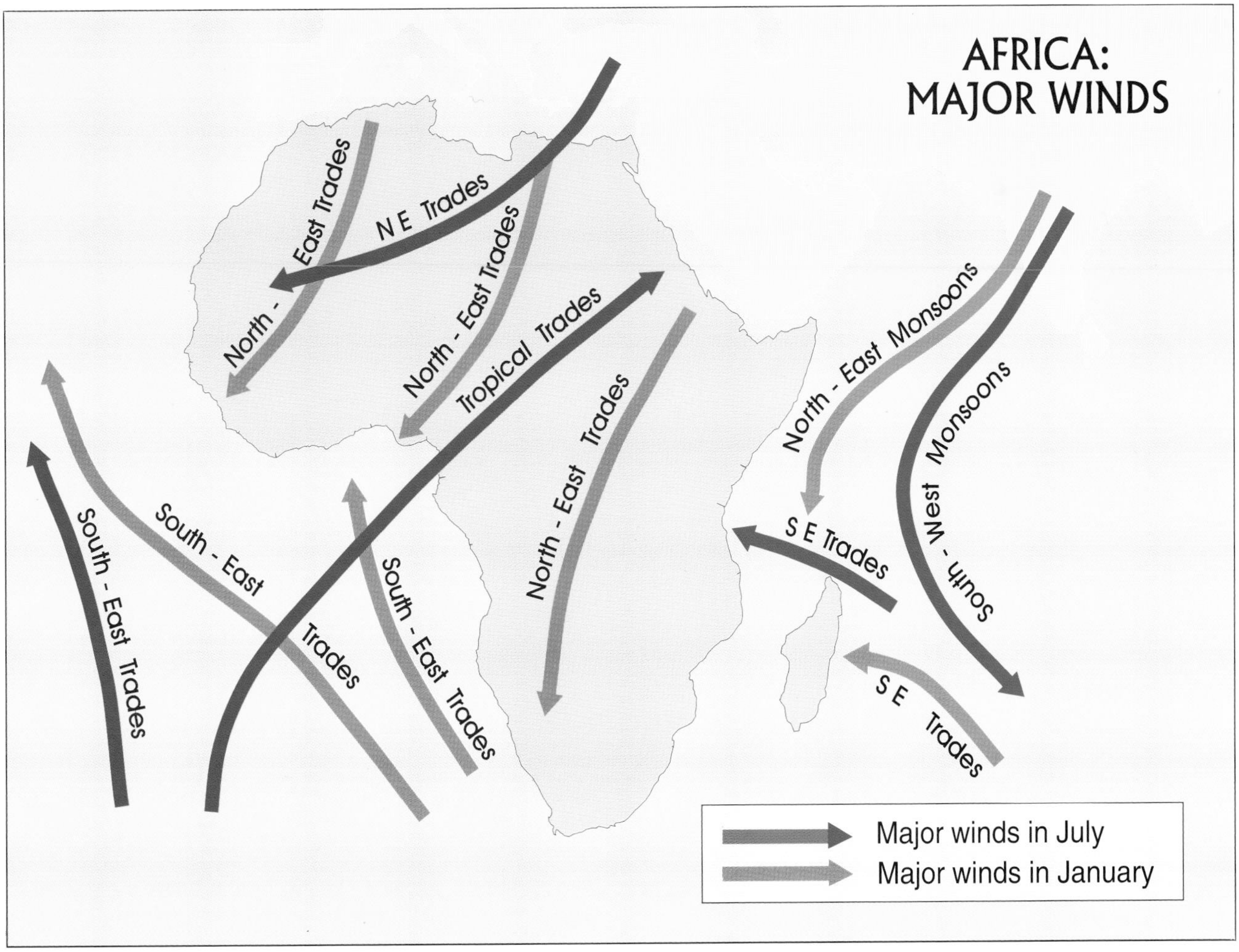

AFRICA: MAJOR WINDS

North - East Trades
NE Trades
North - East Trades
Tropical Trades
North - East Trades
North - East Monsoons
South - West Monsoons
S E Trades
S E Trades
South - East Trades
South - East Trades
South - East Trades

Major winds in July
Major winds in January

Left: *Lake Nakuru is one of the numerous soda lakes located in the Great Rift Valley of East Africa.*
Top: *The lower Orange River passes through arid country in southern Africa.*
Above: *The yellow-necked spurfowl* Francolinus leucoscepus *is found in African savanna and forest habitats.*

CHAPTER 1

THE SAVANNA MOSAIC

The name savanna means different things to different people but when used in the African context it conjures up images of great open plains covered in grass, with a scattering of flat-topped thorn trees and traversed by vast herds of game animals. This image is only partly correct, because savanna encompasses a much broader range of vegetation although grass is always the common denominator. More than one-third of Africa's land surface is dominated by savanna. Many different factors, such as rainfall, temperature and soil nutrients, determine the nature of the savanna regions. Rainfall is seasonal and often erratic, with drought a constant threat.

The savannas form the transitional zones between areas of high and low rainfall, lying between dry land and the tropical forests. In a relatively narrow belt fringing the tropical forests of western and north-central Africa and extending eastwards around Lake Victoria is an area that receives more rain than other savanna areas but not as much as the forests themselves. This is not a uniform belt but fingers and patches of forest extend into the surrounding grasslands. Another narrow belt of drier savanna lies between the Sahel in the north and the savanna/forest fringe in the south, extending from the Atlantic coast eastwards to the Ethiopian Highlands. This belt of tropical grassland becomes drier from south to north.

Originally it is believed that much of this region was covered by dry forest but most of this has been destroyed by man, and today

Background: *Impala,* Aepyceros melampus, *frequent open woodland savanna.* **Right:** *The vulturine guinea fowl* Acryllium vulturinum, *a denizen of the east African savanna.*

only open woodland remains. Sadly, many savanna areas have been greatly modified by the actions of man and his cattle, goats and sheep. The Sahel belt, and parts of the Horn of Africa, are sometimes referred to as northern dry savanna, but we have included this area in the chapter on drylands. Then there are the great expanses of savanna that extend from the Indian Ocean to the Atlantic, and southwards from the Zaïre Basin to merge into the Kalahari Desert and the South African plateau. The latter is Africa's only expanse of sparsely treed temperate grassland but man has put much of this region under the plough and built on it, and most of what remains has been overgrazed by domestic animals.

The landscapes and geological structures of the savannas are as varied as their wide distribution would indicate but most are dominated by seemingly endless plains, in areas broken by rolling hills and rugged inselbergs. They are bisected by rivers, many of which flow only during the rainy season, and seasonally filled floodplains that are not only important for the wildlife but also play a critical role in sustaining large numbers of humans. The soils of the African savannas are on the whole low in nutrient minerals and organic materials. During the dry season natural and man-made fires are a frequent savanna phenomenon and serve to return nutrients to the soil. In fact during the dry months the African savanna horizons are almost continuously blurred by the great clouds of smoke billowing into the sky. Many savanna areas are susceptible to erosion by both wind and rain as soon as the ground cover (mainly grasses) is removed, usually as a result of overgrazing by domestic animals.

The climate of the African savannas is characterised by short rainy seasons, with the amount of rain decreasing gradually the further one moves away from the equator. The length of the wet season is at its greatest close to the equator but is shorter as one moves northwards and southwards. The showers fall in the summer when the tropical rainbelt, which "migrates" north and south with the movement of the sun, drops its welcome load on the parched earth. Rain often falls in torrential downpours and thunderstorms occur frequently at this time of year. Moisture locked in the soil dur-

Above: *A typical savanna scene in southern Africa.*
Right: *One of several lushly grassed calderas that lie between lakes Edward and George in western Uganda.*
Far right: Stapelia gigantea, *a distinctive savanna species.*

ing the rains evaporates rapidly at the onset of the dry season and plant growth is greatly reduced, or stops completely. Dry season nights in the northern and southern savannas are often very cold and frost is not unusual but closer to the equator there is less variation.

THE VEGETATION

The vegetation of the savannas is to a greater or lesser extent dominated by the grasses, on which most of the animal life tied to this biome depends. There are many different grass species that can grow on virtually all soil types, even those with very low nutrient levels. They range in size from tiny species a few centimetres tall, to great waving giants of 2 m and more. Grasses growing in the higher rainfall savannas tend to be taller and more luxuriant but in drier parts the grasses are usually shorter and finer in structure. Savanna grass species can withstand the long dry months, respond rapidly to the first rainfalls of the summer, recover amazingly quickly after fire and many species can tolerate seasonal inundation. Most grass species have extensive fibrous root systems that are a further aid to survival. Even when heavily

cropped, many species can grow rapidly by producing different types of horizontal stems from which new shoots grow – surface runners known as stolons and sub-surface stems called rhizomes. Some species survive being trampled by pushing out roots from the nodes, or stem joints.

Grasses have also developed ways of ensuring that seed survives the long, dry dormant period and also to avoid being destroyed in the frequent fires. Most species produce large quantities of seed that lie dormant in the soil but the red oat grass (*Themeda triandra*), a widespread savanna species, has seeds that literally drill their way into the soil.

The African savannas include areas of treeless grassland, open grassy areas with a scattering of trees and bushes, and woodland (such as miombo) of varying densities but always with a virtually uninterrupted ground cover of grass. Much of the West African savanna has been greatly modified by the actions of man and his livestock and what was formerly dry forest is now open woodland. Within this zone there is a gradual transition from the higher rainfall southern savanna which is mosaiced with gallery forest and other densely wooded areas, as well as grassland, to the drier and more open country merging into the Sahel. Typical trees include *Isoberlinia doka*, *Monotes kerstingii* and *Terminalia macroptera*. There are also areas dominated by *Combretum-Terminalia* woodlands and in the more northerly stretches the *Acacias* tend to be abundant, as do the *Commiphoras*.

The savannas covering large areas of eastern Africa include open, sparsely treed grassland as found in the Serengeti/Maasai-Mara ecosystem, and large tracts of sparse grassland with abundant *Acacia-Commiphora* thickets. In the southwest there are areas of climax evergreen woodland and open woodland types. The southern dry savannas have large expanses of *Combretum-Terminalia*, *Brachystegia* and *Acacia* woodlands.

A number of tree species, some of them spectacular in appearance, have very wide distributions within the savanna zones and they include the baobab *(Adansonia digitata)* and the sausage tree *(Kigelia africana)*. The massive trunk (up to

Above: *Elephants congregate to drink.* **Left:** *A yellow baboon adolescent "on watch". Both elephant and baboon are typical savanna residents.* **Above right:** *The giraffe* Giraffa camelopardalis *is restricted to dry savanna woodland.* **Below right:** *The pygmy mouse* Mus minutoides *is one of the tiniest savanna mammals.*

28 m in circumference) with its lava-like covering of soft bark, makes the baobab one of Africa's most easily recognisable trees. They grow mainly in hot and dry savanna woodland and live to great ages, frequently well over 1 000 years. Fruit bats are very important pollinators of this species. Because of their age, size and appearance baobabs have given rise to many legends. Some tribes believe that these often hollow trees are inhabited by spirits and that anyone plucking their large white flowers will be killed by a lion, whereas others believe that drinking a brew made from their seeds will provide protection from crocodiles.

The sausage tree is best recognised when in flower or fruit, as both are large and impressive. The flowers, some 15 cm in diameter, are cup-shaped, deep red in colour and with yellow veining on the outer surface. It is the fruit, however, that gives the tree its common name. They are sausage-shaped, grey in colour, reach a maximum length of 1 m and weigh as much as 10 kg. Anyone foolish enough to contemplate resting or camping under a fruit-laden sausage tree would be advised to wear a crash helmet! Very few animals feed on these fruits, except on occasion the elephant.

THE MAMMALS

The African savannas have an amazingly rich mammal fauna. It is here where the great herds of antelope and zebra concentrate, and with them the attendant predators. Up until the early decades of this century all the savannas of the continent were populated by vast resident and migratory herds of game but ever-growing human and cattle populations and the advent of modern firearms greatly reduced the numbers and in some instances diversity. The worst-hit areas were the savanna zones of West Africa.

THE PLANT EATERS

About half of all existing ungulate species are endemic to Africa – a total of 87. Many of these have a total or partial association with the African savanna. The country with the greatest antelope diversity is Kenya with 37 species. Sudan and Tanzania have 34 each and Zaïre has 30 species. The savannas of West Africa support fewer species of large herbivores than similar areas in eastern and southern Africa. For example there are no zebra, blue (brindled) wildebeest (*Connochaetes taurinus*), impala (*Aepyceros melampus*), sable (*Hippotragus niger*), steenbok (*Raphicerus campestris*), oryx (*Oryx gazella*) or greater kudu (*Tragelaphus strepsiceros*). However, several species are "shared", including the hartebeest (*Alcelaphus buselaphus*), roan (*Hippotragus equinus*), kob (*Kobus kob*), waterbuck (*Kobus ellipsiprymnus*), topi (*Damaliscus lunatus/korrigum*), oribi (*Ourebia ourebi*), common duiker (*Sylvicapra grimmia*), buffalo (*Syncerus caffer*) and giraffe (*Giraffa camelopardalis*). Most of the ungulates that occur in the different savanna regions are represented by distinct subspecies, which are particularly pronounced in species such as the hartebeest and topi.

A question that is frequently asked about the massed herds and the large number of species living in close association, is how they are able to avoid severe competition for food. For example, at certain times of the year there are more than 400 ruminants feeding on each hectare in some areas of savanna in the Serengeti/Maasai-Mara ecosystem. Not all savanna residents are grazers; there are also the browsers feeding from bushes, trees and shrubs, then there are the mixed feeders that both graze and browse. By feeding on different types of plants and plants at different stages of growth or development each species fits into its own niche. Most herbivores (plant-eaters) on the savannas are ruminants, that is they chew regurgitated food, usually referred to as cud. Vertebrates, including the herbivores, are unable to manufacture the enzymes that break down the cellulose walls of plant cells but their gut is inhabited by a vast assemblage of bacteria and protozoans which undertake this task. In order to facilitate the work of these micro-organisms, the ruminants first hold the plant food in "fermentation tanks" in the stomach and once the enzymes start unlocking the nutrients the

animal regurgitates the vegetation into its mouth and further chews it so that the enzymes have a greater surface area on which they can work. Species that do not chew cud include plains zebra (*Equus burchellii*), elephant (*Loxodonta africana*), warthog (*Phacochoerus aethiopicus*), square-lipped rhinoceros (*Ceratotherium simum*) and the hook-lipped rhinoceros (*Diceros bicornis*). The ruminants, or cud-chewers, have a stomach with four chambers that allows them to feed rapidly and store a large quantity of food to be re-chewed and digested later when they are able to keep an eye on potential predators. Many species are grazers but each selectively feeds on a specific range of grasses, or only feeds when the grass is at a certain height. Savanna grasses are able to withstand heavy grazing and when they are cropped to the ground new shoots emerge. If we take the example of the plains zebra and the blue wildebeest (*Connochaetes taurinus*) we can best illustrate how they can both feed together without competing with each other. The zebra can utilise drier and tougher grasses by cutting them between its upper and lower incisors, whereas the wildebeest, like all antelope with incisors only in the lower jaw and a hard biting pad on the upper jaw, harvests grasses that are not as tough as those taken by the zebra. Although the zebra processes food faster than the wildebeest in its single-chambered stomach, the

four-chambered stomach of the wildebeest is much more efficient at extracting nutrients.

Another abundant and widespread ruminant is the buffalo (*Syncerus caffer*), Africa's only wild cattle species. They tend to feed on fairly coarse grasses, so making shoots and finer grasses available to other species. The topi/tsessebe (*Damaliscus lunatus*) eats tall and coarse grasses usually ignored by other species, with several antelope such as the impala (*Aepyceros melampus*), Grant's gazelle (*Gazella granti*), and Thomson's gazelle (*Gazella thomsonii*) favouring finer grasses. The last three species mentioned are mixed feeders and grass forms a varying part of their diet. The Thomson's take mostly grass but the other two, particularly during the dry season, include considerable browse in their intake. The diets of all species usually differ to a greater or lesser extent during the wet and dry seasons.

Left: *The plains zebra* Equus burchellii *has a wide distribution on the savannas of southern and eastern Africa (no zebras are found in western Africa).* **Above:** *The warthog* Phacochoerus aethiopicus, *a familiar savanna herbivore.* **Below:** *D'Arnaud's barbet,* Trachyphonus darnauddii.

The many species that utilise browse as their principal source of food are also able to share similar resources by feeding at different levels. The giraffe has the greatest height advantage as it can reach tree leaves, buds and flowers up to 5 m above the ground. In areas where giraffe are abundant many trees, particularly *Acacias*, are shaped and moulded by the feeding of these tall mammals. As with all the antelopes, and the buffalo, the giraffe has a four-chambered stomach and is a ruminant. Although once abundant and widespread in mixed *Acacia* and grassland savanna, they now only survive in isolated populations, with the most severe reduction in numbers having taken place in West Africa. In the dry *Acacia* savannas of East Africa the gerenuk (*Litocranius walleri*), with its long neck and legs, is able to reach tree and bush leaves at a greater height than many mid-sized browsing antelope and it increases this advantage further by frequently standing on its hind legs and using the front legs to pull branches to within reach of its mouth.

The giant eland (*Tragelaphus derbianus*), common eland (*Tragelaphus oryx*) and greater kudu (*Tragelaphus strepsiceros*) are the largest of the browsing antelope but they usually avoid feeding competition by favouring slightly different habitats. The eland species are highly mobile and

Above: *Impala* Aepyceros melampus *prefer open woodland savanna but avoid completely exposed grassland.*

rarely stay in one area for any length of time. The kudu on the other hand is more sedentary.

The elephant (*Loxodonta africana*) has influenced the structure of the African savannas more than any other species. They occupy, or have done in the past, virtually the entire spectrum of habitats that the continent has to offer. They feed on coarse grasses, tear out shrubs, ring-bark and push over trees. In this way they help to convert forest and dense woodland into open woodland, with more grass cover which in turn increases the impact of fire. More intensive fire results in the death of most trees but the tough grass roots, or rhizomes, survive and vast areas stand as virtually treeless grass-covered plains. With these elephant-influenced changes some species decrease in number, or disappear, whereas a number of grazing species find new range opened to them. Much of this natural pattern has however changed with the great reduction in elephant numbers, the increasing influence of man on the environment, and the inability of many elephant populations to move out of game parks. Whereas in the past they were able to move over vast areas, allowing vegetation to recover, today most savanna populations are confined and if elephant numbers are allowed to increase unchecked they destroy habitats, not only for themselves but for many other species as well. To prevent this destruction, the authorities in a few conservation areas, such as South Africa's Kruger National Park and the Hwange National Park in Zimbabwe, undertake regular culling programmes that maintain elephant numbers at levels believed to be optimal.

Even with the great diversity of feeding patterns it would not be possible for the savannas to sustain the great herds without some other factor playing a role to prevent over-exploitation of available food resources. This is where migration comes into play. True migration is a two-way seasonal journey that many animal species undertake to feeding grounds, or to where water is available for those species that need to drink regularly. Africa has many examples of migration involving savanna species but there are two that warrant particular mention: the well-known blue wildebeest movements in the Serengeti/Maasai-Mara complex and the little-mentioned movement of white-eared kob (*Kobus kob leucotis*) that takes place at the base of the Boma escarpment in south-eastern Sudan.

The migratory blue wildebeest population of the Serengeti ecosystem in north-western Tanzania and south-western Kenya forms the largest existing, discrete population of antelope in Africa. The Serengeti/Maasai-Mara ecosystem was largely grassland but during the past 100 years it graduated into large areas of dense woodland and then back again into open tracts of grassland. In 1961 it was estimated that some

TOURISTS AND THE "BEEST"

The Serengeti/Mara ecosystem which lies on either side of the border between Kenya and Tanzania is the scene each year of one of the world's great natural wonders: the migration of hundreds of thousands of blue wildebeest (Connochaetes taurinus). *During the rains the wildebeest herds are widely dispersed over eastern Serengeti but at the onset of the dry season little surface water is available. As the animals have to drink regularly they are forced to move westwards to permanent water. One of the areas to which they move is close to the Mara River, in the Maasai-Mara National Reserve. Large herds must swim across this river to reach new pastures. There are certain traditional crossing points where the wildebeest can scale the banks, and it is an awesome sight to watch thousands of wildebeest swathed in clouds of fine dust standing tightly packed at the river's edge until they finally plunge into the waters of the Mara. Large groups of youngsters that have forded the river stand on the steep bank bleating for the mothers that have not yet crossed. In desperation many of the young animals throw themselves back into the slow-moving waters. Wave after wave of animals arrive at the river's bank, in a seemingly never-ending stream.*

A hazard is posed by crocodiles who take the occasional wildebeest, but one of the greatest threats to the animals is the increasing number of tourists who come from all over the world to view the migration. Everyone is eager to get the best view and the drivers jockeying for position sometimes block the exit points, forcing the animals to attempt the river crossing at unfamiliar places. They panic and some drown. Occasionally the animals fail to scale the steep banks and return exhausted to rest before attempting the crossing again. The tourists are usually unaware of the tragedy that their presence has caused but if they travelled some two kilometres downstream they would witness a great gathering of vultures, griffons and marabous feeding on the carcasses of the wildebeest drowned by the ignorance of the human interlopers. It is not unusual for more than 100 animals to drown this way in one episode.

Above: *A vervet monkey,* Cercopithecus aethiops, *feeding on nectar from the flowers of the wild mango tree.*
Below left: *The martial eagle* Polemaetus bellicosus *is one of the largest and most spectacular of the savanna bird species.*

260 000 wildebeest were present within the system. However, the outbreaks of rinderpest that kept the herds in check decreased during the 1960s, and in the 1970s there was a change in the seasonal rainfall patterns. Greater falls were experienced during the dry season, which increased the available supply of grass. The wildebeest continued to increase in numbers until 1977 but since then the population has stabilised to between one million and 1.5 million animals, the number that the system can maintain. In the Serengeti the wildebeest spend the months of December to April (wet season) on the short grass-covered plains of the south-east, but from May to July they move to the woodlands and medium-length grasslands in the west. During the dry season, which extends from August to November, they move to the northern woodlands. With the onset of the rains they return to the short grasslands in the south-east. As the population started to increase, so they gradually expanded their range northwards across the Kenyan border into the Maasai-Mara National Reserve. Although the vast majority of the population takes part in the annual migration, substantial numbers remain on the wet-season grasslands. Enough animals leave, however, to ensure that the grasses can recover. At about the time when wildebeest numbers were increasing, the population of Thomson's gazelles (*Gazella thomsonii*) was higher than today's figure of about 500 000 but competition for food has caused a reduction in their numbers. Although the dry-season range of the wildebeest lies mainly within conservation areas, large tracts of the wet-season range and parts of the migration route are not protected and there are increasing conflicts between the herds and human settlement and cattle ranching. The wildebeest are also finding themselves hemmed in to the north of the Maasai-Mara by increasing tracts of land being planted out to wheat. Close to the onset of the dry-season migration adult bulls establish territories in which they gather varying numbers of cows with which they mate. However, these territories are of very limited duration and last only for a few days during pauses in the migration.

THE COOPERATIVE HUNTERS

The lion (Panthera leo) *is the only truly social cat and also the only felid that undertakes cooperative hunting. The usual social unit, or pride, includes one or more adult males – of which one is dominant – and a number of lionesses, sub-adults and cubs. Pride size varies from area to area and probably depends on the abundance of prey species.*

Most hunting takes place at night, with greatest prey capture on moonless nights. Lions do hunt around sunrise and sunset but they avoid virtually all activity during the hot midday hours. Within the pride the lionesses do most of the hunting but the males usually take first turn at feeding from a kill. In fact in a study undertaken in the Etosha National Park (Namibia) it was found that males only joined the females in four per cent of hunting opportunities. It has been argued by some authorities that what appears to be cooperative hunting is in fact a case of each individual working on its own and taking advantage of any beneficial situation that may arise from the hunt. On the other hand a researcher working in Etosha has found a complex division of labour amongst females participating in hunts. Usually the larger and heavier animals lay in ambush and caught prey chased towards them by other lionesses, in what appeared to be coordinated actions.

When hunting, lions attempt to get as close to potential prey as possible, using even the sparsest cover before charging, and chase distances rarely exceed 200 m. Lions eat an amazing variety of prey species, ranging in size from mice to young elephants, and from porcupines to buffalo. Medium to large ungulates make up the bulk of their diet in most areas. These include giraffe, blue wildebeest, oryx, impala, kob, springbok, plains zebra and warthog. Prey preferences vary from area to area and even from pride to pride when occupying adjacent territories. In the Kalahari Gemsbok National Park some lions have learned how to hunt porcupines and on the northern Namibian coast one pride learned how to hunt Cape fur-seals (Arctocephalus pusillus) *on the beaches.*

Apart from actively hunting their own prey, lions are not averse to appropriating kills made by other species, such as cheetah and spotted hyaena. This occurs more commonly in areas where prey biomass is higher, such as in the Serengeti/Mara ecosystem.

Below: *A lion and cubs with zebra kill.*
Photo: Pat J Frere

The calves are usually dropped just before, or at the onset of, the rainy season as the herds are returning to the lush new grasses in the south-east of their range.

Another substantial migratory blue wildebeest population (about 20 000 animals) spends the dry season in the Nairobi National Park (Kenya) and then with the onset of the rains they disperse southwards onto the unprotected Athi-Kaputei Plains. However, with the encroachment of human settlements and the intensification of cattle farming these routes are becoming increasingly disrupted. Wildebeest in savannas to the south are also subject to seasonal movements but never on the same scale that is found in eastern Africa. The wildebeest of the Serengeti/Mara system share their range with large numbers of Thomson's and Grant's gazelles (*Gazella granti*), topi (*Damaliscus lunatus*), impala (*Aepyceros melampus*) and eland (*Taurotragus oryx*), as well as great numbers of plains zebras.

The white-eared kob of south-eastern Sudan numbered some 840 000 in 1985 but the ongoing civil war in that country has prevented more recent counts. It is generally felt, however, that because of the isolated nature of the area where they occur and the low human population density, numbers have probably been maintained. This vast aggregation, with densities of up to 1 000 animals per square kilometre at times, centres on the grassland at the base of the Boma Escarpment. The kob move away from the floodplains during the rains but return with the onset of the dry months, covering some 1 500 km during the migration. As with the blue wildebeest and their crossing of the Mara River, the kob are forced to swim across a river during the migration. At the same time large numbers of topi (up to 500 000) move some 400 km to join the kob on their wet season pastures. A subspecies of Thomson's gazelle, known as the Mongalla (*Gazella thomsoni albonotata*), also follows the general migration but uses grassland adjacent to those grazed by the kob and topi.

The West African plains game animals have been greatly reduced in numbers as a result of habitat loss, the combined influences of drought, man-induced phenomena and large-scale hunting for meat. By far the majority of plains species surviving in this part of the continent are now restricted to conservation areas, and even there poor management provides little security. Travellers passing through these West African savannas during the latter part of the last century and in the early 1900s reported vast herds of such species as kob (*Kobus kob kob*), western hartebeest (*Alcelaphus buselaphus*

major), scimitar-horned oryx (*Oryx dammah*) and addax (*Addax nasomaculatus*) as well as several species of gazelle. For example in 1936 a single herd of 10 000 scimitar-horned oryx was observed in Chad. Such aggregations were not uncommon throughout the northern savanna zone of western Africa, but today this oryx as well as the addax are hovering on the brink of extinction. Whereas the West African ungulate herds once roamed throughout the savannas, and during bountiful years deep into the Sahelian zone, today what remains is concentrated in isolated pockets. The most westerly surviving savanna herds are located within Senegal, with viable numbers of roan (*Hippotragus equinus*), giant eland (*Tragelaphus derbianus*) and western hartebeest.

One large species that has survived in substantial numbers in West Africa is the roan, with an estimated 35 000 to 40 000 in the Central African Republic, and some 14 000 in Burkina Faso. The roan is believed to be the most abundant large antelope occurring in Mali. Strangely, this antelope occurs in low numbers in the savannas of eastern and southern Africa.

Below left: *Grant's gazelle* Gazella granti *ram.*
Below: *The springhare* Pedetes capensis *occurs in large numbers in the east and southern African savanna regions.*
Right: *The snake lily* Haemanthus puniceus.

Plains zebras are common on the savannas of southern and eastern Africa and they may form large herds, sometimes numbering several thousands, but they always retain the unity of the small family herds within these large gatherings. Both this species and the blue wildebeest frequently form mixed herds. One advantage experienced by large herds of plains game is the presence of many individuals alert to the ever-present threat of predators. The eyes of most grazers are set well up on the head, so that even when feeding they are able to see above the grass. When a large predator is observed and it is perceived to pose a threat the grazers can escape by running off at high speed.

However, it is not only the large herbivores that consume the abundant grasses and the other plants of the savannas. There are vast but less visible hordes of small species, including hares (*Lepus* spp.), springhares (*Pedetes capensis*), rodent molerats, mice and rats. Many of these animals are nocturnal and spend the daytime in burrows but they emerge at night to feed. The springhare, a small kangaroo-like rodent, occupies large areas of the southern and eastern savannas, where it feeds on grasses, including the roots and rhizomes, which it digs out with the long claws of the front feet. In some areas they reach very high densities and have considerable impact on the grass cover. The ground squirrels, of which there are four species, occupy the drier savannas and emerge during the daylight hours to feed on grasses, roots, bulbs and seeds. There are also several species of mouse that feed during the day, including the striped mice of the genera *Rhabdomys* and *Lemniscomys*. These, and a number of nocturnal mouse species such as the gerbils (*Gerbillurus* spp., *Tatera* spp.) and the multimammate group (*Praomys/Mastomys*), react to good seasons with an abundance of food by increasing their breeding tempo. These veritable population explosions soon result in an over-exploitation of available food and the populations crash to much lower levels.

Another group of savanna dwellers, the fossorial molerats, rarely come to the surface but where they reach high densities they consume vast quantities of roots and other plant parts, including those of grasses. Some small savanna rodents are specialist feeders. There are those that take mostly seeds, such as the fat mice (*Steatomys*). The climbing mice (*Dendromus*) eat seeds and insects, many of the gerbils favour grass seeds, and grassland members of the genus *Otomys* feed mainly on green plant material. So it is not only the large herbivores that have evolved feeding patterns to avoid serious competition for food – the humble, less visible savanna dwellers do so too.

Although primates are most abundant and diverse in forested habitats, several species have adapted to life on the woodland savannas. Two members of the family **Lorisidae**, the thick-tailed bushbaby (*Otolemur crassicaudatus*) and the lesser bushbaby (*Galago moholi*), spend most of their time in trees, emerging at night to feed on the sap of *Acacia* trees, insects and other items. Much of their time is spent foraging arboreally but ground movement is not uncommon. The call of the thick-tailed bushbaby is one of the typical sounds of the bushed savannas of eastern and southern Africa and bears a resemblance to the scream of a human infant.

However, it is the large troops of diurnal, ground-foraging baboons that are most frequently observed on the African savannas. The taxonomists differ on how many species there actually are but we tend to agree that the chacma (*Papio ursinus*), yellow (*P. cynocephalus*) and olive (*P. anubis*) baboons should all be grouped together as subspecies within *Papio cynocephalus*. A fourth baboon, the Guinea baboon (*Papio papio*), is restricted to the extreme western point of the West African savanna and is very poorly known. The savanna baboons all share a similar social structure, living in troops ranging from ten to more than 100 individuals, within a home range that includes a number of tall trees or rocky cliffs where they sleep at night, out of reach of predators. Troops are controlled by one, or occasionally two, dominant males, with other adult males being subservient. All the males are dominant over the females. Only dominant males get to mate with oestrus females, although other males can mate with non-receptive and young females. Baboons are omnivores, including some animal food in their diet although it is dominated by plant food.

The patas monkey (*Erythrocebus patas*) is highly adapted for its terrestrial lifestyle, with long legs and a slender body that allows it to run at great speed. They live in troops, each with only one dominant male, and feed on a variety of plants, as well as including insects in their diet. It occupies large home ranges and is restricted to the drier savannas of western and eastern Africa. The more widespread vervet monkey (*Cercopithecus aethiopicus*) also spends a considerable amount of time foraging on the ground but a troop never moves more than a few hundred metres from trees and they never occupy the open savannas favoured by the patas.

Below: *A cheetah,* Acinonyx jubatus, *with an oryx kill. Photo: John Carlyon.* **Above right:** *The black-backed jackal is one of the smaller savanna predators.*
Above far right: *The greater kudu* Tragelaphus strepsiceros.

The Predators

If the African savannas are renowned for their great herds of herbivores, they are no less famous for the array of predators that feed upon them. It is in this biome that the lion (*Panthera leo*), cheetah (*Acinonyx jubatus*), leopard (*Panthera pardus*), wild dog (*Lycaon pictus*) and spotted hyaena (*Crocuta crocuta*) dominate the top of the food chain. Unfortunately, with the reduction in their natural prey the large predators, as well as some of the smaller species, turn to domestic flocks and herds for their food. In this way they come into conflict with the interests of man and they are hunted ruthlessly. The large predators have disappeared from vast areas of their former range. The wild dog has been hardest hit, with perhaps as few as 2 000 surviving in the whole of sub-Saharan Africa.

The wild dog is a highly specialised hunter which forms packs averaging from 10 to 15 animals. When hunting the animals start to move slowly towards their intended quarry. As the selected prey animal starts to move away the dogs increase their pace, some animals pressing the pace to be replaced by others as they tire. Once an intended prey animal has been selected the pack is rarely distracted from it and the chase can continue for several kilometres. They take a

very broad spectrum of prey animals but medium-sized antelope such as impala are important and blue wildebeest and plains zebra are favoured in some areas.

The cheetah is another large predator that has been greatly reduced in numbers and range. Like the wild dog, this cat has a slender greyhound-like build and over short distances it can reach speeds exceeding 80 km/h. Unlike the canid it does not have the stamina to maintain a chase for more than a few hundred metres, however. In addition to the pressures it faces from man, the cheetah usually fares badly in areas where other large predators such as lion and spotted hyaena occur, as they frequently rob them of their kills. Despite its speed the cheetah only succeeds in capturing a relatively small percentage of the animals it attempts to run down.

Although the spotted hyaena frequently scavenges from the carcasses left by other predators and from animals that have died of other causes, they are also very efficient hunters. Although it occurs throughout the savanna zones and is still common in some areas, numbers have been greatly reduced in poisoning campaigns and by shooting. Hunting levels among spotted hyaena vary from area to area but most kills are made by packs of three to 30 animals. They take a wide range of prey, including young and adults of many antelope. Large packs will harass and try to chase lions from their kills.

However, it is the lion that sits at the top of the food chain on the savannas, at least in those areas where man has not moved in with his cattle. As with the wild dog and the spotted hyaena, the lion has a very well developed social system. They live in prides which vary considerably in size, within the range of three to 30 individuals. Depending on pride size there may be between one and four adult males, several adult females including one dominant animal, and a number of sub-adults and cubs. The bulk of their diet is made up of medium to large mammals, particularly ungulates such as buffalo, eland, greater kudu, blue wildebeest and plains zebra. They are also not averse to eating carrion and chasing other predators from their kills.

Many smaller predators are also associated with the savannas, including three species of jackal, the bat-eared fox (*Otocyon megalotis*) and two social mongoose as well as a number of solitary species, the civet (*Civettictis civetta*), four smaller cats, the honey badger (*Mellivora capensis*) and the striped polecat (*Ictonyx striatus*). Several other mammals of the savannas deserve mention, including the aardvark (*Orycteropus afer*) and the smallest member of the hyaena family, the aardwolf (*Proteles cristatus*). Although many other species include termites in their diets, these two mammals rely almost exclusively on these small insects for nourishment. The aardvark with its great spade-like front claws is able to excavate into even the hardest "castles of clay" constructed by termites. The aardvark is considered to be a "keystone species" because of its importance to so many other species. This large (40 kg to 70 kg), unique animal plays a crucial role in maintaining savanna habitat diversity by digging numerous burrows and holes which provide shelter and ideal breeding environments for a great variety of other savanna-dwelling animals.

THE BIRDS

The diverse nature of the African savannas and the great range of habitats they offer has ensured that the bird fauna is incredibly rich. This is the domain of the great flocks of seed-eating birds, the scavenging vultures, the birds of prey, bustards and the largest of all – the ostrich (*Struthio camelus*). The ostrich inhabits the savannas and drylands, avoiding densely vegetated areas where its advantage of great running speed would be lost. Ostriches can maintain speeds exceeding 50 km/h for long distances but despite this they frequently fall prey to such predators as the cheetah, and the young chicks are caught and eaten by such carnivores as the black-backed jackal (*Canis mesomelas*). Ostriches usually live in small flocks of four to 30 birds and feed on a range of seeds, green plant parts, flowers and occasionally insects. They are often seen in the company of such species as plains zebra, blue wildebeest and oryx where each benefits from the alertness of the other as an anti-predator early warning system. A family that is well represented on the savannas is that of the long-legged and long-necked bustards (Family **Otididae**), which range from about half a metre in height to over 1.3 m in the case of the Kori bustard (*Ardeotis kori*).

Below left: *The vulturine guinea fowl* Acryllium vulturinum. **Above:** *The helmeted guinea fowl* Numida meleagris *scratching for seeds.* **Below:** *Rüppell's griffon,* Gyps rüppellii. **Below right:** *The grey turaco (go-away bird)* Corythaixoides concolor.

They are usually solitary foragers but small flocks of some species may gather at a rich food source. All species eat insects, other invertebrates and some plant food, including seeds, but the larger bustards will take small vertebrates when the opportunity arises.

A number of francolin species and two guinea fowl are associated with savannas, the latter being the vulturine guinea fowl (*Acryllium vulturinum*), which forms large flocks and is restricted to the drier scrub and river fringes of East Africa, and the much more widespread helmeted guinea fowl (*Numida meleagris*). The most frequently observed francolin of many East African savanna areas is the yellow-necked spurfowl (*Francolinus leucoscepus*) but as with all members of this family they rarely move far from bush cover.

Among the more obvious and visible savanna birds are the vultures; circling on the air thermals in search of carrion, at predator kills, or sitting in trees. This group of large to medium-sized birds have found ways of avoiding competition for food, with each species feeding on a different part of a carcass. Species such as the whitebacked vulture (*Gyps africanus*), the Cape griffon (*Gyps coprotheres*) and Rüppell's griffon (*Gyps rüppellii*) have long beaks and necks and a rasp-like tongue that aids in feeding on muscle tissue and internal organs. The large whiteheaded vulture (*Trigonoceps occipitalis*) and lappetfaced vulture (*Torgos tracheliotus*) have massive beaks suited to tearing skin and tendons. All the vultures mentioned so far have bare or almost bare heads and necks. This is because if they were well feathered they would soon become clogged with blood and other fluids from the carcasses. Two species that have thinner and more lightly built beaks, as well as feathers on the head and neck, are the Egyptian vulture (*Neophron percnopterus*) and the hooded vulture (*Necrosyrtes monachus*). As they feed mainly on scraps around a carcass they do not get the head and neck soiled as the other species do. Another bird that is commonly associated with the savannas and frequently feeds at carcasses with vultures is the marabou stork (*Leptoptilos crumeniferus*). This is yet another species with a featherless head and neck.

There is a great diversity of birds of prey on the savannas, ranging from the long-legged ground-hunting secretary bird (*Sagittarius serpentarius*), to the massive martial eagle (*Polemaetus bellicosus*) and numerous kestrels, goshawks, sparrowhawks, falcons, kites and others. One would think that with such an array of feathered predators there would be severe competition for food but as with many other groupings this is greatly reduced by specialisation or generalisation. There are the snake-hunters, the bird-eaters, those that specialise in catching and eating rodents or larger mammals, those that feed mainly on insects, and those that will take any prey they can overpower. Even the species which eat similar food, for example the bird-

Top: *Southern ground hornbill* Bucorvus leadbeateri.
Above: *Yellowbilled hornbill* Tockus flavirostris.
Right: *Grey hornbill* Tockus nasutus.

THE HORNBILLS

The hornbills (Family Bucerotidae) *are medium-sized to large birds ranging in length from about 40 cm to 90 cm, and all are characterised by a large, down-curved beak. Some hornbills are restricted to forest and riparian woodland but a wide array of species occupies the numerous savanna habitats.*

The redbilled hornbill (Tockus erythrorhynchus), *the yellowbilled* (Tockus flavirostris) *and the grey hornbill* (Tockus nasutus) *have extensive distributions and all favour* Acacia *and dry broad-leafed woodland savanna. A few species have more restricted distributions, such as Monteiro's hornbill* (Tockus monteiri), *which is endemic to the savanna woodlands of north-western Namibia. The largest of all hornbills are the southern ground hornbill* (Bucorvus leadbeateri), *which occurs in southern and eastern savannas, and the Abyssinian ground hornbill* (Bucorvus abyssinicus) *of the northern savanna zone. These birds are the size of turkeys and, as their name implies, they spend much of their time foraging on the ground. They roost in trees at night. They have a varied diet and eat lizards, young birds, small mammals and invertebrates. They are often seen turning over and breaking up elephant droppings in search of, amongst others, dung beetles. The smaller hornbills also eat a wide range of food items but frequently include fruits and berries on the menu. After mating the female hornbill enters a selected tree-hole in which she lays and incubates her eggs. Once the female has entered the hole the male collects mud and uses this to seal the entrance, leaving only a narrow slit through which he can feed his mate while she and the eggs remain safe from predators. During the incubation period, which is from 30 to 50 days depending on the species, she undergoes a complete moult. Once the chicks have hatched she breaks out of her "safe haven" and the entrance is resealed in order to protect the fledglings. She is now able to assist the male in feeding their ravenous offspring.*

Above: *The barred owl* Glaucidium capense, *one of many owl species that inhabit the savanna. Photo: John Carlyon*

hunters, may use different techniques to catch their prey; the harriers fly low over scrub and long grass snatching up small birds as they rise in panic, whereas the falcons take birds in the air following a steep aerial stoop.

Without doubt, though, it is the small seed-eating species that are the most abundant. One species, the redbilled quelea (*Quelea quelea*), occurs throughout the savanna grasslands where it feeds on seeds, mainly of grasses, and lives in flocks that may be so large they beggar description. Such large flocks, frequently numbering millions of birds, require large quantities of seeds and they have to be largely nomadic to ensure that they always have access to adequate food supplies. When these flocks descend on human crops the results are devastating. Millions of tons of grains are consumed by these feathered "locusts" each year. Because of the vast numbers, predators don't even make a dent in the populations. When on the move the birds fly very close together and the flock turns as one, forming a near-solid mass that could serve to intimidate or confuse predators.

THE REPTILES

Africa's two largest tortoises inhabit the savannas: the leopard tortoise (*Geochelone pardalis*) in the south and east and the spurred tortoise (*Geochelone sulcata*) in the dry wooded grassland and Sahel belt from the Atlantic to the Ethiopian Highlands. There are also a number of smaller species including several hinged tortoises (*Kinyxs* spp.), which are able to close the rear part of the carapace (shell) to protect the hind legs and tail. Snakes include the widespread python (*Python sebae*) and puff adder (*Bitis arietans*), both of which wait under cover for suitable prey to come within catching distance. The python relies on its great strength to constrict its prey but the puff adder injects small mammals with poison that soon kills them. Many snakes living in the savanna rely on speed to capture fast-moving rodents, lizards and in some cases other snakes.

A very wide diversity of lizard species occupy the numerous niches offered by the savannas. Many species are long and slender and can move rapidly, escaping threats by taking cover under rocks, in holes or beneath bark. There are also ground- and tree-dwelling geckos (Family **Gekkonidae**), and members of the **Agamidae** family, some of which are ground-dwellers, some restricted to rocky habitats and a few which spend most of their time in trees. Another

group of lizards that is well represented, the skinks (Family **Scincidae**) also occupy many different savanna niches. The largest lizards encountered on the savannas are the monitors (Family **Varanidae**), which frequently reach lengths greater than one metre. Despite their size they are fast-moving and efficient predators, taking nestlings, small rodents, other reptiles and invertebrates.

THE INVERTEBRATES

Many insect species have considerable impact on the African savannas, including the great plant-devouring swarms of migratory locusts (*Locusta migratoria*) that can darken the sky for hundreds of square kilometres and the moving carpets of "army worms", the caterpillars of moth species such as *Spodoptera exempta*, which can clear entire areas of grass within a very short time. It is the termites, however, that play probably the most dramatic and ongoing role of all insects in the savanna soils. Many species construct large and complex "castles of clay" that may house millions of termites in a well-structured and ordered city. The amazing thing is that the entire population of each colony is the offspring of a single pair of adults. The colony can be compared to the human body, in that one part cannot survive on its own if removed from its usual environment. Each is so exclusive to its role in life that it is totally reliant on the colony "body". For example, the workers are blind and unable to breed, and the soldiers are armed with huge jaws that prevent them from feeding themselves so that they have to be fed by the workers. The queen is by far the largest member of the colony – she is so obese that movement is virtually impossible and her sole role in life is to produce thousands of eggs each day. Most of the time she produces sterile offspring but at certain times she can trigger changes in her pheromone secretion so that large numbers reach sexual maturity. At the onset of the rains these winged termites head out into the dangerous world on their nuptial flight.

Those that survive the attentions of numerous predators form male and female pairs and set about establishing new colonies. Termites are constantly moving plant material (some are grass collectors, the so-called harvester termites, while others cultivate fungus gardens on beds of wood and other plant materials) from the surface and the soil. The cellulose found in the plant material is broken down by organ-

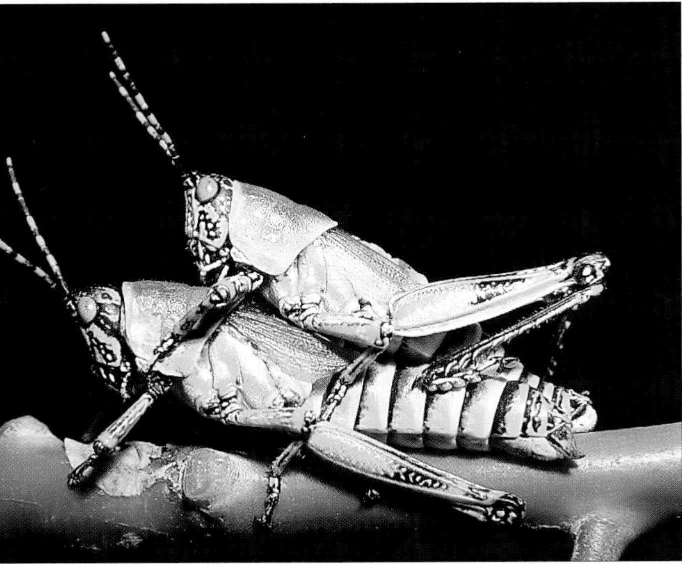

Far left: *The stone grasshopper* (Trachypetrella *sp.) is at home on the great savanna plains.* **Left:** *The mound of the termite* Macrotermes *– a common sight on the African savannas.* **Below left:** *Elegant grasshoppers* (Zanocerus elegans) *are common savanna residents.* **Below:** *The giraffe* Giraffa camelopardalis *is restricted to dry savanna woodland.*

isms in the termite's gut, or by the fungus gardens, and over time is recycled back into the system. The grass and other plant material harvested by termites usually far exceeds that eaten by the large herbivores. The tsetse fly, of which the principal savanna species is *Glossina morsitans*, has been called Africa's greatest conservationist because it transmits sleeping sickness (trypanosomiasis) to both man and his livestock when sucking their blood, and in this way prevents their spread into prime game areas. Although some game species are carriers of the protozoan parasites they do not develop sleeping sickness, and all have a natural immunity. With the advent of modern insecticides some areas have been cleared of tsetse flies, enabling man to move in with his animals so causing the game numbers to dwindle.

THE FUTURE

There are still large areas of savanna country that are well preserved but in some regions, such as West Africa, there has been considerable destruction because of the demands created by a large and rapidly expanding human population. Problems include tree cutting for fuel, overgrazing by domestic herds which reduces food available to wild species, and a proliferation of modern firearms that has led to the decimation of many of the great herds.

Most of Africa's principal national parks and game reserves are located in the savannas. Some of these, particularly in the south, are well managed but others exist on paper alone. It is becoming increasingly obvious that biodiversity can only be adequately preserved in formal conservation areas, unless human population growth can be drastically curbed. This seems highly unlikely, however. Even the presence of huge savanna conservation areas does not guarantee that biodiversity will be sustained. The Serengeti/Mara ecosystem protects the great herds of blue wildebeest to a large extent but increasing demands are made by pastoralists with their cattle herds and expanded cultivation of wheat to the north of the Maasai-Mara. In West Africa some of the parks have uncontrolled human settlements within their boundaries. In Chapter 8 the threats faced by the African environment and its biota are examined in greater detail.

CHAPTER 2

THE AFRICAN DRYLANDS

Africa can lay claim to the largest true desert in the world, the Sahara (about one-fifth of the continent's surface area), one of the oldest, the Namib, and vast tracts of arid land. In fact, depending on the definition one prefers, well in excess of 60 per cent of the continent's surface consists of low-rainfall areas. The Sahel belt which forms the buffer between the Sahara Desert and the moist lowlands and forests of West and Central Africa stretches from the Atlantic Ocean in the west to the River Nile in the east. Virtually the entire Horn of Africa is dry land, extending in patches and fingers into Kenya. In the south the Kalahari Desert covers almost the entire country of Botswana and spills over into neighbouring territories. Its southern fringes extend to the arid central plains of South Africa: the Karoo, Bushmanland and Namaqualand which reach towards the western and southern seaboards. The word "desert" usually conjures up a vision of seemingly endless expanses of mighty "oceans" of sand dunes but the deserts also contain great flat plains, mountain and hill ranges, and seasonal pans that hold water for only a few weeks once in several years. Permanent waterholes (oases) and rivers which penetrate deserts allow man to settle in an otherwise hostile environment. What constitutes desert or drylands? The usual definition relates to the amount of rain received in any particular area but as with many things there does not seem

Background: *Sand dunes are probably the most photographed landscape feature of deserts, but vast areas of the Namib and Sahara deserts are covered by gravel plains, mountains and rocky outcrops.* **Right:** *The armadillo lizard* Cordylus cataphractus *in defensive posture. This species occurs in the Southwest Arid Zone of Africa.*

to be consensus on exact quantities. Desert is characterised by extremely low rainfall, frequently less than 100 mm per year, whereas semi-desert and arid zones usually receive less than 250 mm each year but never more than 500 mm per year. For example, several localities in the Sahara have mean annual rainfall figures of less than 20 mm, such as Murzuq with 8 mm and Ghat with just 13 mm. But rainfall in all the arid lands of Africa is erratic in occurrence and unpredictable in quantity. Several years may pass with below the meagre average fall and then one shower could equal the total of the previous five years. Arid lands also suffer great temperature extremes with a baking hot day leading into a bitterly cold night. Despite their inhospitable nature the drylands are home to a diverse and interesting spectrum of plants and animals, many of which are highly adapted to withstand the rigours of desert life.

The following accounts deal with the Sahara and Namib deserts in some detail, followed by an overview of the remaining drylands.

THE SAHARA DESERT

The word "Sahara" is simply the plural of *sahra*, which is Arabic for "desert". The Sahara is in effect the remains of a very old rock shield, made up of granites, gneiss, quartzites and schists, with its origins rooted in the Precambrian era. Much of the region we now know as the Sahara must have been a huge range of mountains that was reduced to a peneplain by erosion and weathering during the period known as the Paleozoic. In fact today more than 50 per cent of the world's greatest desert consists of mighty plains and large, shallow depressions. Overlying the granitic deposits are sedimentary rocks of more recent origin that were laid down over millions of years when the sea frequently inundated the land. The marine floodings of the Paleozoic era left many strata of sandstones and limestones that now remain as great eroded plateaus and isolated pinnacles and columns standing out on the open plains.

As the Mesozoic era slid into place, changes in climate resulted in vegetation growth that included forest and woodland, of which the only evidence today is the presence of fossilised, or silicated, wood. Once again the ocean levels rose and flooded all the lower lying areas. They remained inundated until the start of the Eocene period. The tertiary rocks of the Sahara are primarily deposits that had their origins on land, were swept along by rivers and streams from such ranges as the Atlas and eventually laid down in great scree fans to be compacted into sandstones, chalks and marls over millions of years. These scree fans were deposited from west to east for over 2 000 km with chalk forming the upper layer in most cases. Some areas remain intact as great open uplands known as *hamadas*, but elsewhere water erosion has resulted in the creation of numerous "moonscape" outcroppings. In the far east, sandwiched between the Nile and the Red Sea, is the Nubian Desert, a narrow plateau dominated by limestone trenched with numerous wadis.

The Atlas Mountains, lying at the north-western fringe of the Sahara, were formed during the Tertiary era when the alpine folding process resulted in extensive volcanic activity in the Sahara. This was to last from the mid-Tertiary until the beginning of the Quaternary era. The great Saharan peneplain was compressed, resulting in extensive faulting which allowed lava to escape to the surface. Evidence of this volcanic action can be found in several mountain ranges, particularly those in the central regions. Of the volcanoes themselves little remains except laval plugs which originally lay in the volcanic pipes. Altitude in the Sahara ranges from the 3 325 m-high Tarso Taro in the Tibesti Mountains to the Qattara Depression in north-western Egypt, which lies more than 100 m below sea level in places.

The Sahara is dominated by barren stony plains and plateaus and isolated mountain ranges, but it is the sand-oceans that usually capture the human imagination. There are three principal dune belts which stretch from the north-east to the south-west, ranging in size from about 24 000 km^2 to over 62 000 km^2. The sand-seas can be divided into two

Far left: *Well weathered granitic rock.* **Left:** *Weathering of rock by water, wind-blown sand, and heating and cooling produces amazing scenery in deserts.* **Below:** *Fossilised tree trunks are evidence of a moister climate in the past.*

types: the mobile, ever-moving fields and the static fields. The sands are mainly of alluvial, or river-borne, origin carved from the rock, carried along and deposited in the basins and on the plains over many millions of years. The great rivers that rose from the central Saharan mountain ranges were formed during the Quaternary era. Some geologists suspect that the Saharan sands were formed as recently as 250 000 years ago with sediments being flushed into the Mediterranean Sea by rivers, particularly during flooding. Now strong winds push the sands back in the direction of their southern origins. The great sand-seas serve one critical role in that they act as vast reservoirs for the storage of water.

Satellite images and photographs taken by United States astronauts indicate that vast underground aquifers lie beneath the sand-covered basins throughout the Sahara. During periods of higher rainfall and substantial water flow, particularly over the past 200 000 years, these basins were filled and the water percolated through the sand to lie below the surface. In Egypt a number of experimental wells have been dug in the desert (96 per cent of Egypt is covered by desert) and agronomists have established an experimental farm, with

Below: *The vegetation of the dry interior of South Africa has been greatly modified by many years of overgrazing by domestic stock.* **Right:** *A mountain scene in the Algerian Sahara in the vicinity of the Haggar. Photo: Peter Wyss*
Bottom right: *Scorpions are widespread and diverse in the drylands of Africa. This is* Parabuthus planicauda.

amazing initial results. Some experts believe that Egypt could put 200 000 acres of desert land under cultivation for 200 years with available supplies of underground water. No one, of course, predicts what will happen after 2200 AD!

Obviously, at least in parts, the Saharan soils are fertile but the low rainfall and lack of surface water prevents extensive vegetation growth. Apart from the ancient links between Africa and South America during the era of the super-continent of Gondwanaland, a common factor still exists. Some scientists believe that as much as 12 million tons of dust is raised each year by winds blowing over the Sahara Desert and its Sahelian fringe and drawn into the Amazon Basin by great storms that rage about 25 times per annum. The dust is then carried to the forest floor by moisture-laden air which deposits about 450 g of phosphate per acre to increase fertility in a nutrient-poor substrate.

The Sahara was not always dry however, and over the past 65 million years its borders have changed position many times. The most recent dessication started about 5 000 years ago when North Africa was a productive "bread-basket". Not all can be blamed on climatic changes however, as the impact of man in the form of wood-cutting, overgrazing by domestic livestock and cultivating marginal land has accelerated the rate of desertification. As the last Ice Age began to wane some 12 000 years ago, shifting weather patterns introduced a moist climate to North Africa and the Sahara took on a new guise. Areas covered today by harsh desert land were inhabited by hippos, elephant, giraffe and a now-extinct giant buffalo, amongst others. In the remote massif of Tassilin-Ajjer (meaning the plateau of rivers), located in the southern Algerian Sahara, a great assemblage of prehistoric paintings testifies to the rich fauna of those times.

Rainfall in the Sahara, as with all desert regions, is extremely low and in some areas rain may not fall for several years. The interior receives the lowest falls, with rainfall increasing towards Sudan as well as to the north and south. When it rains, heavy showers may result in dry watercourses (*wadis*) carrying raging torrents several hundred kilometres through the desert. However, the flow never lasts more than a few days. A zone of tropical cloud develops during spring, spreading over much of the southern Sahara by August. By December the clouds are but a memory, however. A second cloud belt forms over the Mediterranean and advances into the desert's northern fringes in winter but retreats in the summer. Cloud "bridges" may briefly link the two belts. Absolute desert, with virtually no rainfall and an absence of plants, occurs in Tanezrauft, west of Ahaggar, in the Ténéré and in the Libyan Desert. In some areas, such as Biskra and Ouagla, large shallow lakes, known as *shotts*, appear during the cooler winter months. These are formed by rising ground water which evaporates during the warmer months, so that the lakes take the form of dry and salt-lined depressions during the summer. The highest temperatures are usually recorded along the northern fringe, which is frequently buffeted by the hot wind known as the *scirocco, samum, khamsin* or *gibli*. Probably the most unpleasant feature of the Saharan climate is the ever-present threat of sandstorms, which reach their peak frequency in the spring, particularly April and May.

Lying at the southern rim of the Sahara Desert is the Sahel, a belt of dryland that stretches from the Atlantic Ocean coast in Senegal to Sudan in the east, encompassing some 20 per cent of the African land mass. This belt is, in effect, a southward extension of the Sahara that has been subjected to severe drought and abuse by man. From 1968 to 1973 well over 3 million cattle died, formerly perennial rivers ceased to flow and lakes began to retreat from their shorelines. This dry period was followed by years of good rainfall but during 1984 and 1985 drought again devastated this desert fringe and mass starvation of animals and humans followed.

Above: *The Namib has many highly adapted endemic plant species. This is the "Halfmens"* Pachypodium namaquanum.

Much of the Sahel belt has been occupied in the past by nomadic peoples who were well adapted to the climatic vagaries of their environment. The nomads and their livestock followed the rains, retreating southwards during dry periods. This is no longer possible, and the results of the last drought were horrific. As terrible pictures of the dead and dying were beamed into the homes of millions of people living in the developed world, there was a clamour for action. Billions of dollars of relief money were pumped into the region, but sadly the money has had little effect. Nomads were encouraged to cease their wanderings and settle at fixed points, resulting in massive overgrazing, destruction of trees (as much as 90 per cent of energy consumed in Sahelian countries comes from burning wood) and depletion of water resources. As the plant cover is depleted, retention of solar heat at night is reduced, thus in turn reducing moisture produced during plant transpiration.

Desertification is a natural process in many areas but the rapid increase in human population has greatly accelerated the spread of drylands throughout Africa.

THE NAMIB DESERT

The Namib Desert extends for more than 2 000 km along the south-western coastline of Africa, from the Olifants River in the Western Cape, South Africa, to San Nicolau in Angola. It forms a narrow belt, in most places less than 200 km wide, that is sandwiched between the Atlantic Ocean and the western escarpment. The eastern boundary of the Namib Desert is difficult to define but it is usually taken as the 1 000 m altitudinal line (above sea level). This desert, sometimes claimed to be the world's oldest, is believed to have seesawed between arid and semi-arid for at least 80 million years and there have been periods when water was much more abundant than it is today. The landscape features that can be observed now have been modified and changed greatly over time by water, wind, cooling and heating. Dune fields that developed during the Tertiary era have solidified and are now covered by fields of much more recent origin. The feature that has the greatest influence on the desert as we know it today is the presence of the cold Benguela Current, which was already fully established some 5 million years ago. The portion of the sand dune field that extends between Lüderitz and Swakopmund was probably only formed after this current had stabilised.

Above: *Sand dunes in the Namib Desert.*

Open gravel plains are dotted with rocky outcroppings, or inselbergs, of granite, quartzite and schists, and bisected by normally dry riverbeds. Only two rivers carry water into the Atlantic Ocean throughout the year; the Cunene in the north which rises in the Angolan highlands and the Orange in the south, with its source in the mountains of Lesotho. Others, such as the Hoanib, Ugab, Swakop and Kuiseb rivers, flow only when rain falls in the interior and then usually only for short periods. However, strong subterranean water supplies support large trees and shrubs that would not normally survive in this arid environment, allowing non-desert fauna to penetrate an otherwise hostile region.

A number of rivers, such as the Tsauchab and Tubas, have had their paths to the sea blocked by the dune fields. Sand dunes cover a large part of the Namib Desert and two principal fields are recognised. The most extensive one reaches from the Kuiseb River in the central part of the desert southwards to the Orange River, which forms the boundary between South Africa and Namibia. The northern dune field is narrower and lies between Torra Bay in Namibia and the Curoca River in Angola. The Namib dunes are made up almost entirely of quartz grains.

From the point of view of fauna, the Namib Desert is one of the richest in the world in terms of species as well as endemics. This statement is particularly applicable to the dune fields. Two factors, both linked to climatic factors, ensure the survival of this faunal assemblage – moisture obtained from fog and wind-blown detritus. As with all deserts, rainfall in the Namib is extremely meagre and irregular, with as little as 15 mm per year falling along the coast and up to 100 mm in the interior.

Because of the great length of this desert different rainfall regimes apply in various parts of the Namib. The Angolan Namib receives its rains in summer, whilst the southern Namib has winter falls. The South Atlantic Anticyclone pressure system directly influences the Benguela Current, maintaining cool water inshore, ensuring the frequent development of fog, the maintenance of high coastal humidity and the steep climatic gradient from the coast into the interior. Great banks of fog frequently move inland from the coast overnight, often for more than 50 km, reaching its greatest density at an altitude of between 300 m and 600 m. Raised areas such as the inselbergs and sand dunes act as fog "traps" and it is these areas that display the greatest diversity. Many species have evolved to make use of this source of moisture.

Strong winds serve to blow fog onshore and transport fragments of plant and animal detritus deep into the desert both from the coast and the interior. Many invertebrates, as well as some small vertebrates, rely to a large extent on detritus as their main source of food.

TWO UNIQUE NAMIB DESERT PLANTS

NARA *(Acanthosicyos horrida)*

One of the most characteristic plants growing in the Namib Desert, the nara is a member of the cucumber (cucurbit) family and it grows in sandy areas wherever its very long taproots can reach underground water. The green, virtually leafless stems ensure greatly reduced water loss and undertake the process of photosynthesis. It is a dioecious species, with the male and female plants being separate. Although the male plants produce flowers throughout the year, the female produces one crop of prickly melons (about 150 mm in diameter) which ripen by late summer. The great prickly masses provide ideal shelter for many small animals, and the flowers and fruits are an important source of food for numerous insects, small rodents, oryx, black-backed jackal and brown hyaena. From prehistoric deposits it is known that man exploited the fruits as a food source, and even today some local people harvest them for the fruit pulp and seed.

WELWITSCHIA *(Welwitschia mirabilis)*

Although this strange desert-dwelling plant is grouped with the conifers (pine trees), it also has a number of characteristics in common with the flowering plants. To the non-botanist it bears little obvious resemblance to a pine tree, except for the fact that both the male and the female plants carry cones, those of the female being by far the largest. The top of the stem is concave and tapers in the ground to a length of about 3 m. The plant carries only two leaves, but because of their tattered nature there usually appear to be more. The leaves grow continuously and in dry years increase in length by between 10 and 20 cm. In good years when moisture is more abundant they may grow by as much as 10 cm per month. The roots extract moisture directly from the ground (usually dry watercourses, which they favour) and the leaves absorb some water from the fog. It is known that medium-sized plants are several hundred years old so large examples could be well over 1 000 years old.

Above right and centre: *The flowers and fruit of the nara.* **Right:** Welwitschia mirabilis. *Amazingly enough, this plant only has two leaves that continue to grow through its very long life. They become tattered and shredded, giving the impression that it is a multi-leafed species.*

Above: *The hamadryad or hamadryas baboon* Papio hamadryas *occupies semi-desert country in Ethiopia, Sudan, Somalia and a limited area of the southern Arabian Peninsula, but its distribution is limited to those areas with drinking water.*

OTHER DRYLAND AREAS

Two other regions of aridity in Africa require mention, the **South-west Arid Zone**, which apart from the Namib Desert includes the Kalahari and the interior of central and western South Africa, incorporating the Karoo, Bushmanland and Namaqualand; and the **Horn of Africa** which includes all of Somalia, eastern Ethiopia, Eritrea, Djibouti and outliers in northern Kenya.

The Kalahari Desert falls within the South-west Arid Zone, and although it is now a large semi-desert it was once much more extensive and linked with the drylands of north-eastern Africa. Sands of Kalahari origin occur in the Congo Basin, Angola and western Zambia but these areas are now covered by more extensive vegetation and receive more generous rainfall than the Kalahari proper. The Kalahari Desert covers most of the country of Botswana, spilling over into eastern Namibia and the northern reaches of South Africa, with a toe-hold in western Zimbabwe. Much of the area consists of open sand plains, with areas of low sand dunes, isolated inselbergs, dry riverbeds that flow only after their catchments have received unusually good rains and great salt pans, such as the Makgadikgadi system in the centre of Botswana. Western areas receive annual rainfalls of between 100 mm and 250 mm but this increases in the east to some 500 mm in bountiful years. As the amount of rain usually exceeds the 100 mm desert limit, vegetation is correspondingly more abundant and represented by open woodland (with many *Acacias*), thicket, scrub and abundant seasonal grasses.

As one moves to the southern fringes of the Kalahari the number of trees start to decrease, except along seasonal watercourses, and low, sparsely distributed scrub and lower grass levels become obvious. In the recent past grass was much more abundant in the Karoo, Bushmanland and Namaqualand than it is today.

Before the arrival of the European settlers and their herds of domestic animals, the dry plains were home to great nomadic herds of the now extinct quagga (*Equus quagga*), black wildebeest (*Connochaetes gnou*), red hartebeest (*Alcelaphus buselaphus*) and springbok (*Antidorcas marsupialis*). They followed the rains which brought fresh grass growth to the parched flatlands. As the settlers moved deeper into the interior and each claimed his piece of land, game numbers declined drastically and the domesticated hordes of livestock were confined. Low scrub started to replace the dwindling grass stocks and desertification progressed at an accelerated pace to the south and east. Most of these drylands consist of seemingly endless plains broken by the occasional hill range of either volcanic or sedimentary origin and many dry watercourses. Only one large river, the Orange, cuts its way north and west to pour its silt-laden waters into the Atlantic Ocean.

The drylands of the Horn of Africa include one small area towards the horn's tip receiving less than 100 mm, but much

Left: *Grevy's zebra* Equus grevyi *was once widespread in arid areas of eastern Africa but as with many species, numbers have declined drastically.* **Below:** *The Namaqua chamaeleon* (Chamaeleo namaquensis) *is an unusual member of the chamaeleon family in that it is mainly terrestrial.*

of the region records between 100 mm and 400 mm of rain in average years. As with the rest of Africa, this region has experienced numerous climatic changes. It has become progressively drier during the course of the past 6 000 years, with increases in domestic stock numbers, as in other dryland regions, aggravating the situation.

Although at one time the drylands of the South-west Arid Zone and those of the Horn of Africa were linked – as is evidenced by the presence of species such as the oryx (*Oryx gazella*) and Kirk's dik-dik (*Madoqua kirkii*) in both areas today – the latter now barely extends below the equator in Kenya and marginally into northern Tanzania.

As with the drylands already discussed this region is not uniform but consists of a range of landforms, soil types and vegetation: the northern uplands which include the Carcar Mountains and bear some common ground with the Ethiopian Highlands; the area that centres on the deep, infertile soils of the Ogaden but stretches far beyond; and the arid, windswept coastal strip extending southwards from Obbia. By far the greatest areas are vegetated by *Acacia* and *Commiphora* scrubland, particularly as one moves southwards from the Ogaden.

DESERT SURVIVAL

Plants and animals living in the desert regions of the world have evolved to survive extremes in temperature and limited access to moisture. Many species of desert plants are ephemeral, that is they are short-lived, only germinating when the meagre rains fall and producing seeds before the dessicating winds destroy the parent plants. The seeds of these plants are very hardy and can withstand extremely harsh conditions, often lying dormant for many years. For months, even years, barren plains are virtually bare of plant life, then light rain begins to fall and within a few days carpets of living colour appear.

Just as rapidly the plains return to their blend of browns and greys. Some plants are able to survive on the little moisture present in the air. At night the temperature drops, and although the moisture content of the air remains the same, the relative humidity increases, causing dew to condense on plants and other surfaces such as rocks. In the Namib Desert the frequent fogs that roll inland from the Atlantic Ocean hold great benefits for plants which have evolved to make use of this regular supply of water. A number of plant species are able to absorb fog droplets rapidly through the leaves and in this way supplement the moisture that can be absorbed through the roots. One such species is a small, succulent-leaved shrub, *Trianthema hereroensis*, which only grows within the fog belt. Because of this reliable source of life-sustaining water it is able to produce flowers and seeds on a continuous basis. Other species have no mechanisms that allow for absorption of water other than through the roots, such as the common dune grass *Stipagrostis sabulicola*, but because of an extensive and shallow-lying root system they are able to draw sufficient water from fog-moistened and dew-dampened surface sand.

A widely occurring Saharan grass species, *Aristida pungeus*, also has a very extensive root system that allows all of the minimal moisture to be utilised. Lichens are a symbiotic relationship between fungi and algae, with the former providing structural support and the latter providing the source of energy through photosynthetic food production. They occur in almost all habitats throughout the world, but some have evolved to utilise the fogs of the Namib to great effect.

One species in particular, *Teloschistes capensis*, is foliose and reaches a height of 100 mm. It grows in a very restricted belt close to the coast and lives in unique and extensive "forests". Many lichen species are crustose, lying flat on the ground, or rock, surface and are found in all of Africa's drylands. Succulent plants, that is those species with thick, fleshy leaves, absorb and store water during the brief periods when rain falls, such as the widespread aloes. Many succulents also have swollen stems and/or tuberous roots that further serve to preserve water between prolonged periods of drought. Other species have no leaves, or greatly reduced ones such as found in most *Euphorbias*, to reduce water loss. Still others have thick, waterproof "skins" and a few have leaf pores which can be tightly closed during the hotter hours when water loss is at its greatest. These water-storing plants are found in many forms in all of Africa's drylands, although in the Sahara they are best represented along the narrow, humid Atlantic coastal belt.

In areas with less rain large trees and bushes are mainly restricted to watercourses where their long roots can reach down to subterranean water, with such species as *Acacia erioloba*, *Acacia albida* and *Ficus sycomorus* found in the Namib and Kalahari, with the less spectacular *Tamarix aphylla* and *Acacia tortilis* growing in the Sahara. Species of *Acacia* and *Commiphora* are widespread in Africa's drylands.

As with the plants, desert-dwelling animals have had to evolve ways to overcome extremes in temperature and a shortage of water. Many smaller species escape temperature extremes and dessication by burrowing below the surface. The air in a burrow acts as insulation and in the case of small mammals it is moistened by their breath. Some, such as the jerboas (*Jaculus* spp.) of the Sahara and the hairy-footed gerbils (*Gerbillurus* spp.) of the Namib and Kalahari, excavate tunnels to which they can return after foraging. The entrances are usually blocked when the animal is resident as this serves to maintain temperature and humidity levels. In the case of gerbils in the Namib it has been found that burrow entrances are often excavated at sites where oryx (*Oryx gazella*) have urinated, thus preventing the collapse of the tunnel mouth. In areas where the terrain is not conducive to burrowing, animals will seek shelter amongst, or below, rocks and in crevices.

The widespread hyraxes (*Procavia* and *Heterohyrax* spp.) feed during the cooler morning and late afternoon hours but shelter from the heat of the day and the cold nights deep amongst insulating rocks. There are many small rodents and several insectivores, including a number of elephant shrews (*Elephantulus* spp.), which use rock shelters. Most species are nocturnal but the elephant shrews frequently forage for insects during the day. They wait in the shade of the rocks, darting out to capture an unsuspecting beetle or grasshopper

Below left: *Many species of aloes occur in the drylands of Africa. This is a tree aloe,* Aloe pillansii. **Above:** *The springbok* Antidorcas marsupialis *is the only gazelle occurring in the southern drylands.* **Below right:** *Temminck's courser* Cursorius temminckii.

and rushing back to devour it under cover. Even these delightful animals have to penetrate deep into the crevices during the hottest hours.

Many species of reptiles and invertebrates also escape heat and loss of body moisture by burrowing, or living amongst rocks, but they have the added advantage of having hard, impermeable outer body coverings that help to minimise water loss. Many of the flightless tenebrionid beetles occurring in drylands have added "insurance" against water loss. They produce waxy secretions that serve not only to keep moisture in the body but also to reflect solar radiation. The Namib is believed to have more species of wax-producing tenebrionids than any other desert. Some beetles have very long legs and by "stilting", that is raising themselves above the ground surface, they can minimise contact with the hot sand. Mention should be made here of a number of sand dune dwelling tenebrionid beetle species that have evolved to make the maximum use of the Namib fogs. The "head-standing" species *Onymacris unguicularis* is diurnal, burrowing under the sand at night, but as the heavier fogs usually occur during the early morning hours they have to make their way laboriously to the top of the dune slipface. They

then turn to face into the fog-laden wind, with the body raised in the rear so that the water droplets run down to the mouth. Species in the genus *Lepidochora* excavate shallow trenches in the sand which lie perpendicular to the fog-bearing winds, with the ridges on either side of the trench absorbing more moisture than the surrounding sands. They then return down the trench extracting moisture from the ridges.

Other species of animals do not need to drink but obtain sufficient moisture from their food, while many excrete wastes that are very concentrated so little body water is lost. Kidneys of many desert-dwelling mammals are able to concentrate urine very efficiently and thus reduce the amount of water lost. During the digestion processes excess amino acids are broken down to produce ammonia, which is toxic if retained in the body, so it is combined with other substances to produce harmless urea or uric acid. In the case of birds, insects and most reptiles uric acid is crystallised in the body, further preventing the loss of essential water.

Many species of birds migrate out of areas during periods of climatic extremes, which in terms of Africa's drylands means high temperatures and drought. In times of rain and food abundance large numbers of certain bird species move in from the desert fringes, with these movements being less dramatic in drylands receiving higher rainfall and with better vegetation cover. Most species that are not migratory usually stay within flying distance of water, such as the larks, finch-larks, bustards and the sandgrouse. The sandgrouse species are regular drinkers, usually in the morning and late afternoon (at least one species drinks after sunset), and great numbers may be observed at these times. As sandgrouse frequently nest away from sources of water, males slake their thirst and then soak their breast feathers so they can carry the water back to the chicks. The ostrich (*Struthio camelus*) occurs in all African drylands and it has evolved to be able to drink very salty water where nothing else is available. As in the case of seabirds, the ostrich has a specialised nasal gland that excretes excess salts.

Many large mammals, such as the antelope, living in the drylands rely on their mobility to migrate to areas of greater water and food availability. The oryx (*Oryx gazella*) migrates from areas of shortage to areas where there is fresh plant growth stimulated by rain, but it has also evolved to tolerate high body temperatures, a process known as adaptive heterothermy. This permits a mammal, which normally maintains a constant body temperature, to allow its body temperature to fluctuate in response to environmental pressures. The oryx can tolerate high body temperatures as the temperature of its brain is kept at a lower and more constant level than that of the rest of the body. A network of blood vessels lies

Below: *A lioness* (Panthera leo) *attacking an oryx* (Oryx gazella) *at the edge of a waterhole.*

SANDGROUSE

The sandgrouse, of which 12 of the known species occur in the drylands of Africa, are true desert dwellers. They penetrate even the driest and harshest areas but will fly considerable distances to areas where rain has fallen to exploit short-lived food sources – primarily seeds but also insects such as termites. All species are well camouflaged, which serves to keep them hidden from predators when they are on the ground. They have to drink regularly and when moving between the feeding grounds and waterholes they fly high and rapidly. The males of several species soak the breast feathers in water to carry a limited supply back to the chicks. Some species have relatively limited distributions but others, such as the yellow-throated sandgrouse (Pterocles gutteralis), *have wider ranges. The latter species occurs from the Red Sea in Eritrea to the Kalahari.*

Right: *A male black-faced sandgrouse,* Pterocles decoratus, *showing its handsome plumage.*

below the brain and as the animal pants blood in the nasal sinuses is cooled. An exchange of heat takes place between the veins and arteries so that blood entering the brain is several degrees cooler than in the rest of the body.

A number of invertebrates and some amphibians are able to make use of short-lived (often lasting only a few days) rainwater pools in the drylands. But to ensure that they can develop and breed they have evolved amazingly rapid life-cycles. A number of shrimp-like crustaceans, for example members of the genus *Triops*, lay eggs which can resist dessication and lie dormant for long periods below the surface in shallow depressions that collect water during rain showers. As soon as the water reaches the eggs the next generation must mature and lay eggs before the water evaporates. A small toad, *Bufo vertebralis*, inhabits the inselbergs of the Namib Desert, spending most of its life in deep rock crevices. When the shallow depressions fill with water they emerge to mate and lay their strings of eggs. From hatching to the emergence of the toadlets takes barely two weeks and during this time they have to withstand water temperatures that would kill the tadpoles of many other amphibian species. The largest frog inhabiting Africa's drylands is the bullfrog *Pyxicephalus adspersus* and it survives between rainy seasons by excavating itself an underground cavern and secreting a membranous slime-cocoon which ensures that moisture is not lost. It can remain in this state, without feeding, for several seasons.

DRYLAND MAMMALS

A surprising number of antelope species occur in the African drylands and most of these undertake short- and long-distance migrations in search of fresh pastures. The oryx (*Oryx gazella*) is still fairly abundant in the Namib and Kalahari deserts but two sub-species, the fringe-eared oryx and beisa oryx, which occur in the Horn region, Kenya and north-eastern Tanzania, have been greatly depleted in numbers and range. They are handsome animals characterised by long, pointed horns in both sexes. They are gregarious, living together in small herds, but much larger numbers may come together when moving to fresh pastures. Herds may consist of animals of both sexes and all ages but herds of only cows and calves are also common. Solitary bulls are frequently encountered. Although these animals are predominantly grazers they will also browse, and when available they will eat wild fruits, such as the nara in the Namib and tsamma melons in the Kalahari. During dry periods these fruits are an important source of moisture for many species. Two closely related species, the scimitar-horned oryx (*Oryx dammah*) and the addax (*Addax nasomaculatus*), once ranged widely in the Sahara and the Sahel but both species have been brought to the brink of extinction and only small, isolated populations survive. They have had to compete with ever-growing herds of domestic animals for grazing and have been unable to withstand the pressures of uncontrolled hunt-

ing. The addax is one of the best adapted of all antelope to desert survival.

A group of antelope that are well represented in the arid regions of Africa are the gazelles, but many species have been greatly reduced in numbers. Probably the most abundant is the springbok (*Antidorcas marsupialis*), the only species to occur in the South-west Arid Zone. Springbok once crossed the great arid plains of southern Africa in vast herds, said to have numbered in the millions, in search of food. But today the fencing of farmland and extensive hunting have put an end to these great migrations. Movements of herds of several thousand animals can still be observed, most notably in the Kalahari. Remnant populations of the red-fronted gazelle (*Gazella rufifrons*), Cuvier's gazelle (*G. cuvieri*), Speke's gazelle (*G. spekei*), dorcas gazelle (*G. dorcas*) and slender-horned gazelle (*G. leptoceros*) may still be encountered in isolated parts of the Sahara and Sahel but the long-term survival of most of these species outside well protected conservation areas is doubtful. Two species of arid-area antelope are only found in the desert lands of the Horn of Africa: the thorn-scrub dwelling dibatag (*Ammodorcas clarkei*) and the beira (*Dorcatragus megalotis*). Little is known of the behaviour of either species and the same applies to the endangered hirola (*Beatragus hunteri*), which has a population of some 2 000 in north-eastern Kenya and an unknown number surviving in southern Somalia. The gerenuk, or giraffe-necked antelope (*Litocranius walleri*), related to the dibatag, occurs widely in thorn scrub in the Horn region and in the drier areas of Kenya and north-eastern Tanzania but also extends marginally into adjacent savanna areas. This amazing antelope has an unusually long neck and legs that enable it to browse at levels not accessible to potentially competing species. To add further to this advantage it frequently stands on its hind legs, using the front legs to pull branches down to its mouth.

There are several species of dik-dik, tiny antelope that are well suited to survival in arid country. Three of these species are restricted to the arid areas of the Horn and adjacent areas to the south and one, Kirk's dik-dik (*Madoqua kirkii*), has separate populations in the South-west Arid Zone and north-eastern Africa. Several subspecies of the bubal, or red, hartebeest (*Alcelaphus buselaphus*) are restricted to the drylands but all have been greatly reduced in numbers, particularly in the drylands north of the equator.

Grevy's zebra (*Equus grevyi*) survives in remnant populations in the dry thorn scrub of northern Kenya but it was once found widely in the adjacent drylands to the north. In the south, Hartmann's zebra (*Equus zebra hartmannae*) lives on the fringes of the Namib Desert. Neither zebra species is specifically adapted to dryland living and they have to drink regularly to survive. A number of larger mammals, such as the giant eland (*Tragelaphus derbianus*), common eland (*Tragelaphus oryx*), greater kudu (*Tragelaphus strepsiceros*), blue wildebeest (*Connochaetes taurinus*), steenbok (*Raphicerus campestris*), elephant (*Loxodonta africana*), hook-lipped rhinoceros (*Diceros bicornis*) and giraffe (*Giraffa camelopardalis*), are not commonly associated with true desert but frequently occupy marginal areas and in some cases enter very arid areas following good rains that promote plant growth. All of Africa's large predators occur in the drylands and on the fringes of the true desert, although in greatly depleted numbers. Two species, the brown hyaena (*Hyaena brunnea*) of the South-west Arid Zone and the striped hyaena (*Hyaena hyaena*) of north-eastern Africa and the Sahara, live mainly in areas of low rainfall. The arid zones are mainly populated, but sparsely so, by smaller carnivores feeding mainly on rodents, reptiles and invertebrates.

Some species, such as the fennec (*Fennecus zerda*) and the sand fox (*Vulpes rüppelli*) are restricted to the Sahara, but in the south, as well as north-eastern Africa, some species (for example the bat-eared fox (*Otocyon megalotis*) spill over into the savanna zone.

Although sometimes called the desert cat, the caracal (*Felis caracal*) also occurs in most other African habitats with the exception of the tropical forests. Many of the smaller rodent species are subject to population "explosions" and "collapses", particularly in drylands. Response to good rains and food abundance can be impressive with each female producing several litters in quick succession to gain maximum benefit from this short-lived bounty.

DRYLAND BIRDS

One noticeable aspect of many desert-dwelling birds is the way the colour of their plumage matches their surroundings. One only has to think of the many species of lark and pipit that favour the drylands and blend so well with their surroundings. This coloration acts as camouflage against potential predators, but paler colours are more beneficial in hot climates. The coursers, such as the double-banded courser (*Rhinoptilus africanus*) of the south-west and north-east, will breed even during the harshest seasons, as will many of the sandgrouse. However, species such as the red-billed quelea (*Quelea quelea*) only breed in large numbers when there have been good rains and grass seed is abundant. Wherever surface water is available large numbers of doves of several species may be seen, particularly in areas receiving more than 100 mm of rain each year, ensuring adequate seed stocks that make up the bulk of their food. Amongst the larger birds to be seen in the drylands are the bustards, the largest being the kori bustard (*Ardeotis kori*) in the south and the houbara bustard (*Chlamydotis undulata*) in the north. Although most species do not normally live in the driest areas, during times of good rains when plant growth results in an abundance of insects, bustards may move in to take advantage. The bustards are normally solitary or seen in small flocks, but after heavy rains in the Kalahari more than 50 kori bustards have been spotted within sight of one another. Several owl species are associated with the African drylands, but none are exclusive to them. Most are pale-coloured forms. They include the barn owl (*Tyto alba*) and spotted eagle-owl (*Bubo africana*), both of which have extensive ranges, and the desert eagle-owl (*Bubo ascalaphus*) of the Sahara. Diurnal raptors are rare in true desert areas but relatively abundant in other drylands. As is the case with many other birds, numbers of certain raptor species may increase in arid areas following good rains, which stimulates the numbers of prey animals such as small rodents, lizards and invertebrates. As the food resource decreases numbers of raptors decrease accordingly. The largest of all birds, the ostrich (*Struthio camelus*), is widely distributed in the drylands although in the Sahara, Sahel and the Horn of Africa they have been severely reduced in numbers by hunting.

Left: *The springbok is the only gazelle found in the southern drylands.* **Below:** *The redcrested bustard (korhaan)* Eupodotis ruficrista *occurs in drylands as well as savanna.*

DRYLAND REPTILES

If any group of vertebrates has succeeded in becoming "master" desert-dwellers it has to be the reptiles. They have colonised the sand dunes and the open plains, the rocky hills and the salt flats. The tortoises are well represented in the drylands, with such species as the "starred" tortoise (*Psammobates oculifer*), "tent" tortoise (*Psammobates tentorius*) and speckled tortoise (*Homopus signatus*) occupying parts of the south-west, although being absent from the true Namib. The large, spurred tortoise (*Geochelone sulcata*) ranges right across the Sahel from the Atlantic to Ethiopia in the east and along the southern fringe of the Sahara. Whereas most of the other tortoises escape the heat of the day by burrowing under the sand or seeking out meagre shade, the spurred tortoise cools its head, neck and forelegs with its saliva when its body temperature goes over 40.5 °C. On the Sahara's northern fringe several species of tortoise occur, including the so-called Greek tortoise (*Testudo graeca*).

The most noticeable of the dryland reptiles are without doubt the lizards. Many species, such as the skinks, lacertids, agamas and cordylids are active during the daylight hours but most of the geckos emerge to hunt their invertebrate prey at night. Lizards, like the tortoises, are poikilothermic – that is their body temperature is controlled by their surroundings and not by their internal body mechanisms. This is why one frequently sees lizards sunning themselves in the early morning. As soon as they have absorbed sufficient heat they begin to forage and carry out their other activities, but as the temperature rises they either burrow in the sand, enter rock crevices or take shelter under other cover, only to emerge once temperatures start to fall. If exposed to high temperatures most reptiles soon die. The lizards belonging to the genus *Uromastix* occur in the northern drylands, primarily the Sahara, and are able to accumulate fat reserves in the tail that can carry them through particularly dry periods. Several species of gecko are also believed to have evolved this survival mechanism. The armadillo lizard (*Cordylus cataphractus*) occurs in rocky areas of south-western South Africa and has a unique method of defence. If caught in the open by a predator it rolls on its back and bites its own tail, leaving its attacker facing an impenetrable ball of sharp, spiny scales. The web-footed gecko (*Palmatogecko rangei*) of the Namib sand dunes "swims" below the sand surface, sheltering there during the day and emerging to hunt on the surface at night.

Snakes are poorly adapted to the high temperatures experienced in the drylands but they escape by sheltering in crevices or under rocks and in some cases by burying themselves in sand. They also benefit from their ability to produce highly concentrated urine and their animal diet, which is high in moisture. Vipers are well represented in African deserts and include the horned viper (*Cerastes cerastes*) of the Sahara, horned adder (*Bitis caudalis*) of the South-west Arid Zone and the side-winding adder (*Bitis peringueyi*) of the Namib sand dunes. Several species of viper that live in sandy areas bury themselves by sweeping the body from side to side and only the eyes and the nostrils remain above the surface. In this way they are protected from the sun and invisible to approaching lizards, or other prey animals. Many species of snakes found in higher rainfall areas also occur in dryland margins but rarely penetrate the driest regions.

Below left: *The rough-scaled gecko* Pachydactylus rugosus, *a species of the South-west Arid Zone.* **Top:** *The Karoo sand snake* Psammophis notostictus. **Above:** *The tenebrionid beetle fauna of the Namib Desert is very rich and many of these beetles have developed amazing survival techniques, particularly in their exploitation of moisture.*

DRYLAND INVERTEBRATES

A wide variety of terrestrial invertebrate species inhabit the drylands. Many of these small animals are highly vulnerable to dessication but they are, to a large extent, able to resist water loss by evaporation because their exoskeletons are impervious to water vapour. Protection is provided by a thin secreted layer of wax that coats the exoskeleton. We have already discussed the importance of this wax layer to a great number of the tenebrionid beetles that inhabit the Namib and other deserts. Although scorpions occur in many different regions of Africa, they are particularly well represented in the drylands. Many escape the midday heat by excavating tunnels, or seeking shelter under rocks, or in rock crevices. Spiders are not as obvious in drylands as they are in, for example, tropical forests because most species are nocturnal

and are seldom seen. Many species live in silk-lined burrows, others shelter below rocks or in grass tussocks.

Two insects that exact a great toll on the vegetation of African drylands and savanna are the desert locust (*Schistocerca gregaria*) and the migratory locust (*Locusta migratoria*). Desert locusts normally live solitary lives but every few years (there is no predictable pattern) shortages of food force these large grasshoppers to gather into areas with green plants. This concentration of locusts stimulates hormone changes in the animals that results in a generation of swarming locusts. The interesting thing is that although they are the same species, the young of the swarming generations differ in nearly all ways from the young of the solitary generations. Once the hoppers of the swarming generation metamorphose into adults they form huge swarms that may extend over hundreds of square kilometres, being carried by winds to areas of low pressure where moisture levels are higher and green plant food more abundant.

Termites are found in virtually all African habitats, including the drylands, and their plant-eating habits have enormous impact on the vegetation, particularly in those species that feed mainly on grass. A study undertaken in the central Namib Desert has shown that grass-eating termites on the plains are responsible for the harvesting of as much as 80 per cent of an entire season's grass crop.

THE FUTURE

Deserts by their very nature usually keep man at bay, but the search for minerals such as oil has exposed vast tracts of dry land to potential exploitation. The extraction of fossil water stocks, particularly in the arid regions of southern Africa and to an ever-increasing extent in the Sahel and the northern and eastern fringes of the Sahara is sure to have medium- and long-term detrimental effects. However, the core of the Sahara and large tracts of the Namib are relatively untouched and will probably remain so for some considerable time. What is most disturbing are the inroads and destruction taking place in the remaining drylands, such as the Sahel, the Horn of Africa, the Kalahari and the interior of South Africa. The cutting of firewood for fuel has resulted in massive destruction of arid woodland to supply energy to an ever-growing human population. In many areas (for example northern Kenya) charcoal is produced for sale to urban populations far away from the arid zones. As the trees are removed and the rest of the vegetation devoured by ever-increasing herds of domestic animals such as goats, sheep, cattle, donkeys and camels, the soils are no longer held in place by plant roots and the grains are blown away or washed away in rare downpours. In many areas where nomads/farmers were forced to regularly move their stock between permanent water-points in the past, the sinking of boreholes has eliminated the need to move so regularly, thus aggravating soil and vegetation destruction by trampling.

Foreign aid and government policies have caused many nomadic peoples to move to fixed settlements, and the areas lying around these settlements become infertile dust-bowls.

The combination of an ever-growing human population, increasing numbers of competing domestic stock, and regional political and military instability has resulted in massive destruction of wildlife in the drylands. The situation is particularly bad in the Sahel, the Horn of Africa and to a lesser extent in the Kalahari. In the Namib and Kalahari there are several large and well managed national parks and other conservation areas that protect many dryland species, but the parks that exist in other areas to the north are poorly funded and controls are minimal.

Hunting of desert ungulates in the Sahara, Sahel and the Horn is particularly severe. This has been aggravated in the recent past by wealthy individuals from the Gulf States visiting countries in the Horn and the eastern regions of the Sahara to hunt gazelles, bustards and other species, often against the laws of the countries involved. The survival of such dryland species as addax, scimitar-horned oryx, several gazelles, wild asses and others is unlikely unless drastic measures are taken to improve their protection within existing conservation areas.

Below: *Great areas of the African drylands and savanna are prone to periodic crippling droughts.*

CHAPTER 3

THE FORESTED LAND

Many different types of forests are scattered across the length and breadth of Africa. The tropical lowland rain forests dominate the Zaïre Basin and spread westwards to the coast and then fringe the Gulf of Guinea until they are halted by the Dahomey Gap. The Dahomey Gap is a 300 km-wide corridor of dry savanna vegetation that extends to the coast of the Gulf of Biafra and runs through Togo, Benin and eastern Ghana. This savanna belt acts as a barrier to the dispersal of many groups of species. The West African or Guinean rain forests fall within just six countries and it has been estimated that as much as 77 per cent of these forests have been destroyed by the actions of man. Most of them now consist of small isolated patches. All of the western rain forests lie within an area some 1 500 km long and 250 km wide. By contrast the Congolean, or Central African, rain forests still cover vast areas, in fact more than three million square kilometres, of which well over half is located in Zaïre. Destruction of this forest is not as pronounced as in West Africa, mainly because of poor or nonexistent access routes and relatively low human population densities. It is clear that the Guinean and Congolean forest blocks were once linked as they have many plant and animal species in common, as well as many that are unique to one or the other. In a relatively narrow but almost continuous belt that fringes the tropical rain forests from Senegal to the shores of Lake Victoria and then in a sweep to the coast in northern Angola is a buffer that separates the savannas from the rain forests. Much of this belt contains a

Background: *The woodland mouse* Grammomys dolichurus.
Above: *The crimson acrea butterfly* Acraea petraea.

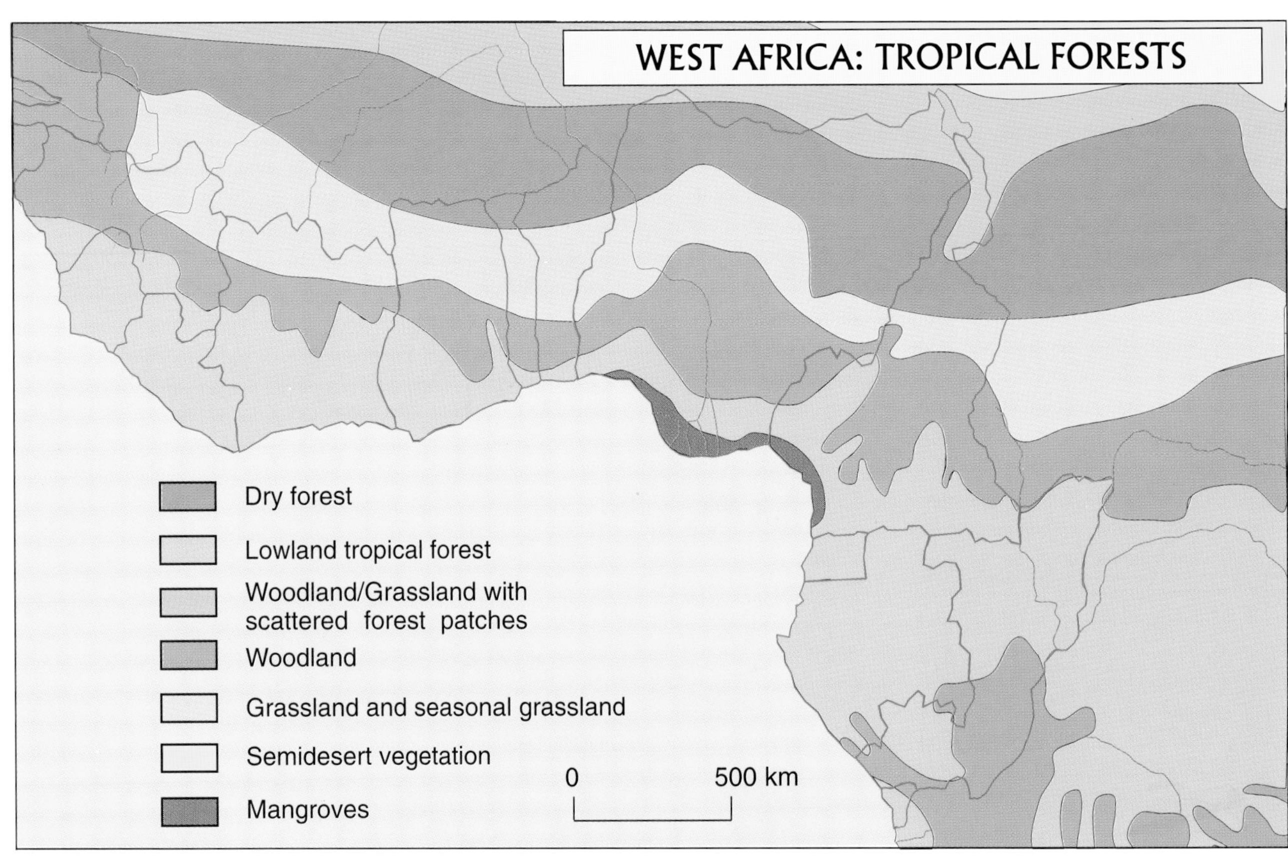
WEST AFRICA: TROPICAL FORESTS
Dry forest
Lowland tropical forest
Woodland/Grassland with scattered forest patches
Woodland
Grassland and seasonal grassland
Semidesert vegetation
Mangroves
0
500 km

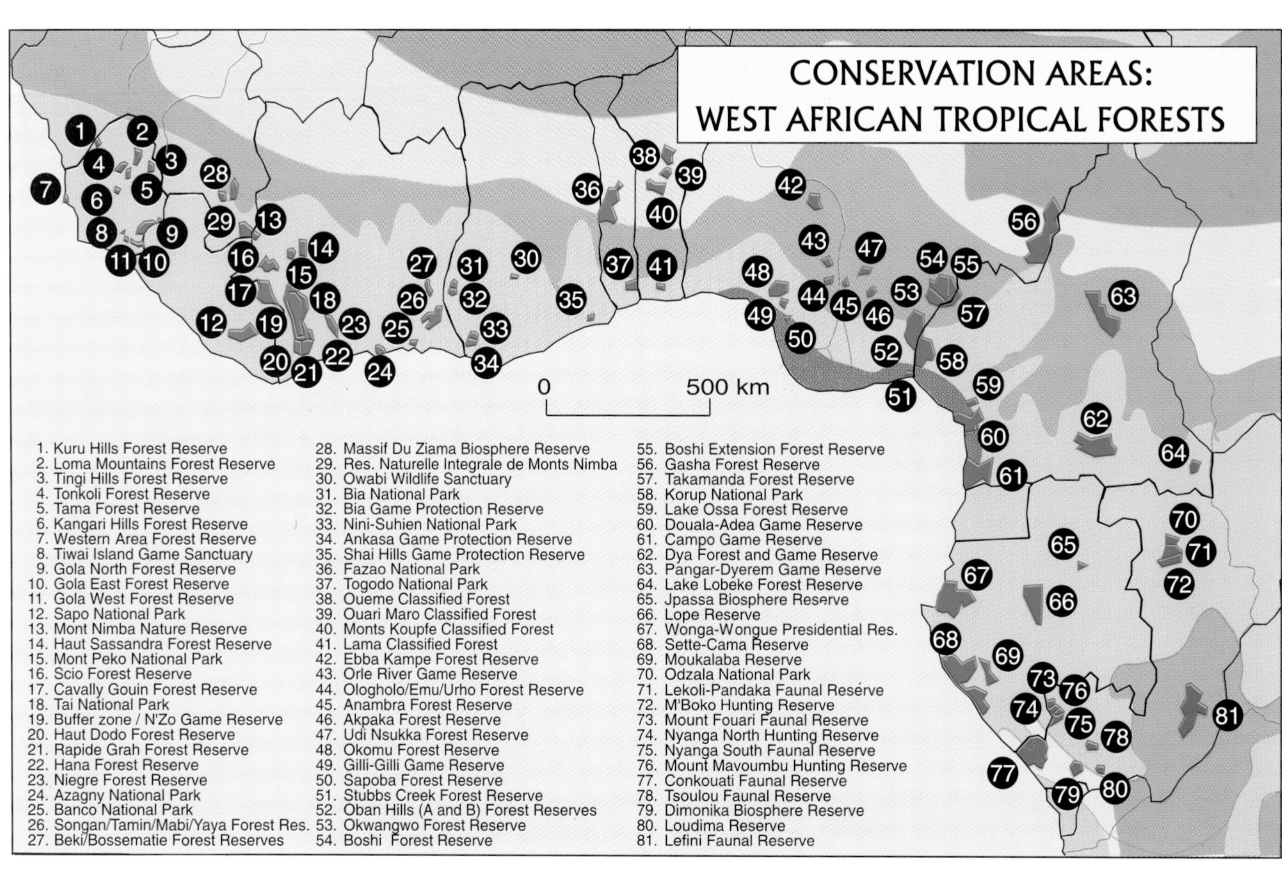
CONSERVATION AREAS: WEST AFRICAN TROPICAL FORESTS
0
500 km
1. Kuru Hills Forest Reserve
2. Loma Mountains Forest Reserve
3. Tingi Hills Forest Reserve
4. Tonkoli Forest Reserve
5. Tama Forest Reserve
6. Kangari Hills Forest Reserve
7. Western Area Forest Reserve
8. Tiwai Island Game Sanctuary
9. Gola North Forest Reserve
10. Gola East Forest Reserve
11. Gola West Forest Reserve
12. Sapo National Park
13. Mont Nimba Nature Reserve
14. Haut Sassandra Forest Reserve
15. Mont Peko National Park
16. Scio Forest Reserve
17. Cavally Gouin Forest Reserve
18. Tai National Park
19. Buffer zone / N'Zo Game Reserve
20. Haut Dodo Forest Reserve
21. Rapide Grah Forest Reserve
22. Hana Forest Reserve
23. Niegre Forest Reserve
24. Azagny National Park
25. Banco National Park
26. Songan/Tamin/Mabi/Yaya Forest Res.
27. Beki/Bossematie Forest Reserves
28. Massif Du Ziama Biosphere Reserve
29. Res. Naturelle Integrale de Monts Nimba
30. Owabi Wildlife Sanctuary
31. Bia National Park
32. Bia Game Protection Reserve
33. Nini-Suhien National Park
34. Ankasa Game Protection Reserve
35. Shai Hills Game Protection Reserve
36. Fazao National Park
37. Togodo National Park
38. Oueme Classified Forest
39. Ouari Maro Classified Forest
40. Monts Koupfe Classified Forest
41. Lama Classified Forest
42. Ebba Kampe Forest Reserve
43. Orle River Game Reserve
44. Ologholo/Emu/Urho Forest Reserve
45. Anambra Forest Reserve
46. Akpaka Forest Reserve
47. Udi Nsukka Forest Reserve
48. Okomu Forest Reserve
49. Gilli-Gilli Game Reserve
50. Sapoba Forest Reserve
51. Stubbs Creek Forest Reserve
52. Oban Hills (A and B) Forest Reserves
53. Okwangwo Forest Reserve
54. Boshi Forest Reserve
55. Boshi Extension Forest Reserve
56. Gasha Forest Reserve
57. Takamanda Forest Reserve
58. Korup National Park
59. Lake Ossa Forest Reserve
60. Douala-Adea Game Reserve
61. Campo Game Reserve
62. Dya Forest and Game Reserve
63. Pangar-Dyerem Game Reserve
64. Lake Lobeke Forest Reserve
65. Jpassa Biosphere Reserve
66. Lope Reserve
67. Wonga-Wongue Presidential Res.
68. Sette-Cama Reserve
69. Moukalaba Reserve
70. Odzala National Park
71. Lekoli-Pandaka Faunal Reserve
72. M'Boko Hunting Reserve
73. Mount Fouari Faunal Reserve
74. Nyanga North Hunting Reserve
75. Nyanga South Faunal Reserve
76. Mount Mavoumbu Hunting Reserve
77. Conkouati Faunal Reserve
78. Tsoulou Faunal Reserve
79. Dimonika Biosphere Reserve
80. Loudima Reserve
81. Lefini Faunal Reserve

mosaic of different forest types interspersed with more open woodland and savanna elements. Tropical montane forests clothe the slopes of many peaks and ranges in eastern Africa, such as those on the Ruwenzoris, Virungas and Mount Elgon, as well as the Cameroon Highlands and those highlands centred on Mount Nimba. There are also montane forests and cloud forests associated with the Ethiopian Highlands, isolates in south-eastern Africa and along the western escarpments of Angola. Small isolated patches of mainly evergreen forest cling to gorges and the more sheltered sites on such mountain ranges as the Drakensberg, Cape Folded Belt and the Soutpansberg in South Africa.

The temperate forest patches of the Atlas Mountains are isolated from the rest of Africa by the great arid expanses of the Sahara Desert and the associated trees have closer affinities to those of Eurasia than of Africa. As with many African forests, the Atlas forests have been greatly modified and in some cases destroyed by the actions of man.

There are vast tracts of woodland associated with many savanna areas but the most extensive and least affected by man are those located in a broad coast-to-coast belt in south-central Africa. These savanna woodlands take on many structures and forms, with patches of tall trees and dense thickets of smaller trees and bushes, liberally interspersed with more open country. Most trees are semi-evergreen or deciduous and leaf-shedding and flowering become synchronised with the clear seasonal climatic changes. In the drier areas the woodlands have a lower diversity of tree species and they gradually phase into the open wood- and grasslands. Another factor that plays a significant role in shaping the species composition and structure of this type of woodland is fire. Frequent fires result in the destruction of many tree species and the area eventually converts to open grassland with widely scattered fire- and drought-resistant trees. There are also the gallery forests, which are largely dominated by evergreen species and grow in relatively narrow belts along rivers in higher rainfall areas. Drier and more open riverine forest and woodland is found along watercourses, usually in association with savanna.

Below: *A flare of colour in dry woodland in western Tanzanian miombo.* **Below right:** *Swamp forest. There are extensive areas of this type of forest in such countries as Zaïre, the Congo Republic and Cameroon. Photo: Penny Meakin* **Bottom:** *The female fruits of* Podocarpus latifolius, *the yellow-wood tree, on the slopes of Mount Kenya.*

Left: *Although many forests are made up of a rich diversity of tree species, Africa also has many "mono-species" forests such as this* Ficus sycomorus *stand.*
Below: *The reed and tree frogs of the genus* Hyperolius *are abundant in African marshlands and many tropical lowland forests. This beautiful example was photographed in the Kibale Forest of western Uganda.*

Another forest form is restricted to the tidal-washed mangrove swamps of the Atlantic and Indian ocean coastlines. These forests are mainly restricted to sheltered areas of the coast and river estuaries where wave action is not so aggressive. Tree diversity is very small (six species in the west and nine in the east) and none are shared between the two coastlines; those on the west coast have greater affinities to the mangroves of the east coast of South America than with eastern African forms. All mangrove tree species have evolved adaptations to living in zones of high salinity. Mangroves are found in patches from Senegal to northern Angola on the west coast, and on the east coast the principal forests reach from Kenya to the KwaZulu/Natal province of South Africa. The largest block lies on the delta of the Niger River and covers an estimated 500 000 ha.

Some patches of trees or tree-like plants are frequently referred to as forests, but these are in fact little more than woodland patches. They include stands of tree *Euphorbias*, such as one located in Lake Nakuru National Park in Kenya.

THE TROPICAL RAIN FORESTS

The tropical rain forests are the richest environments on the land surface of the earth, offering ideal conditions for the vast array of plants and animals that inhabit their warm, moist depths. The African tropical forests are not as species-rich as those of South America and South-east Asia, but nevertheless the diversity is awesome. Tropical rain forests first began to form at the beginning of the Cretaceous era some 140 million years ago, when most of the world had either a tropical or subtropical climate. But the forests of the African tropics are relatively young when seen in relation to the geological timetable. In fact the tropical lowland forests of Africa are probably little more than 10 000 years old.

Before the last Ice Age the tropical rain forest covered a much larger area than it does today. The glacial advance reached its peak about 18 000

THE TURACOS

The turacos, touracos, loeries, louries or plantain-eaters as they are variously called, are predominantly forest birds although a few species live in woodland savanna. Estimates on the total number of species vary but probably 22 species can be recognised. They are fairly large birds with lengths ranging from 380 mm to 635 mm, with long broad tails, short, rounded wings and distinct head crests in most species. The beaks are short and stubby and often brightly coloured. They share one peculiarity with the owls and the ospreys and that is the ability to direct the outer toe either backwards or forwards. Turacos climb and run along branches with the agility of squirrels but their flight is relatively weak. These impressive birds are usually noisy and active but because of the nature of their forest habitat they are difficult to observe. The nest usually resembles the flimsy structure constructed by the doves and pigeons, and two to three eggs are usual. Some ten days after hatching the fledglings crawl out onto a branch away from the nest until they are ready to fly. All species feed predominantly on fruit but insects are also eaten; the young are fed regurgitated fruit-pulp. Although most species have fairly extensive distribution ranges, a few are restricted to very small areas.

Below: *The Knysna turaco,* Tauraco corythraix.

years ago, and much of the tropical rain forest was displaced by deciduous forests and woodlands. The rain forests retreated to a few isolated refuges separated from each other by areas of unsuitable habitat. With rises in global temperature the northern ice-cap began its retreat and the isolated forest "islands" expanded into previously inhospitable areas. The present species composition and structure of these tropical forests is primarily a result of recolonisation and recent evolution which has taken place over the past 10 000 years. The fact that these Pleistocene climatic changes were more severe in Africa than in South America and South-east Asia helps to explain why African forests have a poorer diversity of animal and plant species.

What factors make the tropical forests so species-rich? Life in these equatorial greenhouses is powered by two primary climatic factors: abundant and year-round rainfall, and high temperatures which show little fluctuation either on a day-to-night basis or from month to month. The drenching rains fall throughout the year in a narrow belt running just four degrees to the north and south of the equator, and it is in this latitudinal strip that the greatest diversity of life forms live. This high rainfall is delivered by the moist, unstable equatorial maritime winds that arise over the Atlantic and Indian oceans. The further one moves away from this "belt of plenty" the greater the decrease in the height, density and complexity of the forest, until it eventually merges with the great savanna plains. The daily temperature range is narrow because cloud cover is common and the water vapour in the air prevents excessive loss of heat by radiation at night. High humidity levels ensure that the evaporation rate is greatly reduced. Rain forest soils tend to be relatively infertile as a result of the rapid breakdown of humus and leaching of minerals and organic salts by heavy rains.

THE FOREST ZONES

The multi-faceted botanical high-rise of the tropical climax forest consists of a number of distinct layers, or strata, of vegetation. We can divide the space between the forest floor and the open sky into roughly five zones, each occupied by its own range of plant species. If we begin our exploration on the forest floor we first encounter a thin layer of humus – debris that has fallen from the shrubs and trees and animals' droppings and urine, which is rapidly processed by a host of micro-organisms, invertebrates and fungi for re-use as nutrients by forest plants. In this way such nutrients as nitrogen and phosphorus re-enter the soil and are drawn up again by the tree roots and returned to the canopy. The first layer of green plants we encounter are the herbs and tree seedlings, which receive little sunlight, followed by the shrub layer which reaches an average of 3 m above the forest floor. Then there is a layer of small trees with long and narrow crowns enabling each plant to make the most of feeble light, and then a continuous closed canopy of tall trees that have their

crowns exposed to the open air, thus preventing sunlight reaching the lower layers and the forest floor. Rising above the canopy, at scattered intervals, are the so-called emergent trees with their crowns thrusting beyond the canopy. Of course this stratification is not always clearly defined, but the strata described here are indicative of climax tropical lowland forest. The tree canopy is the driving force behind the tropical forest, where 90 per cent of photosynthesis takes place. Most of the canopy trees have flattened crowns and tall, smooth trunks which only bear large horizontal branches towards their upper limits. Many of the trees are broad-leaved evergreens with leaves that are smooth and narrowed towards their tips to allow rainwater to run off rapidly. This prevents the trees from getting waterlogged and weighed down by water to such an extent that branches might snap off. The trunks of most of the trees have smooth bark which allows water to flow freely to the forest floor. The canopy is the zone that is most exposed to outside influences, as the

Above left: Kniphofia thomsonii *in mountain cloud forest on Mount Kenya.* **Top:** *Lowland forest viewed from a clearing. Many of these glades are maintained by the feeding of species such as elephants, or by slash-and-burn agriculture.* **Above:** *A stream passing through a forest clearing created and kept clear by man.*

branches are whipped by strong winds and exposure to solar radiation results in evaporation loss equal to that experienced on the grassland savannas. Temperatures here are frequently 10 °C higher than those experienced on the forest floor during the day, but canopy temperatures are slightly lower than those at ground level at night.

When a canopy forest tree dies, rots and falls, or an elephant feeding on lianas dislodges a rotting branch, lightning strikes and kills a tree or a shallow-rooted tree is dislodged and toppled by strong wind, sunlight floods through to the normally darkened forest floor and encourages the rapid growth of herbaceous plants and shrubs previously suppressed by lack of sunlight, as well as species differing from those found in the surrounding forest. In these glades the temperature of the forest floor rises, evaporation increases and humidity falls so that the humus layer dries out. These changes in conditions encourage plant growth which in turn attracts many species of invertebrates and other animals which thrive in the glades. In fact many species are found only in these sun-bathed clearings. After a few months fast-growing and relatively short-lived pioneer trees start to grow and eventually form their own canopy far below the one created by the forest giants. The low canopy, casting its shadow over the forest floor, recreates the conditions of shade and temperature that trigger the germination of the seeds of the mature forest trees. These giants push steadily upwards until eventually their crowns join those of the surrounding forest. This process may take more than 100 years.

Another vegetation zone which greatly enriches the diversity of the tropical rain forests is the one formed by the epiphytic plants. Epiphytes are non-parasitic plants that grow on the trunks and branches of the forest trees, often in great profusion. They include species from such groups as the orchids, ferns and seedlings of strangler figs. Apart from the vascular plants there are also dense beds of mosses and lichens, and all form an incredibly rich garden in the sky. The epiphytes make a considerable contribution to the productivity of the forest by ensnaring solar energy and increasing photosynthesis levels, filtering nutrients out of the atmosphere, contributing to the humus layer far below and providing habitats for a vast and complex array of invertebrates and some small vertebrates, including tree frogs.

Trees in the rain forests have many characteristics that distinguish them from trees growing elsewhere. We have already mentioned that most canopy species have leathery leaves with pointed "drip-tips" to allow water to run off rapidly, and smooth bark which serves the same purpose. Most of the large forest trees have shallow root systems that would normally leave them vulnerable to toppling during heavy storms, but many have minimised this risk by evolving massive buttress roots which support the tall trunks. Two such species are the greenheart (*Piptadenia africana*) and the afara (*Terminalia superba*). Some trees, particularly in swamp forest, have stilt roots which grow at an angle from the lower part of the trunk and act as supports. Many of the smaller forest trees are cauliflorous. This means

they have flowers and fruits growing directly from the branches and trunk, unlike the "typical" tree which bears its flowers and fruits at the tips of slender twigs, making it very difficult for heavier animals to reach them. Thus forest trees have the advantage of making their flowers and fruits accessible to a much wider range of pollinators and animals who act as unwitting transporters of seeds after eating the fruits.

The strangler figs (*Ficus* spp.) are common and widespread in the rain forests, as well as other forested areas, and they have evolved a novel way of ensuring their survival amongst the luxuriant growth. The fruits of these trees are eaten by many species of birds, fruit bats and monkeys, and the seeds pass through the gut. If they lodge in a tree fork or among one of the epiphytic gardens they germinate. The seedling pushes out long roots which eventually reach the forest floor, but during the long downward journey they wrap themselves around the trunk of the host tree. As the strangler grows it eventually engulfs the unfortunate host, killing it, and the now-independent fig can support itself. These trees are usually hollow and can grow to great sizes.

Another plant that draws the observer to have a closer look is the liana, commonly referred to as the "monkey rope", which provided the legendary Tarzan with his jungle transportation. There are many species of lianas and numerous other creeping and climbing plants in the forests that receive relatively high rainfall. The seeds germinate on the forest

Below left: *The grey parrot* Psittacus erithacus. **Above left:** *The blue duiker* Cephalophus monticola. **Above:** *The red river hog* Potamochoerus porcus *occurs widely within the tropical lowland forests of central and western Africa.* **Right:** *Leopards* (Panthera pardus) *occur in most major African habitats, with the exception of true desert.*

floor and the young plant makes its way towards the canopy where many individuals may intertwine and cause dense tangles. These tangles may become too heavy for a branch to support and it will break, crashing to the forest floor.

MAMMALS OF THE RAIN FOREST

The tropical rain forests of Africa harbour a rich mammal fauna, mainly smaller species that can easily make their way through the forest tangles and thickets. There are, however, a few large species that deserve mention, several of which were only revealed to science within the last 100 years or so. The largest is the forest elephant (*Loxodonta africana cyclotis*), considerably smaller than its savanna-dwelling cousin, with narrower, downpointed tusks and smaller ears, as outward-pointing tusks and large ears would hinder its movement through the foliage. It is believed that the savanna elephant was originally a forest-dweller that was able to occupy the more open habitats when the potential (and now extinct) competitor *Elephas recki* disappeared from the scene. Little is known about the behaviour of the forest elephant because of the nature of its habitat, but it is known that their home ranges are much smaller than those of savanna animals because food is much more abundant and less effort is required to obtain it. The forest elephants play a crucial role in the health of their living space; their feeding serves to open glades and in some cases keep areas permanently clear, allowing the survival of many other plant and animal species. They are also important dispersers of seeds and some plants have evolved seeds that are streamlined so as to ensure easy passage through the elephant's gut. When the elephants are

THE FOREST DUIKERS

Although there is no absolute certainty, it is currently accepted that there are 16 species of "forest" dwelling duiker belonging to the genus Cephalophus. *The doubt arises because some species are very poorly known and some now classed as subspecies may in fact qualify for full species status when further research is undertaken. Some species have been divided into many subspecies; for example 16 are currently listed for the blue duiker. The duikers that occupy the forests and their margins range in size from the yellow-backed duiker* (Cephalophus sylvicultur) *at up to 80 kg, to the diminutive 4 kg blue duiker* (Cephalophus monticola). *In general they are short-legged antelope, with hind legs longer than the front, with stubby, backward-pointing horns that are often totally or largely hidden by a head crest, and a somewhat hunchbacked appearance. In fact the generic name refers to the crest of hairs on the top of the head. Appearance is similar in both sexes. The duikers have the largest brains, relative to body size, of all antelope. Because of the nature of their chosen habitats the duikers are poorly known but most are believed to be solitary, although at least in some species a pair may defend a mutually held territory against intruders of the same species. All of the duikers have well developed preorbital scent-glands, from which a secretion is extruded through a series of pores. These antelope mark regularly and it is believed that this serves a territorial function. In the case of the blue duiker it appears as if they are monogamous, pairing for life and sharing a home range of between two and four hectares. However, the pair spend little time together and they often feed and rest at different times. All duiker produce a single lamb which remains hidden during the first few weeks after birth.*

Some species, such as the blue duiker, appear to be predominantly diurnal, whereas the bay duiker (Cephalophus dorsalis) *is believed to be nocturnal; the yellow-backed duiker may be active at any time. Duikers feed mainly on fallen fruits, leaves, shoots, buds, seeds, bark and fungi, but are unique amongst antelope in that they will readily take insects, chicks of ground-nesting birds, small mammals and even carrion.*

The importance of duiker meat to the rural and urban human populations in the African tropics is immense. In one six-week period the markets in the Zaïrean city of Bukavu sold approximately 46 000 kg of game meat, of which 37 per cent was antelope, the bulk from duiker species. A similar study undertaken in one area of Nigeria revealed that 85 per cent of "bushmeat" samples contained blue duiker.

Below: *The red duiker* Cephalophus natalensis.

killed or forced away from an area, the long-term survival of many of the forest components is threatened and diversity diminishes. No one knows for certain how many elephants survive in the rain forests, but certainly the greatest number live in the Congolean forest block. Probably the largest group in the fragmented Guinean forests consists of about 1 000 individuals in the Tai National Park in the Ivory Coast.

Another large species that occupies both the forest and the savanna is the buffalo (*Syncerus caffer*). As with the elephant the red, or forest, buffalo (*Syncus caffer nanus*) is noticeably smaller than those animals occupying more open habitats, the horns are shorter and more compact and overall body colour ranges from reddish-brown to black. Although they graze in clearings and forest fringes, they take a high percentage of browse, unlike the savanna animals which are almost exclusively grazers.

Restricted to the Ituri Forest and the vicinity of the Semliki River in north-eastern Zaïre is one of Africa's strangest and most recently discovered large ungulate, the okapi (*Okapia johnstoni*). A forest-dwelling relative of the giraffe, it has a shoulder height averaging 1.6 m, with the back angled down towards the rump. The neck is shorter in relation to that of the giraffe but still longer than those of many other browsers, and it has a very long tongue (about 35 cm), further aiding it in reaching high vegetation. Reports of the animal had been filtering out of the Congo (Zaïre) for many years but it was only in 1900 that the first material evidence of its existence came to light. In some areas they occur in fairly high densities, an indication of the abundance of food, which can be reached at heights exceeding 2 m. Even more recently, in 1904, another large, widespread inhabitant of the rain forests became known to the outside world: the giant forest hog (*Hylochoerus meinertzhageni*). This is the largest wild pig in the world, with a weight of up to 235 kg, and apart from inhabiting the lowland rain forests it also occurs in a number of montane rain forests in East Africa. Giant forest hogs do most of their feeding in glades and clearings, and they live together in sounders.

The only other members of the pig family living in forests are the bushpig (*Potamochoerus larvatus*), with the red river hog (*Potamochoerus porcus*) being prevalent in the rain forests. Bushpigs and red river hogs use their hard snouts to root for rhizomes, bulbs and tubers but they also browse and eat fungus and fallen fruits. They will even take animal food when it is available. One other large ungulate, the bongo (*Boocercus euryceros*) occurs throughout the lowland rain forests as well as in small numbers on Mount Kenya. A common and widespread antelope in many forest and woodland types is the bushbuck (*Tragelaphus scriptus*) which is found in suitable habitats throughout Africa. The pygmy hippopotamus (*Choeropsis liberiensis*) is restricted to the Guinean rain forests and may still survive in the forests of the Niger Delta but numbers are greatly reduced as a result of hunting and habitat loss.

Above: *The dwarf galago* Galago demidovii; *this species is restricted to the lowland tropical forests of central and western Africa. Photo: Harry van Rompaey*

Below: *The common chimpanzee* (Pan troglodytes) *is hunted as a source of meat in some areas, as well as being captured for the "underground" market in pets and for medical research. One of the greatest threats chimpanzees face, however, is loss and disturbance of habitat.*

The most successful and abundant of the rain forest antelope are the duikers (Subfamily **Cephalophinae**). They range in size from the 80 kg yellow-backed duiker (*Cephalophus sylvicultur*), which occurs throughout the lowland rain forests, extending southwards into drier forest types, to the tiny blue duiker (*Cephalophus monticola*), which averages only 4 kg in weight. The blue duiker occurs at amazingly high densities in areas with ideal conditions. For example, in one study undertaken in Gabon it was estimated there were 70 of these animals per square kilometre. Only one duiker species dwells outside forests, with the remaining 16 species inhabiting forest and dense woodland. The large Jentink's duiker (*Cephalophus jentinki*), with its dark head, neck and shoulders and silvery-grey body, has a very limited distribution within the Guinean forests. A small, attractive member of this group, also restricted to the western rain forests, is the zebra duiker (*Cephalophus zebra*), which takes its name from the series of dark lines marking its back. The duikers feed mainly on fallen fruit, leaves, fungi and other plant food, but they also take animal food when available. The duikers form a very important source of protein for people living in and around the lowland rain forests and very large numbers are killed. Despite this pressure, and where forests are little affected by man, a few species still survive at high densities. The smallest of all ungulates, the pygmy antelope (*Neotragus pygmaeus*), shares its forest floor home with the duikers in the West African forests, where it can reach high population densities. A closely related but slightly larger species, the dwarf antelope (*Neotragus batesi*), has a wide distribution in the Congolean rain forests.

The rain forests and other dense forests only have one large predator, the highly successful leopard (*Panthera pardus*). In fact this cat occupies virtually all African habitats, except true deserts. Most of their hunting is done on the ground but they are also agile climbers, and they feed on a broad spectrum of prey animals, which helps to explain their success. They have been known to take several primate species including chimpanzees (*Pan troglodytes*) and young gorillas (*Gorilla gorilla*), but most of their prey comprises smaller monkeys, duikers, bushbuck, bushpig and probably giant forest hog, tree hyraxes (*Dendrohyrax* spp.) and a variety of birds and reptiles. The only other felid species living in the rain forest is the rarely seen golden cat (*Felis aurata*), which feeds on rodents, duikers and other small mammals. It probably also takes birds when the opportunity arises.

Rivers that flow through the rain forest in the Congolean region are home to the Congo clawless otter (*Aonyx congica*), the largest of Africa's four otter species. The much more widespread spotted-necked otter (*Lutra maculicollis*) also occupies rivers and other water bodies both within and outside forests. A rare and poorly known carnivore that occurs along eastern rain forest streams is the fishing genet (*Osbornictis piscivora*). This small animal has adapted to catching and feeding on fish and frogs where few other predators or piscivorous birds live. The genets, (*Genetta* spp.), are agile, long-bodied and -tailed carnivores, and several species are recognised. They hunt on the forest floor as well as the trees. Two similar carnivores which spend most of their time hunting in the trees are the African linsang (*Poiana richardsoni*) and the tree civet (*Nandinia binotata*). There is one small carnivore restricted to a tiny area of rain forest in West Africa which carries the name of the country it occupies: the Liberian mongoose (*Liberiictis kuhni*). For many years it was only known from a few skulls and even today scientists have only been able to examine one live animal. The few observations in the wild indicate that it is a social species, as are the members of the mongoose group known as the cusimanse (*Crossarachus obscurus*).

THE FOREST PRIMATES

One group of mammals which is particularly well represented in the rain forests, and in other categories of forests, is the primates. Understandably, this group has captured the attention of scientists and the public alike because human beings also belong to this diverse and interesting group. Some of the studies undertaken on chimpanzees and gorillas constitute the longest continuous research programmes on mammals that have ever been undertaken. The African tropical rain forests are home to one of the most diverse primate communities on earth, with approximately 50 species. Many species are poorly known and scientists are not sure at this stage whether some subspecies or races should in fact be given full species status. In rain forests that have not been too disturbed by man it is sometimes possible to record between seven and ten "true" monkeys, one or two apes (gorilla, chimpanzees and bonobos) and up to five prosimians (dominated by the bushbabies). The Guinean forests have eight endemic primates and a number shared with the forests to

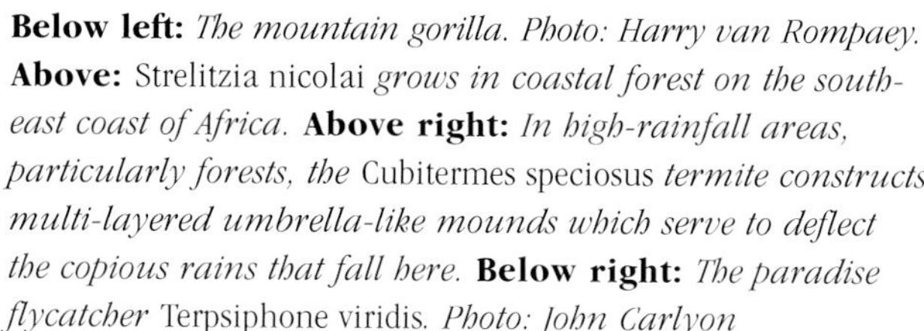

Below left: *The mountain gorilla. Photo: Harry van Rompaey.* **Above:** Strelitzia nicolai *grows in coastal forest on the south-east coast of Africa.* **Above right:** *In high-rainfall areas, particularly forests, the* Cubitermes speciosus *termite constructs multi-layered umbrella-like mounds which serve to deflect the copious rains that fall here.* **Below right:** *The paradise flycatcher* Terpsiphone viridis. *Photo: John Carlyon*

the east of the Dahomey Gap. The country with the greatest primate diversity is Zaïre, which has a total of 32 species and 33 if one includes man. The Ivory Coast, with 17 species, has the greatest diversity within the West African forests.

We will start this overview of the primates with a brief look at the largest of all primates, the gorilla, of which three races are recognised and some authorities believe a fourth warrants recognition. There are, however, two principal divisions: the fairly numerous lowland gorilla, which occurs in two separate populations, the western *Gorilla g. gorilla* and the eastern *G. g. graueri*, and the mountain gorilla (*G. g. beringei*), which is restricted to the forests in the vicinity of the Virunga volcanoes. The western lowland gorilla is still quite common but the eastern lowland form probably does not number more than 5 000 animals. The mountain race is in an extremely precarious position with as few as 600 individuals. Although rumours of a large man-like ape wandering the tropical forests of Africa were in circulation for many years it was only in 1847 in a report in the *Boston Journal of Natural History* that the first scientific description of the gorilla was given. Until very recently the bulk of all research work was done on the endangered mountain race, mainly because they live in the most accessible of the gorilla habitats. Many western lowland gorillas live in habitats that are distinctly unpleasant for the researcher, including swamp forests and dense undergrowth.

Gorillas are large, with adult males weighing up to 180 kg and having a standing height of about 1.7 m. The females are considerably smaller. These mighty primates are strictly diurnal and only start to stir from their slumbers at about six in the morning. By about six in the evening they are lying up again in self-constructed nests. Females and youngsters usually make nests in the trees out of bent branches and leaves but large males, because of their great weight, usually construct nests from plant debris on the ground. Gorillas sleep at different sites every night. They live in groups of two to 30 individuals, with an average of 16 for the mountain race. The lowland animals tend to run in slightly smaller groups. These groups are very stable and each is dominated by a large silverback male. The name refers to the silver-grey hairs that cover the backs of mature males. Other silverbacks may briefly associate with a group but soon move on and may establish a home range adjacent to the former group. Here the male will try to attract females. Nearly all female gorillas leave their group on reaching maturity and soon join a new group or link up with a solitary silverback.

As with many animal species living in the tropical forests, there is no recognisable birth season for gorillas. A female first gives birth to a single young (weighing about 2 kg) from about eight years of age, but it takes a male about 11 years to reach silverback status. Each group range tends to be quite small – in one study of mountain gorillas ranges averaged eight square kilometres in size. Ranges can vary considerably, however, according to the abundance of food and pressures put on the gorillas by human activities. Because of the great abundance of food, including leaves, shoots and stems, they only need to cover a few hundred metres a day. In swamp forests they will wade into the water to harvest great clumps of water weeds. The lighter youngsters and occasionally females will climb into the canopy to feed, but the heavier adults feed mostly on the forest floor. When feeding, gorillas strongly favour the glades and patches of secondary forest where the bulk of their food plants grow. Many of these glades are created by forest elephants but some old patches were once cleared by man for growing crops. After they have rested for a few years they provide suitable feeding grounds for the gorillas. Studies on the mountain gorillas have shown that they feed in the glades for most of the year, but when the bamboo is pushing out new shoots some groups feed almost exclusively on this seasonal windfall.

The second largest African primate, the common chimpanzee (*Pan troglodytes*), occurs in rain forests north and east of the Zaïre (Congo) River and then westwards to the Dahomey Gap. There is a separate and highly fragmented population in the forests of West Africa. As with the gorilla there are three recognised races, with a total of more than 200 000 individuals surviving in the wild. Although most chimpanzees live in rain forest they do extend into forest-savanna mosaics and montane forests up to 3 000 m.

Populations live in loosely organised groups of some 30 to 80 animals that lack definite leadership and usually form several separate subgroups. These are not stable and there is considerable movement between groups. Most subgroups have between two and 10 individuals but in one study almost half contained between two and four animals. They have a much broader diet than the gorilla, taking fruit, leaves, seeds, flowers, bark, insects, birds' eggs and meat. Active hunting has been recorded and includes smaller monkeys (there are a few records of cannibalism), young forest antelope, birds and reptiles. One study in Gabon showed that the troop under observation made up 68 per cent of their diet with fruit, 28 per cent with other plant parts and 4 percent from animal food. Their use of tools is well documented. They use cleaned grass blades and twigs to extract termites from their colonies, and in one study a group was found to be using stones to hammer open hard nuts. They spend between six

Below far left: *The violet turaco* Musophaga violacea.
Above left: *The potto* Perodicticus potto, *a primitive primate that is restricted to the forests of the Guinea-Congolean Block.*
Above: *The genets are a successful group of small forest carnivores.* Genetta tigrina *is shown here.*

and eight hours foraging each day and much more of their time is spent feeding in the trees than the gorillas. Also the distance they cover each day is usually greater, with a record of up to 15 km.

Totally isolated from the distribution range of the common chimpanzee is the bonobo (*Pan paniscus*), also known as the pygmy chimpanzee. Despite this there is little difference in size between the two species. They only occur in the rain forest of Zaïre to the south of the Congo and Lomami rivers, but the exact limits of their distribution are unknown. Until fairly recently they were considered to be a race of common chimpanzee but their clear physical and behavioural differences are now felt to constitute full species status. Their diet is similar to that of their northern and eastern relatives.

Two medium-sized primates which fulfil a similar role to the savanna baboons but in the rain forests are the mandrill (*Mandrillus sphinx*) and the drill (*Mandrillus leucophaeus*). They do most of their foraging on the ground and live in large troops in the forests in the most western region of the Congolean block. In some areas, such as the montane forests of East Africa, savanna baboons (*Papio* spp.) also occupy these well-wooded habitats but frequently feed in adjacent savanna and open woodland. Like the common chimpanzee, bonobo and young gorillas they feed at most levels within the forest "high rise", but all spend much of their time feeding on, or close to, the ground. With so many species of smaller primates spending much of their time in the trees they have to face the same problems of food division as the grazers and browsers of the savannas.

There are three basic divisions of "true" monkeys: the colobus group, the mangabeys and the guenons. The last group has by far the most species. The colobus monkeys are predominantly leaf-eaters which have evolved complex stomachs to extract the maximum nutrients from their simple diet. Some of the colobus monkeys are restricted to the tropical lowland rain forests but others range beyond and are found in montane forests of eastern Africa. There is some confusion about their taxonomy as there are many regional and isolated variants. One of the best known is the eastern black-and-white colobus (*Colobus guereza*) with its black and white fur and in some races a bushy white-tipped tail. The red colobus (*Colobus badius* group) spends much of its time feeding at the highest level of the "high rise". The olive colobus (*Colobus verus*) feeds on leaves at lower levels in the forest. Because of the simple nature of their diet they have small home ranges and high densities may be reached in some locations. One anatomical feature that sets the colobus monkeys aside from the other groups is the lack of thumbs. The mangabeys tend to feed at lower levels in the trees and they will also descend to the ground to forage. The collared mangabey (*Cercocebus torquatus*) includes a high percentage of tough-skinned fruits and nuts in its diet.

The largest group, the forest guenons belonging to the genus *Cercopithecus*, are all characterised by long tails, slender limbs and short faces. A few species occur outside the lowland rain forests and occupy forest land on mountains to the east and south, such as the "blue" monkey (*Cercopithecus mitis/albogularis*) which is represented by many races. The very widespread vervet, or green, monkey does not occur in the tropical lowland forest but shows a preference for drier forest types and savanna woodland. As several species may occur together competition for food is largely avoided by feeding at different levels in the forest, selecting different food items and using different techniques to find it. The red-tailed monkey (*Cercopithecus ascanius*) feeds mainly on fruits but other species will feed mainly on flowers, buds and other plant parts. Nearly all will, however, include items in their diet other than those in which they specialise or favour.

A final group of primates are the prosimians, including the bushbabies (such as *Otolemur* and *Galago*), the potto (*Pero-*

dicticus potto) and the angwantibo (*Arctocebus calabarensis*). Most species are restricted to the lowland rain forests but a few occupy drier woodlands in association with savannas. They all include insects, small vertebrates, fruit and tree resin in their diet and unlike the other forest primates they do all of their foraging at night.

SMALL MAMMALS

It is not possible to discuss all of the small mammal species that roam the forest floor and the different layers of the green "high rise" but one group that must be mentioned is the **Megachiroptera**, or fruit bat. The fruit-eating bats, of which there are many species, occur outside the tropical rain forest zone but this is where they reach their greatest diversity. This of course can be explained by the year-round abundance of fruit, on which they feed. Many, if not all of these bats, crush ripe fruit pulp in the mouth, swallow the juice and spit out most of the pulp and seeds. The food that is swallowed passes rapidly through the simple gut and any seeds are left unharmed by the digestive juices. Apart from fruits a few species also feed on flowers to obtain nectar and juices. Why then are these flying mammals so crucial to the health of the forest? Firstly, they are of critical importance for the dispersal of many tree seeds – both by spitting them out and passing them in the faeces. Some trees have evolved to rely to a large extent on this method of seed dispersal. Those that feed from flowers also serve as pollinators. Some fruit bat species live in small colonies but the straw-coloured fruit bat (*Eidolon helvum*) forms great aggregations that may number many thousands. Many species of insectivorous bats (**Microchiroptera**) also occupy forest habitats. The tree hyraxes (*Dendrohyrax* spp.) are small distant relatives of the elephant that have taken to an arboreal way of life, emerging at night to feed on leaves, twigs and bark.

A few forest species have found a way to move from tree to tree by gliding. One of these is the anomalurus (*Anomalurus peli*), a rodent with a total length of almost 90 cm, and with extensions of skin running between the front and hind legs. When it wishes to glide from one tree to the next it simply launches itself into space and spreads its legs. In this way it is able to move about the forest without having to struggle through dense foliage, or first descend to the ground. There is also a rich squirrel fauna, with specialisation in feeding in order to avoid undue competition. The largest of all the squirrels is *Protoxerus stangeri*, which is exclusively arboreal. The smaller rodents, particularly rats and mice, are very well represented, with many forest-floor dwellers but also several that feed and live at different levels in the vegetation. Climbing mice of the genus *Dendromus* are found in many habitats, but the woodland mice (*Grammomys* spp.) are restricted to forest and dense woodland and spend most of their time in the trees and undergrowth. Several species of the small squirrel-like dormice (*Graphiurus* spp.) occur in forests of several types, where they spend most of their time aloft. The giant rats (*Cricetomys* spp.), which can weigh as much as 3 kg, live in burrows on the forest floor. They forage for fallen fruits and seeds which they carry back to their shelters in large cheek-pouches.

THE BIRDS

Several hundred species of birds are totally, or partially, restricted to African forests. A few species, for example the crested guinea fowl (*Guttera edouardi* and *G. pucherani*), the endangered white-breasted guinea fowl (*Agelastes meleagrides*) of the Guinean forest block, the black guinea fowl (*Agelastes niger*), several francolin species (Family **Phasianidae**) and the interesting Congo peacock (*Afropavo congensis*) spend their time foraging on the forest floor, scratching among the leaf litter and humus. The Congo peacock lives in the eastern area of the tropical lowland rain forest and it was only revealed to the outside world in 1936. All of these fairly large "floor birds" feed on a mixture of plant and invertebrate food.

Most forest birds that move and feed above the forest floor forage singly, in pairs or in mixed-species flocks. These mixed-bird flocks are largely a phenomenon of the tropical forests. As they move through the forest feeding each species seeks out its own favoured food and the level at which it is found. This behaviour disturbs the foliage and causes insects

Below left and above: *Frogs of the genus* Hyperolius *in the Kibale Forest, western Uganda.*

to emerge, making them available to the birds in the foraging flock. Because fruit is so abundant in the forest many forest birds are fruit eaters. The hornbills, of which many species are restricted to a forest habitat, use their long beaks to reach for fruit growing on thin twigs that would not bear their weight. Their large beaks also make it easier for them to reach fruits in dense foliage. A group of colourful fruit eaters are the turacos (Family **Musophagidae**) of which about 20 species are recognised as occurring in the forests and woodlands of Africa, foraging at most levels of the forest. Although these and other species of forest birds have brightly coloured plumages when seen in sunlight, in the depths of the forest these colours do not stand out. Compared to the tropical rain forests of South America and South-east Asia, Africa has a very poor parrot fauna but one of the best known is the grey parrot (*Psittacus erithacus*), a bird which sits behind bars in many homes around the world because of its ability to mimic language and many other sounds. Another parrot that lives in the forest canopy is the collared lovebird (*Agapornis swinderianus*).

Apart from the mammalian predators there are also a number of birds of prey and owls that hunt in the forests. The most impressive, and widespread, is the crowned eagle (*Stephanoaetus coronatus*), a large (up to 90 cm from beak tip to tail tip) hunter of monkeys and tree hyrax (taken when sun-basking). In clearings, glades and more open forest they will also take duikers, young bushbuck and guinea fowl from the forest floor. The bat hawk (*Machaerhamphus alcinus*) also has a wide distribution in forested areas and as its name implies hunts bats at dusk when it emerges to forage from its daytime roosts. Although they will hunt at different levels in the forest, they frequently wait for their prey above the canopy and then catch it in flight. The forest also harbours a number of species of sparrowhawks, long-tailed, round-winged bird hunters that are able to dive, dodge, and wheel in the dense forest growth.

Within forest and woodland habitats there are many species of owls, some of which are common and widespread, and others – such as the Usambara eagle-owl (*Bubo vosseleri*) and the Sokoke scops owl *(Otus ireneae)* – which are restricted to very limited forested areas.

THE REPTILES AND AMPHIBIANS

The reptiles and amphibians are well represented in African forests and woodland, with many species being restricted to these habitats. Particularly in the case of the montane forest species, many are found only in very limited areas. Within the tropical forests the equable temperatures and high level of humidity favour the abundant herpetofauna. As with all other animal groups occupying the forest, the different reptiles and amphibians make use of all strata available to them. Some live a subterranean existence, such as the burrowing python (*Calabaria reinhardti*), whereas other snakes such as the Gaboon adder (*Bitis gabonica*) and the rhinoceros adder (*Bitis gabonica rhinoceros*) live on the forest floor, their skin pattern and coloration providing one of nature's finest examples of camouflage. These large (up to 1.8 m), fat snakes feed mainly on large rodents and ground birds such as francolin which they bite with their very long (up to 4 cm) poison-injecting fangs. The beautifully, but cryptically, marked royal python (*Python curtus*) is another denizen of the forest floor that waits in ambush alongside trails for its prey, which includes the smaller duiker species and large rodents. Unlike the adders, the pythons kill their prey by constriction. There are numerous snake species that spend most, or all, of their time hunting prey in the understorey and as high as the canopy. The tree vipers, of the genus *Atheris*, are unique to their family in that they have taken up a completely arboreal existence hunting small rodents and tree-dwelling frogs. One of the most successful and diverse of the arboreal reptile families has to be the chamaeleons. Although some species occupy savanna woodland and there are even a few ground-dwelling species, the majority are found in forests, particularly those located in the tropics. No one is certain exactly how many species there are, with estimates ranging from 70 to more than 100, varying in size from the diminutive Marshall's leaf chamaeleon (*Rhampholeon marshalli*) at 50-90 mm, to some that exceed 36 cm. They vary greatly in coloration as well as the form and structure of their head "decorations". *Chamaeleo fischeri* has a "battering-ram" extension on the snout, and others such as the three-horned chamaeleon *(Chamaeleo oweni)* and Jackson's chamaeleon *(Chamaeleo jacksoni)* have several hornlike projections on the head. Still others have well developed crests and dewlaps. All of the tree-dwelling chamaeleons have clawed, grasping feet and prehensile tails. Most species feed on invertebrates, dominated by insects, but some of the larger species, such as Meller's chamaeleon (*Chamaeleo melleri*) include small birds, reptiles and frogs on their menus.

Other lizards that are abundant in some tropical forests are the members of the genus *Holaspis* that move through the trees by gliding for short distances and the day-active geckos of the genus *Lygodactylus* which range in size from 60 mm to as much as 350 mm.

Although this is not usually considered to be tortoise country, two species of hinged tortoise (*Kinixys erosa* and *K. homeana*) occupy the lowland rain forests of Africa. The first mentioned, the serrated hinged tortoise, is associated with forest streams in which they swim and dive to obtain food – unusual behaviour indeed for a "land" tortoise.

It is in the tropical forests that the tree frogs come into their own, as they occupy all habitats from the undergrowth to the uppermost reaches of the canopy. Although the frog fauna of the forests of South-east Asia and South America are much richer than those of Africa, there is still great diversity in both genera and species. Amongst the most numerous are the small, colourful members of the genus *Hyperolius* but among the most brilliantly coloured are the *Cardioglossa* species. There are also larger species such as those belonging to the genera *Leptopelis*, *Chiromantis* and many others. It is not only the arboreal species that occupy the forest – there are also numerous amphibians lying in the ground litter and the shallow soil, as well as in the streams and swampy areas. They include the world's largest frog, appropriately named *Conrana goliath*, which lives along forest streams in the western Congolean zone, and several species of the legless, wormlike, subterranean caecilians that are found in moist forests throughout the tropics. The rain frogs (*Breviceps* spp.) are squat, bulldog-like creatures that spend much of their time in self-excavated burrows, usually in damp soil. The large eggs are laid in shallow holes, and it is in these that the froglets complete their development, never having come into contact with open water. Another interesting species is the viviparous toad *Nectophrynoides occidentalis*, which is only known to occur in the forests on the slopes of Mount Nimba in the Guinean zone. The vast majority of forest-dwelling frogs, particularly the arboreal species, are very vocal but despite this they are usually difficult to locate.

THE INVERTEBRATES

As in virtually all other habitats, it is the invertebrates that dominate the forests, most noticeably those in the tropics. This is truly the realm of the invertebrates! They range from the subterranean world to the highest points of the canopy and everywhere in between. A fantastic array of habitats and micro-habitats is available to them: rotting vegetation, leaf litter, growing vegetation, the epiphytic gardens and dropped fruits, to name just a few. The consistently high temperatures allow the metabolism of tropical forest invertebrates to function at a high rate, which reflects in the large size of many species. It is in this rich environment that one encounters giant butterflies (the swallowtail *Drurya antimachus* of West Africa reaches a wingspan of some 200 mm) and moths, king-size beetles, stick insects, millipedes, centipedes, snails, earthworms and spiders. The favourable conditions allow many of these creatures to complete their life-cycles more rapidly than related species in areas of temperate climate. This allows them to reproduce more frequently, often producing as many as 12 to 20 generations in a single year. This probably increases the chances of genetic variation, which could result in the speeding up of species evolution. This may help explain why there is such an incredible species diversity in tropical forests. The high humidity is also a very important factor in promoting the flourishing populations of species that would dessicate in drier environments. There are numerous species of snails, including a number of true giants, such as *Achatina fulica*, which often reaches lengths greater than 150 mm. Although usually associated with more arid environments, scorpions are often abundant in the forests and some species attain lengths of up to 250 mm. There are also many species of vegetarian millipedes and predatory centipedes, again with considerable size variation and a few that warrant places in the record books. There are many species of ants and termites, some species living in

Left: *The gold-banded forester* Euphaedra neophron.
Below left: *The variable mimic* Hypolimnas anthedon.
Top: *A nymph "froghopper", or spittle-bug, constructing its shelter of foam bubbles. This individual was photographed in the Budongo Forest in Uganda.*
Above: *A mantis feeding on another mantis.*

small colonies, still others forming vast complex communities, at all levels within the forest. There are the predatory ant hordes, the "gardeners" and "farmers", the builders and "squatters", the scavengers and thieves, in other words an ant species to fill every niche. Certainly there are several species that can deliver very painful bites to the unwary. There are termites that construct "umbrellas" over their mounds to protect them against the copious rains and ants that "stitch" leaves together to shelter their eggs and larvae. Although the tropical lowland forests are particularly rich in invertebrate species, all other forest types have their fair share of creeping, crawling and flying creatures but diversity and biomass is generally at its lowest in the drier types.

THE FUTURE

Forests play a vital role in maintaining water and nutrient cycles and soil stability, and acting as major sources of biological diversity. On one 0.64 ha plot of forest at Korup in south-western Cameroon 138 different species of trees have been recorded. Undisturbed forests form the most complex climax vegetation that can be supported by the environmental conditions prevailing in a particular region. Africa's tropical forests are, in general, poorly explored by the scientific community and inventories of biodiversity are largely incomplete. Despite the critical importance of forests to the well-being of planet earth man has been working hard at exploiting and destroying this biome at an ever-increasing rate. The Romans and other Mediterranean-based civilisations were largely responsible for the almost wholesale destruction of the temperate forests of the Atlas Mountains and coastal North Africa. By the year 1500 European explorers and settlers were starting to seek out resources throughout the world, but exploitation and destruction of Africa's tropical forests started in earnest only in the late nineteenth century. Vast areas of forest, particularly in West Africa, were cleared to make way for the plantation cultivation of such crops as cocoa, palm oil and rubber. There has also been increasing exploitation of trees for their timber, both to feed the export market and to meet ever-growing internal demand. As the human population grows at staggering rates this exploitation continues to escalate, not only for the timber and other natural resources but also for living space and land to grow subsistence crops. There are implications here for both the global and local environment. On the local scale climate can be influenced, resulting in lower rainfall, the shallow and infertile soils become leached and eroded, water cycles can be altered and this all results in unprecedented loss of biological diversity. In Ivory Coast it has been estimated that some 6.52 per cent of all forests are cleared annually, that is about 250 000 ha. In little more than a decade virtually no forest will remain. Nigeria is losing its forests at a rate of about 5 per cent each year, that is 350 000 ha; and although the State Forest Department tries to manage the forests scientifically so little remains it is highly unlikely that sustainability can be achieved. In Zaïre, with over 100 million hectares of natural forest land and destruction levels at only 0.2 per cent, there is still considerable hope that suitable levels of conservation and sustainable exploitation could be achieved. This also applies to the Congo Republic and Gabon, which have almost 42 million hectares of natural forest and clearing levels of just 0.1 per cent.

Sadly, much of the West African tropical forest holdings are destined to disappear within the next few decades, as human population growth spurs on ever greater demands for space and resources. Although there are a number of proclaimed conservation areas that are located in, or incorporate part of, forests in this region, many are poorly managed and have thousands of peasants living within their borders or close by. Wood cutting, poaching and cultivation go on largely unchecked within many reserves. Even within the large Congolean forest block conservationists cannot afford to become complacent.

CHAPTER 4

THE AFRICAN HIGHLANDS

Africa has no great mountain ranges comparable with Asia's Himalayas and South America's Andes, but the mountains and high plateaus of this continent are no less fascinating. Some of the mountainous areas are extensive but they are widely scattered and include those of volcanic origin, those resulting from folding of the earth's crust and others which have been influenced by faulting. Most of Africa has existed as a single, rigid block since the Precambrian era and strongly folded rocks of fairly recent origin are only found in the extreme north-west (the Atlas Mountains) and the continent's south-western tip (the Cape Folded Belt). The Cape Folded Mountains, as well as the Drakensberg, were being formed during the Triassic era. The Atlas Mountains were formed during the Tertiary era when the alpine folding process resulted in extensive volcanic activity in the Sahara. This activity only ceased at the start of the Quaternary era. At this time a great mountain range emerged linking north-western Africa and the Iberian Peninsula (Spain), effectively cutting off the Mediterranean Sea (or as it is referred to during that era, the Tethys Sea), with the latter eventually drying out. But by the end of the Miocene the Atlantic again flowed into the Mediterranean. In the Sahara there are only two mountain ranges of note, the Hoggar and the Tibesti, which were discussed under the chapter on drylands. They are both a result of

Background: *Sunrise over Mount Kenya, viewed from the Aberdare National Park. Photo: Pat J Frere.* **Right:** *The Cape eagle-owl* Bubo capensis *shows a preference for rugged, mountainous terrain. Outside South Africa this species is known as Mackinder's eagle-owl.*

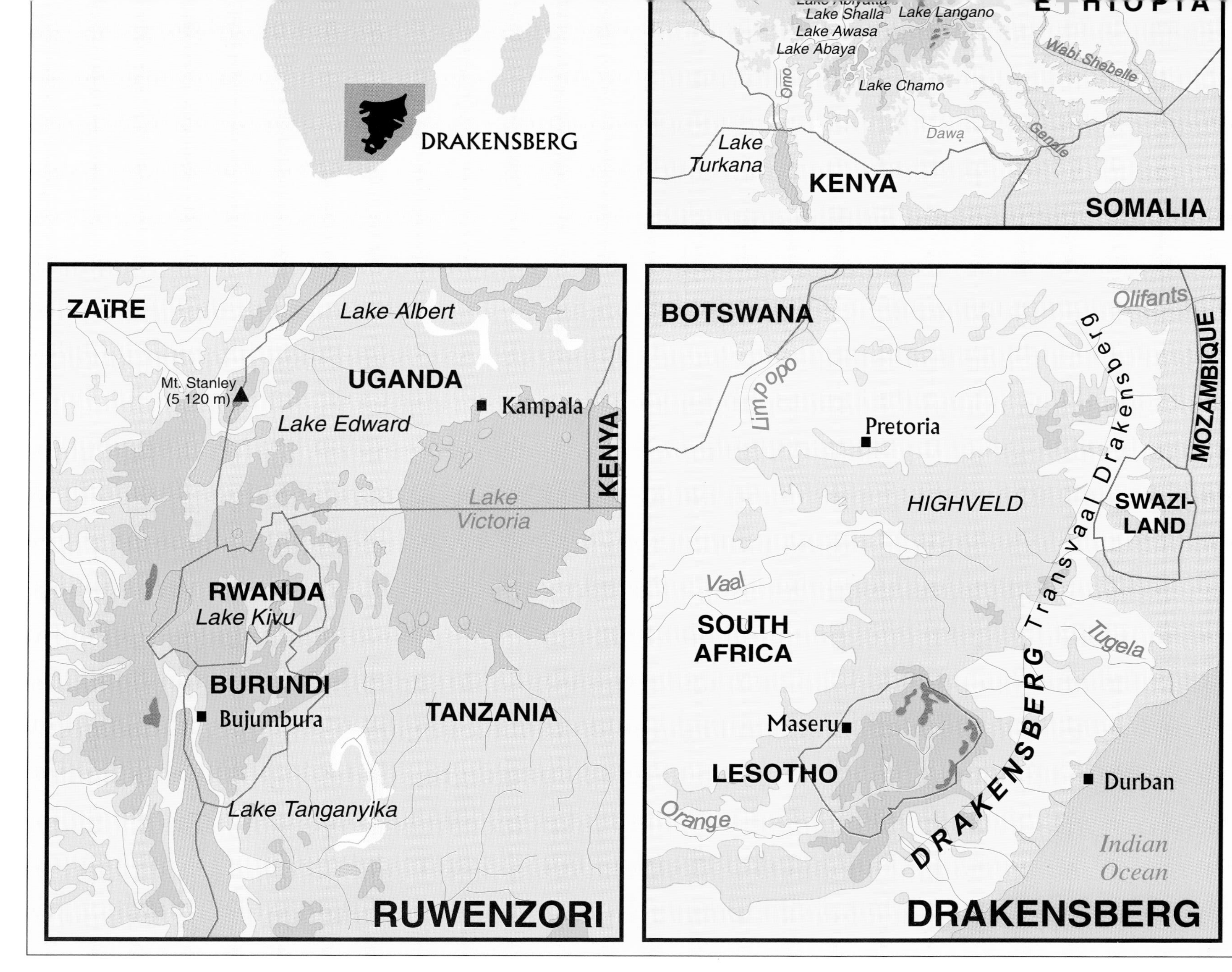
DRAKENSBERG
Lake Shalla
Lake Langano
Lake Awasa
Lake Abaya
Omo
Lake Chamo
Wabi Shebelle
Dawa
Genale
Lake Turkana
KENYA
SOMALIA
ZAÏRE
Lake Albert
UGANDA
Mt. Stanley
(5 120 m)
Kampala
Lake Edward
KENYA
Lake Victoria
RWANDA
Lake Kivu
BURUNDI
Bujumbura
TANZANIA
Lake Tanganyika
RUWENZORI
BOTSWANA
Olifants
Limpopo
Pretoria
MOZAMBIQUE
HIGHVELD
Transvaal Drakensberg
SWAZI-LAND
Vaal
SOUTH AFRICA
Tugela
Maseru
LESOTHO
Durban
Orange
DRAKENSBERG
Indian Ocean
DRAKENSBERG

AFRICA: MONTANE REGIONS

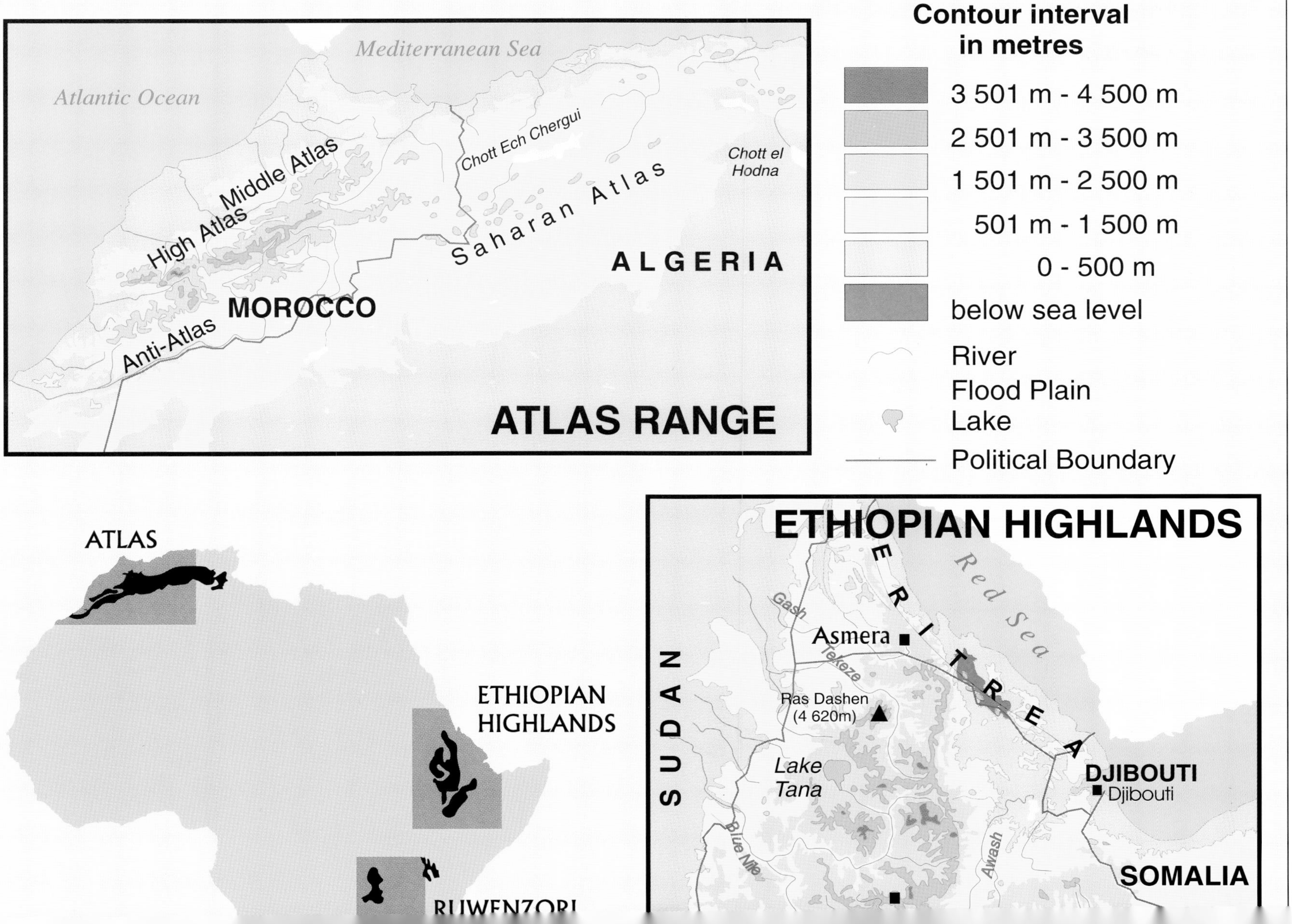

Contour interval in metres

- 3 501 m - 4 500 m
- 2 501 m - 3 500 m
- 1 501 m - 2 500 m
- 501 m - 1 500 m
- 0 - 500 m
- below sea level
- River
- Flood Plain
- Lake
- Political Boundary

ATLAS RANGE

Atlantic Ocean
Mediterranean Sea
High Atlas
Middle Atlas
Anti-Atlas
MOROCCO
Saharan Atlas
Chott Ech Chergui
Chott el Hodna
ALGERIA

ATLAS
ETHIOPIAN HIGHLANDS
RUWENZORI

ETHIOPIAN HIGHLANDS

SUDAN
ERITREA
Asmera
Gash
Tekeze
Ras Dashen (4 620m)
Lake Tana
Blue Nile
Red Sea
Awash
DJIBOUTI
Djibouti
SOMALIA

Above: *Mount Kenya looking across from the Aberdare Range; both are of volcanic origin.* **Right:** *The growth of moss "gardens" is encouraged by high moisture levels.* **Far right above:** Helichrysum nandense *growing at 3 600 m on Mount Kenya. Photo: Pat J Frere* **Far right below:** *Senecios sp. on Mount Kenya.*

faulting, and upthrusting of lava derived from volcanic activity. The highest peak, Tarso Taro, rises to 3 325 m in the Tibesti Mountains. West Africa consists mainly of plains and low uplands with only two montane areas of any note: the Cameroon Highlands lying in the north-western corner of the Congolean Forest Block and the smaller area of highland in the west of the Guinea Forest Block. The latter area extends from the 1 752 m-high Mount Nimba on the Guinea, Liberian and Ivory Coast border and then westwards into Guinea, with other associated mountain country being the Ziama Massif and Fouta Djallon. The Cameroon Highlands are centred in the country of Cameroon but spill over into north-eastern Nigeria and the offshore island of Bioko lying in the Bight of Biafra. The southern area of high land is of volcanic origin and volcanic peaks include mounts Cameroon, Malabo (on Bioko), Kupe and Manenguba. To the north of the latter lie the Bamenda Highlands, which are of largely non-volcanic origin.

The largest areas of high land lie to the east of the continent, however. The greatest area of land with an altitude exceeding 2 000 m lies entirely within the country of Ethiopia and is known appropriately as the Ethiopian Highlands, the "roof of Africa". It is a vast volcanic basaltic dome made up of different layers of lava that is believed to have had its earliest origins some 75 million years ago. All volcanic activity ceased some four to five million years ago and during the Pliocene and Pleistocene eras glaciers dominated the highest mountains. Eventually the dome was split during the formation of the Great Rift Valley, which roughly follows an imaginary line drawn from Djibouti at the junction of the Red Sea and the Gulf of Aden, to the Ethiopian capital of Addis Ababa and then in a south-westward swing to Lake Rudolf. The northern part of the fractured dome is much more extensive than the area in the south. The highest peak, Ras Dejen (4 543 m), lies in the Simen Mountains not far from the newly independent state of Eritrea. Much of the dome consists of great, rugged escarpments which separate the hilly plateaus from the terraced lowlands.

Moving southwards along the Great Rift Valley we begin to encounter some of Africa's most romantic peaks, many of which are of relatively recent volcanic origin. Volcanic mountains are created as a result of lava, cinders and other debris following a fault line or breaking through the earth's surface in huge quantities. By the very nature of their structure volcanoes are generally short-lived in geological terms and erosion is rapid. In this way many old volcanoes have made their appearance and eroded away over the last 30 million years or so but others still spend much of their time with their "heads" in the clouds. Africa's highest mountain, Kilimanjaro (5 896 m), is little more than 750 000 years old and is actually a cluster of three peaks. Kibo (Uhuru) is the tallest and flanked on the west by the 3 962-m Shira and in the east by Mawenzi at 5 149 m. Kibo's most extensive eruption is believed to have taken place as recently as 36 000 years ago. There is a glacier of some four square kilometres but this is receding. Snow is also a feature on the highest points of Mount Kenya and the eight Virunga volcanoes. This range reaches a maximum height of 4 507 m and lies between lakes Edward and Kivu. Other mountains of volcanic origin in the area are Mount Meru, Mount Elgon and the Aberdares.

A feature of Africa's tropically located volcanoes is the rich soils on their slopes and in their surroundings, which of course directly influences their associated vegetation. Because of this high fertility they attract large numbers of human cultivators. Two of the Virunga volcanoes have been recently active, with Nyamulagira erupting several times since 1894 when it was first sighted by Europeans. Then in 1977 Nyiragongo spewed blazing lava that burned its way through forest and subsistence farms. The activities of this string of volcanoes have played a major role in shaping the structure of this part of the Great Rift, by blocking rivers that once fed into the Nile and Lake Edward and probably creating Lake Kivu, which pours its surplus waters southwards into Lake Tanganyika. Although the Virungas form part of the 1 500 km-long chain of high land running down the eastern boundary of Zaïre and spilling into Uganda, Rwanda, Burundi and Tanzania, most of the mountains are the result of upthrust

bedrock and are not volcanic. They include such ranges as the Ruwenzoris, Itombwe and Migula, with the highest point soaring to 5 100 m. This mountain belt is also known as the Kivu-Ruwenzori Highlands or as the heights of the Albertine Rift. If one travels south-eastwards from Kilimanjaro and then back to the south-west in a shallow arc, one encounters several smaller mountain ranges, including the Usambaras, Nguru, Ukaguru, Uluguru, the Uzungwa Escarpment and finally the Southern Highlands adjoining Lake Malawi. The highest peak in the latter range is Rungwe, an extinct volcano, at 2 959 m. Although none of these mountain blocks is large, many are home to species found nowhere else.

The southernmost extensive montane region in Africa, with the highest peak south of Kilimanjaro (Thabana Ntlenyana at 3 482 m), is the Drakensberg which extends from the Eastern Cape through KwaZulu/Natal and deep into the Eastern

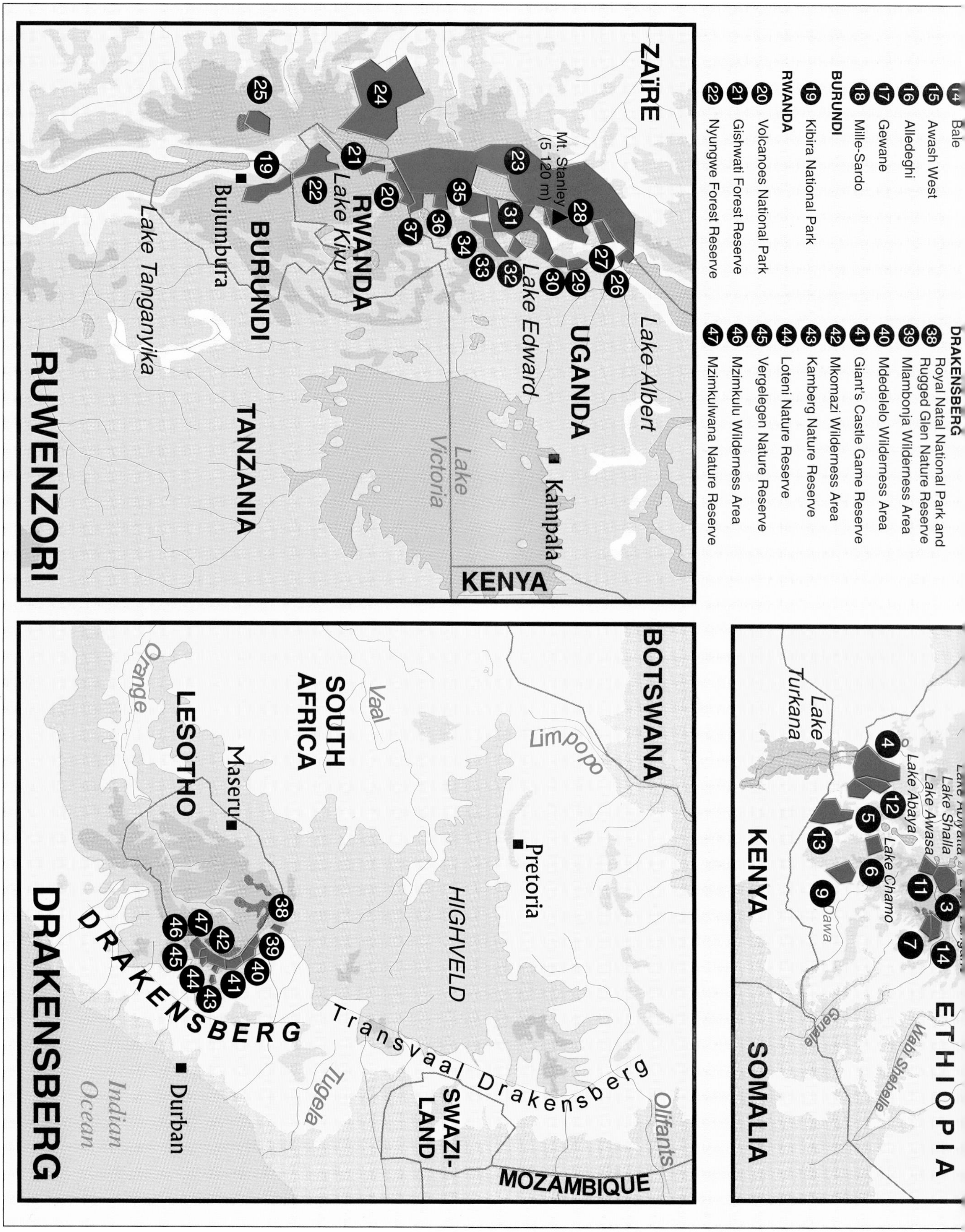

14 Bale
15 Awash West
16 Alledeghi
17 Gewane
18 Mille-Sardo

BURUNDI

19 Kibira National Park

RWANDA

20 Volcanoes National Park
21 Gishwati Forest Reserve
22 Nyungwe Forest Reserve

DRAKENSBERG

38 Royal Natal National Park and Rugged Glen Nature Reserve
39 Mlambonja Wilderness Area
40 Mdedelelo Wilderness Area
41 Giant's Castle Game Reserve
42 Mkomazi Wilderness Area
43 Kamberg Nature Reserve
44 Loteni Nature Reserve
45 Vergelegen Nature Reserve
46 Mzimkulu Wilderness Area
47 Mzimkulwana Nature Reserve

ETHIOPIA
Lake Shalla
Lake Awasa
Lake Abaya
Lake Chamo
Wabi Shebelle
Dawa
Genale
Lake Turkana
KENYA
SOMALIA

ZAÏRE
Lake Albert
UGANDA
Mt. Stanley (5 120 m)
Kampala
Lake Edward
KENYA
Lake Victoria
RWANDA
Lake Kivu
BURUNDI
Bujumbura
TANZANIA
Lake Tanganyika
RUWENZORI

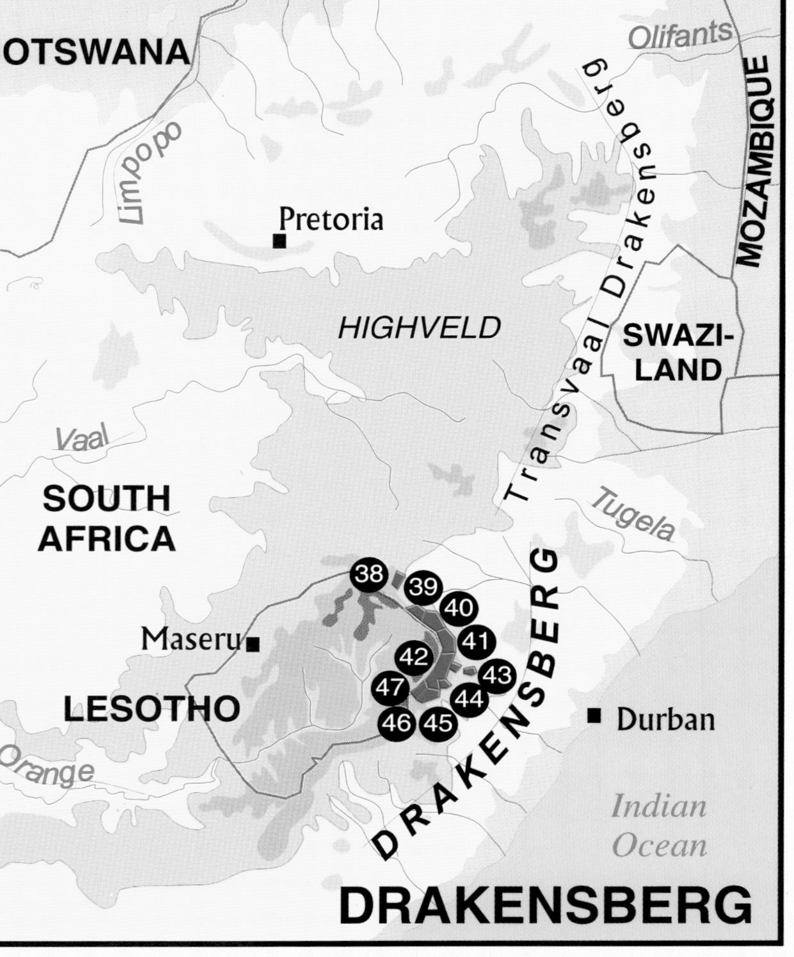

AFRICA: CONSERVATION AREAS IN THE MONTANE REGIONS

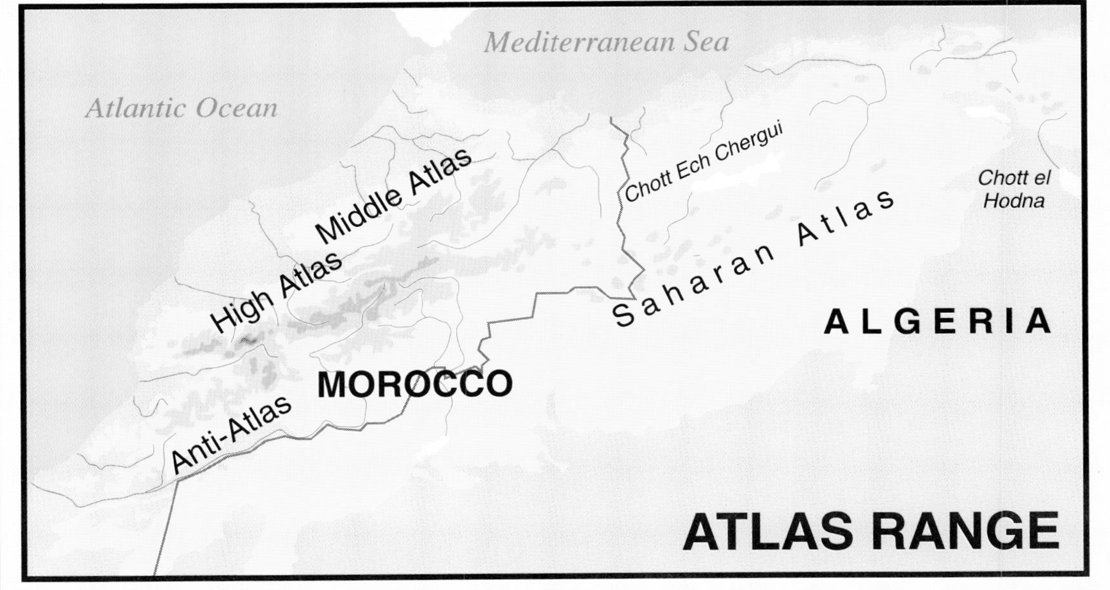

Contour interval in metres

- 3 501 m - 4 500 m
- 2 501 m - 3 500 m
- 1 501 m - 2 500 m
- 501 m - 1 500 m
- 0 - 500 m
- below sea level
- River
- Flood Plain
- Lake
- Political Boundary

CONSERVATION AREAS

ETHIOPIA (National Parks)

1. Awash
2. Simien Mountains
3. Abiyatta - Shalla Lakes
4. Omo
5. Mago
6. Nechisar
7. Bale Mountains
8. Yangudi Rassa

ETHIOPIA (Wildlife Reserves)

9. Yavello
10. Harrar Elephant

ZAÏRE

23. Virunga National Park
24. Kahuzi Biega National Park
25. Luama Hunting Reserve

UGANDA

26. Toro Game Reserve
27. Bwamba Forest Reserve
28. Ruwenzori Mountains National Park
29. Kibale National Park
30. Kibale Corridor Game Reserve
31. Queen Elizabeth National Park
32. Kyambura Game Reserve
33. Kasyoha-Kotomi Forest Reserve
34. Maramagambo-Kalinzu Forest Reserve

Transvaal, all provinces of South Africa. The range totally dominates the small kingdom of Lesotho and a large part of Swaziland. The name is derived from the Afrikaans and means "dragon mountains", but the Zulu refer to the range as *uKhahlamba,* "the barrier of upright spears", which is much more appropriate. The Drakensberg consists of a number of geological strata, including the Molteno and Red Beds, and the Cave Sandstone, but the dominant features are the basaltic deposits of the Stormberg Series, particularly along the vertical wall of the great escarpment in KwaZulu/Natal. Layer after layer of lava poured to the surface over tens of millions of years and in Lesotho there are areas where the laval belt is some 1.5 km deep and forms the cap of the sub-range known as the Lebombos. The northern extension of the Drakensberg consists mainly of very ancient sedimentary rocks.

THE BEARDED VULTURE

The bearded vulture, with a wingspan of 2.6 to 2.8 m, a weight of 5 to 6 kg and a length (beak tip to tail tip) averaging 1.1 m, is one of Africa's largest flying birds. These birds occur in scattered and isolated populations in high mountain country including the Drakensberg, suitable habitat in eastern Africa, the Ethiopian Highlands and the Atlas Mountains. Elsewhere, they occur in the high ranges of Eurasia. During the last century they bred in the eastern extension of the Cape Folded Mountains but no longer do. It is estimated that there are some 120 breeding pairs in the southernmost population, with unknown numbers elsewhere, although it is considered to be fairly abundant in Ethiopia. They show a preference for breeding in hollows on high cliffs, often in association with montane grassland and low scrub. In the Drakensberg they breed in the winter months of May to July. The bearded vulture forages in open country where it searches for carcasses. Bones are broken by dropping them from great heights onto rocks. Favoured sites (known as ossaries) may accumulate large numbers of bone fragments.
Photo: *Penny Meakin*

Above: *The Drakensberg range extends for some 1 000 km. This picture was taken in the Natal block of the Drakensberg. Photo: John Carlyon*

A short distance to the south-west of the Drakensberg one encounters the eastern outlier of the Cape Folded Belt, which stretches westwards for about 800 km to the vicinity of Cape Town and then pushes northwards for some 350 km. Throughout their length these mountain ranges run parallel to the coast, separating the narrow coastal plain from the arid plains of the interior. These mountains consist of sedimentary rocks, dominated by Table Mountain Sandstones, that were

subjected to massive folding and tilting. The only comparable mountains in Africa are the Atlas of Morocco in the extreme north-west. There are also extensive highland areas, associated with the western escarpment, in Namibia and Angola.

MOUNTAINS AND CLIMATE

Mountains play a critical role in influencing wind patterns and rainfall, not only in the vicinity of the peaks and ranges but often for great distances beyond. Despite the small surface area of Africa covered by mountains their impact in this regard is considerable.

The higher the altitude on a mountain, the lower the air density and oxygen levels. Low-density air cannot hold much moisture so humidity levels are low and air clarity is greater than at lower altitudes. Low-density and low-pressure air does not absorb much heat from the sun but it does permit the passage of more ultraviolet rays than does denser, low-altitude air. Winds blowing in mountains can reach great speeds because of reduced frictional drag, and this results in an accelerated rate of evaporation which further cools the air. As we will see later many species of plants and animals have evolved means of overcoming the problems of high-altitude living. When moisture-laden winds come into contact with a

Top and above: *Lichens are usually abundant and diverse in Africa's mountains.*

mountain or a range of mountains, they are forced to rise in altitude so that the moisture load cools and condenses and falls as rain. But on the leeward side, that is the slopes having no contact with the rain-producing prevailing winds, there is little condensation and a drier zone develops within the so-called rain-shadow. On those higher mountains located in the equatorial zone there are usually belts, or at least patches, of cloud forest. It is so named because at the altitudes where it grows air temperatures are cooler than at lower altitudes and this causes water in the air to condense so that a veil of mist is present most of the time. The amount of rain and the season when it falls varies from mountain to mountain and range to range. Much depends on the location of the mountain and the movement of the rain-bearing winds. Assekram, in the Saharan Hoggar range, receives an annual average rainfall of 164 mm, which is high for the desert but extremely meagre when compared with other ranges. The upper heights of the Cape Folded Belt receive on average more than 3 000 mm per year, whereas the Rungwe complex to the north of Lake Malawi is drenched by up to 4 000 mm each year. The amount of rain falling obviously has a massive influence on the fauna and flora.

Snow is a permanent feature of only a few African mountains, such as Kilimanjaro, Kenya and the Ruwenzoris, but seasonal snows fall on the ranges of the Atlas, Drakensberg and the Cape Folded Belt.

MOUNTAIN VEGETATION

Because of their scattered distribution and the isolated nature of Africa's mountains the vegetation of montane regions in different parts of the continent varies considerably. Obviously, the height of a mountain dictates the range of habitats that are available for occupation by animals and plants, as does the amount of rain.

Since the mountainous regions of Africa are so isolated, each has evolved its own distinctive flora and associated animals. Each of the highland areas has affinities with surrounding lower-lying areas. A number of vegetation zones can be recognised on mountains and these are linked to latitude and altitude. Because of the influences of rainfall and the "rain-shadow" these zones are rarely uniform and evenly spaced. Zonation is particularly marked in the Ethiopian Highlands and on the higher ranges and peaks of eastern Africa, such as mounts Kenya and Kilimanjaro. The following brief accounts present an overview of the vegetation found growing on Africa's principal mountains.

The **Cape Folded Belt**, located at the southernmost tip of Africa, lies almost entirely within the Cape Floral Kingdom, and rises at its highest point to 2 325 m on the Seweweekspoortberg. It consists of a number of interlinked chains made up of mixed heathland (fynbos) that is dominated by species of *Ericas* (heathers), *Restios* and *Proteas*. Large trees are rare but remnant stands of two species of cedar (*Widdringtonia cedarbergensis, W. schwarzii*) are still found, although forest is largely restricted to isolated rocky gorges. Elements of the Cape heathland vegetation occur in the Drakensberg and on the mountains of eastern Africa. The vegetation of these mountains has been covered in greater detail in Chapter 5.

The **Drakensberg** range in southern Africa is dominated by grassland and savanna types, with shrubland and isolated forest pockets. Of the approximately 1 800 plant species recorded 300 are endemics, that is they are not found outside this range. More than 200 000 ha of these mountains fall within conservation areas.

Ethiopian Highland vegetation bears a number of resemblances to that of the equatorial mountains to the south. The great escarpments separate the hilly plateaus from the terraced lowlands. A belt of montane forest which reaches an altitude of about 3 000 m includes such tree species as *Juniperus procera, Hagenia abyssinica, Olea chrysphylla* and *Podocarpus* spp. In those forested areas receiving more than 1 400 mm of rain each year there are also stands of bamboo. However, these once-extensive forests have been severely depleted and modified by human actions, which include cutting for fuel and clearing for subsistence agriculture. Then from a lower limit of about 2 900 m to an upper limit of some 4 000 m one encounters the moorland, or ericaceous belt, which includes such species as the tree heather (*Erica arborea*) and St John's wort (*Hypericum revolutum*). The highest altitudes have an impoverished Afroalpine vegetation which is largely dominated by grasses and interspersed by giant lobelias (*Lobelia rhynchopetalum*). Despite the high altitude and inhospitable climate, these areas have been heavily used by domestic stock, although there are several important conservation areas within the highlands, for example Simen Mountains (225 km^2) in the far north and the Bale Mountains (2 200 km^2) in the south.

The highest mountains in eastern Africa are treated here together. They include **Kilimanjaro**, the continent's highest mountain, as well as the **Virungas**, **Ruwenzoris** (Mountains of the Moon), **Aberdares**, **Elgon**, **Kenya** and **Meru**. With the exception of the Ruwenzoris all are of volcanic origin and all are richly endowed with plant species. Although they share many genera, many species and subspecies are endemic. The first and lower zone consists of mixed forest, with mainly evergreen species on the wetter slopes and semi-deciduous ones on the "rain-shadow" side. There may also be extensive stands of juniper and podocarps, most notably in the drier regions, as can be seen on the northern slopes of Mount Kenya. As one moves higher one enters the upper-montane or cloud forest, consisting mainly of a low, dense canopy of relatively small trees, with branches thickly swathed in ferns, bryophytes, epiphytic orchids, lichens and others. With the exception of Kilimanjaro all these mountains have belts and patches of tall bamboo (*Arundinaria* sp.) within, or in close association with the montane forest zone. Beyond the forest lies a zone of ericaceous scrub, or heathland, which includes low scrub and in many cases taller heath species such as *Erica arborea*. This vegetation type is particularly well developed between 3 000 m and 3 500 m on the Ruwenzoris. It is however in the next vegetation zone, the Afroalpine, where one finds those plants best adapted to

Right: *A* Nerine *in flower in a glade on the Ruwenzori range in East Africa.* **Below:** *High rainfall and near-continuous cloud cover ensures abundant moisture for plants growing at high altitudes, resulting in greater diversity.*

withstand very low temperatures, strong winds and other extremes. Plants in this zone include the giant lobelias (*Lobelia* spp.) and the giant senecios (*Dendrosenicio* spp.) which grow patchily on all mountains, except in the Ruwenzoris where they form dense stands covering extensive areas. The giant senecios are slow growers and flowering intervals may be as long as 20 years. The stems and buds are insulated by the dead and living leaves, with the buds producing a thick, sticky substance that further serves to protect the growth points from the extreme cold. Mixed scrub also occurs at this level, often dominated by *Helichrysum* spp. and on the drier slopes by tussock grassland.

The vegetation of the **Cameroon Highlands** is dominated by montane forest and grassland, with at least 45 endemic plant species occurring on Mount Cameroon alone. The **Guinean highland**, centred on Mount Nimba, has extensive areas of tropical forest but human activities such as logging, mining and subsistence agriculture are making severe inroads, even in conservation areas. Two thousand species of plants have been recorded from Mount Nimba.

In the Saharan ranges of **Hoggar** and **Tibesti** vegetation is sparse, but because they receive slightly higher rainfall than the surrounding desert there are some plant species here which also occur along the Mediterranean seaboard, including stunted specimens of cypresses and myrtles.

Finally, the vegetation of the **Atlas Mountains** has been modified by the activities of man over thousands of years but there are still many forested areas made up mainly of Holm oak interspersed with Barbary thuya, *Juniper* spp. and scattered stands of Aleppo pine. There are also extensive areas of low heath- and scrubland, with the south-easterly facing slopes being influenced by the "rain-shadow", but many areas have been severely overgrazed by domestic stock.

MAMMALS OF THE HIGHLANDS

Although some mammal species are found on many different mountains and mountain ranges, many species and subspecies are restricted to very limited areas. Some species are commonly associated with lower altitudes and venture into the mountains to feed. Elephants (*Loxodonta africana*) occur in the montane and bamboo forests of all the major eastern African mountains and they often enter the ericaceous scrubland and the lower reaches of the Afroalpine. Buffalo (*Syncerus caffer*) also penetrate the upper reaches to feed on the tussock grasses. There has been a sighting of a pack of wild dogs (*Lycaon pictus*) on the Mount Kilimanjaro glacier and there is evidence to show that leopard (*Panthera pardus*) occasionally traverse the highest levels. The versatile common eland (*Taurotragus oryx*) traverses the entire altitudinal range of the Drakensberg. A number of species, such as the giant forest hog (*Hylochoerus meinertzhageni*), buffalo, bushbuck (*Tragelaphus scriptus*) and leopard, occur as residents both in lowland habitats as well is in suitable areas on mountains. In the case of elephants, some animals may be resident on certain mountains, particularly in the equatorial belt, whereas others move in only at certain times of the year.

Top: *The rock elephant shrew* Elephantulus myurus *is one of several species found in association with mountains.*
Above: *The klipspringer* Oreotragus oreotragus *is Africa's only true mountain antelope, showing great agility in seemingly impossible circumstances.*

The only antelope adapted to living in rugged mountainous terrain is the klipspringer (*Oreotragus oreotragus*). It occurs on virtually all the mountains and ranges of southern, central and eastern Africa as far north as the Ethiopian

Highlands, and isolated populations occur on the Jos Plateau (Nigeria) and in the rugged hills of the north-western and north-eastern Central African Republic. They occupy areas of high rainfall as successfully as highlands and canyons on the fringes of the Namib Desert. It is a small antelope, with males averaging 10 kg and females 13 kg (South African figures) and a shoulder height of 60 cm, and the coarse, spiny hair stands erect and not flat as in other species. The structure and nature of the coat is believed to serve as a heat regulator – a distinct advantage at high altitude. Another adaptive feature is the ability to walk and jump on the rubbery tips of the hoofs. They are active throughout the day when it is cool but otherwise do most of their feeding during the cooler morning and late afternoon hours.

Several other species of small antelope are associated with mountainous, or hilly, country. The grey rhebok (*Pelea capreolus*), weighing some 20 kg, is restricted to highlands in South Africa, Lesotho and Swaziland, including the Drakensberg and the Cape Folded Mountains. It lives in small family parties, each attended by a single adult ram, which show a preference for grassed and low-scrub covered slopes, avoiding the steep, rocky areas favoured by the klipspringer. But it has a long, woolly coat that is an adaptation to cold mountain living. The mountain reedbuck (*Redunca fulvorufula*), weighing about 30 kg, is the largest of the "small" upland-dwelling antelope. It has a patchy distribution, with scattered populations found in mountainous and broken hill country in south-eastern and eastern Africa and an isolated population in the northern part of the Cameroon Highlands and adjacent areas of Nigeria. Several species of duikers are found in association with mountains, some occupying both uplands and lowlands, such as the common duiker (*Sylvicapra grimmia*), red duiker (*Cephalophus natalensis* and *C. harveyi*) and the yellow-backed duiker (*Cephalophus*

THE HYRAXES

(ORDER HYRACOIDEA)

There are two groups of hyraxes, the tree-dwellers (Dendrohyrax *spp.*) *and the rock-dwellers* (Procavia *spp.*; Heterohyrax *spp.*). *All have wide distributions and none are restricted to mountains or other high country but they are important denizens of many peaks and ranges in sub-Saharan Africa. The rock hyraxes occupy desert outcrops and high-rainfall mountain slopes and the tree hyraxes occur in many different forest types, including rain and cloud forests on mountains in the tropics, but in some areas they also live among rocks.*

They are small (2-5 kg), stockily built, tailless mammals which have certain anatomical features that align them to the elephant. The fur is thick and varies in colour from region to region, even within the same species, but most are dark to lighter brown. The hair of the tree hyraxes is usually longer but the rock hyraxes (Procavia) *in the Mount Kenya alpine zone also have long hair, an adaptation to their cold home.*

The rock hyraxes are predominantly diurnal, doing most of their feeding during the early morning and late afternoon hours. When they first emerge, as the sun rises, they lie on the rocks before moving off to feed. They live in colonies ranging from four to several dozen individuals, although in areas of food abundance there may be many colonies located in close proximity to each other. Each colony, or group, has a dominant male and female, with the other animals sorting themselves into a pecking order. They take a wide range of plant food. Many predators include them in their diet, such as leopard and Verreaux's eagle. For such a small animal their gestation period of seven months is unusually long, but the young are precocious at birth (150-300 g) and are soon able to run around.

The tree hyraxes are common in the forests on many of the mountains located in the tropics. Unlike their rock-dwelling cousins they are mainly nocturnal, although they will emerge during the day to sun themselves on branches, emerging to feed at dusk. Probably the most startling feature of these forest animals is the cacophony of sound that a beast weighing only a couple of kilograms can produce. It starts as a series of rattling croaks that wind up to a blood-curdling scream and where these animals are abundant, the pre-feeding chorus can be awe-inspiring.

Below: *The yellow-spotted rock hyrax* Heterohyrax brucei *occurs widely in the eastern parts of Africa as far north as Egypt.*

silvicultor). Others are exclusively restricted to mountains, including the black-fronted duiker (*Cephalophus nigrifrons*), which is restricted to bamboo thickets, moorland and montane forest on several of the eastern equatorial mountains and even in the alpine zone in the Ruwenzoris. Abbott's duiker (*Cephalophus spadix*) is limited to montane forest and high-altitude swamps on Mount Kilimanjaro, and also on other isolated ranges as far south as Mount Rungwe near the northern tip of Lake Malawi.

The largest antelope restricted to high-altitude country is the mountain nyala (*Tragelaphus buxtoni*), with the greatest part of the population living at an altitude of 3 000 to 4 200 m between the Harerghe and Bale mountains of Ethiopia. They live in a variety of montane habitats ranging up to the alpine moorlands, in herds averaging eight individuals although larger groups are frequently observed.

Another ungulate which is restricted to the Ethiopian Highlands is the walia ibex (*Capra ibex walie*), with a very small population in the Simen Mountains. This ibex spends virtually all its time between altitudes of 2 800 m and 3 400 m. It shares its habitat with two other high-altitude restricted herbivores, the widespread klipspringer and the gelada (*Theropithecus gelada*), a large grass-eating monkey which forms large troops and is restricted to the extensive grasslands in the highlands. They have thick coats to keep them warm and dry in these high, chilly pastures. The Barbary macaque (*Macaca sylvanus*), the only primate to occur north of the Sahara Desert, lives in the forest and scrub patches on the Atlas Mountains.

Below: *A number of primates live in high montane areas, including this subspecies of the "blue" monkey,* Cercopithecus mitis kolbi, *which lives in the forests on Mount Kenya.*

Several other primates are found at high altitudes but most species also occur in lowland habitats. The savanna baboon (*Papio* spp.), as its name implies, is most widely distributed in non-montane country. However in some ranges, such as the Cape Folded Mountains and the Drakensberg, these large monkeys range widely but tend to favour the lower altitudes. The mountain dwelling subspecies of the gorilla (*Gorilla gorilla beringei*) is restricted to the Virunga volcano region of Rwanda, Uganda and Zaïre and the Bwindi Forest in Uganda, with less than 600 remaining. This highland-dwelling gorilla grows much longer hair than its lowland cousin. All primates that live in mountainous areas – with the exception of the gelada and the savanna baboon – are restricted to forested habitats. Other primates occupying montane forests include the black-and-white colobus (*Colobus guereza*), and several subspecies of the blue monkey (*Cercopithecus mitis*). Some of these have very restricted distributions, including the golden monkey (*C. mitis kandti*) which is only found in a limited area of the Virunga volcanoes.

The only large predator occurring in Africa's montane area is the leopard (*Panthera pardus*), but numbers are usually low as potential prey densities are rarely sufficient to sustain large numbers of carnivores. The success of this cat, in virtually all habitats, is ascribed to its ability to hunt everything from mice to medium-sized antelope. The caracal (*Felis caracal*) is known from several mountain ranges but it spends most of its time at lower altitudes and avoids forest. Only one African carnivore is restricted to high altitudes and that is the Ethiopian wolf (*Canis simensis*), a rare canid that feeds primarily on rodents which it hunts in the montane grassland. At least eight species of rodent living in these grasslands in the Ethiopian Highlands occur nowhere else and some achieve incredible densities. The giant root-rat (*Tachyoryctes macrocephalus*) of the Sanetti Plateau is believed to number some 2 600 individuals per square kilometre. Smaller rodent species and insectivores (particularly shrews and golden moles) are found on all of Africa's principal mountains and ranges. Some species are widespread, whereas others are only found in a specific habitat on one mountain. Those species that occupy the alpine zone tend to have longer fur than their lowland relatives, produce smaller litters and the breeding interval may be longer. Water rats (*Dasymys* spp.) and marsh rats (*Otomys* spp.) are present in the alpine zones of several mountains and in grassland belts at lower levels.

Above: *A black (Verreaux's) eagle* Aquila verreauxii *adult feeding her chick. In most areas this species makes up some 90 per cent of its diet with rock hyraxes (dassies). This large eagle occurs in mountainous and hill country virtually throughout the eastern half of Africa. Photo: John Carlyon*

One of the most visible of the mammals living in rugged highland areas is the hyrax, of which there are several species. They belong to the genera *Procavia*, *Heterohyrax* and *Dendrohyrax*, but the last-mentioned is a tree dweller. The rock-dwelling species are diurnal and live in suitable habitats ranging from sea-level to the alpine zones on some of the highest mountains. The tree-living species are nocturnal and occur in lowland and montane forests.

BIRDS OF THE HIGHLANDS

In general, bird diversity in mountains is low especially at the higher altitudes. In the lower montane zones, particularly where there is mixed forest, the number of species can be quite high. In the Cameroon Highlands at least 22 species are endemic or near-endemic, with some being restricted to one mountain. For example, the Mount Cameroon francolin (*Francolinus camerunensis*) is restricted to the mountain of the same name, between the altitudes of 850 m and 2 100 m. The Usambara eagle-owl (*Bubo vosseleri*) inhabits evergreen montane forest on these Tanzanian mountains. Some of the families that are well-represented in tropical montane forests are the fruit-eating turacos (Family **Musophagidae**), parrots (Family **Psittacidae**), doves and pigeons (Family **Columbidae**) and the sunbirds (Family **Nectariniidae**). The sunbirds are also widely distributed in the ericaceous belt on many mountains and in the Cape Folded Mountains they are abundant, benefitting from the great diversity of ericas and proteas from which they feed.

As one moves higher up the mountains conditions become harsher and the number of species decreases. Birds have the advantage of being able to fly to lower altitudes if conditions, such as extreme cold, threaten survival. Small perching birds keep close to the ground, using even minimal cover to avoid being buffeted by the strong winds that regularly blow at these heights; the larger birds, mainly raptors, are able to ride out all except the strongest winds. Verreaux's eagle (*Aquila verreauxi*) has a wide distribution in the mountain country of southern and eastern Africa, where it hunts the hyraxes which make up more than 90 per cent of its diet. In the Atlas Mountains the golden eagle (*Aquila chrysaëtos*) is the principal large raptor. Probably the most magnificent of all however, is the high-flying bearded vulture (*Gypaetus barbatus*), which has a wide African and Eurasian distribution. In Africa they have a patchy range, living in isolated populations in the Drakensberg, several of the eastern African highlands, the Ethiopian Highlands and the Atlas. Other species of vultures, such as the Cape griffon (*Gyps coprotheres*) of southern Africa and Rüppell's griffon (*Gyps rüppellii*), with a wide distribution south of the Sahara, breed in colonies on steep cliffs in mountainous country but they do much of their foraging in the lowlands. Many smaller raptor species breed and forage wholly, or partly, in the mountains. Most are very widespread, such as the peregrine falcon (*Falco peregrinus*) and the augur buzzard (*Buteo rufufuscus*). The white-necked raven (*Corvus albicollis*) occupying southern highland areas and the thick-billed raven (*Corvus crassirostris*) of the Ethiopian Highlands are the common African montane crows. Two other members of the crow family are found in high mountain areas, the alpine chough (*Pyrrhocorax graculus*) in the Atlas and the chough (*Pyrrhocorax pyrrhocorax*) in the Ethiopian Highlands. These birds live in small flocks

Below: *The rock (speckled) pigeon* Columba guinea *has a wide habitat tolerance and is found in most mountainous areas in sub-Saharan Africa.* **Bottom:** *A species of jumping spider (Family* **Salticidae**) *from a forest pocket in the Soutpansberg range in South Africa.*

and occupy even the highest peaks; in the Asian Himalayas they have been recorded near the top of Mount Everest, the world's tallest mountain.

Although waterfowl are not usually associated with mountains, one that deserves mention is the Abyssinian blue-winged goose (*Cyanochen cyanopterus*) which lives in the Ethiopian Highlands at altitudes greater than 2 400 m. The African black duck has a very wide distribution in highland areas, where it favours fast-flowing streams but it will also utilise standing waters. In the Ethiopian Highlands they have been recorded at water bodies over 3 500 m in altitude.

OTHER MONTANE ANIMALS

Although reptiles and amphibians are usually well represented in the lower zones of African mountains, the higher altitudes have very few species. Endemism, that is species restricted to a particular area, is often strong on African mountains and other highlands. For example, in the Cameroon Highlands there are at least 55 amphibians and 10 reptile species that are found nowhere else. In many cases, but by no means all, the endemics are found in association with forest and denser vegetation where there is a greater abundance of food and higher temperatures.

Chamaeleons are well represented in the montane and lowland forests of tropical Africa, being amongst the best adapted of lizards to an arboreal way of life. They have twig-grasping feet and prehensile tails which enable them to make their way with safety through even the highest vegetation. The grotesquely snouted *Chamaeleo fischeri* is only known from rain forest in the Usambara Mountains. The cordylids, agamas and skinks favour rocky areas on many mountains and ranges. Another diverse group of lizards found on mountains are the geckos, where different species occupy forests as well as rocky terrain where they shelter in crevices.

Snakes are not abundant on mountains but many lowland species penetrate to considerable heights, including the widely occurring puff adder (*Bitis arietans*), bird snake (*Thelotornis kirtlandi*) and the python (*Python sebae*). There are, however, some species that are restricted to mountains, such as the plain mountain adder (*Bitis inornata*), which is only known from a limited area in the Cape Folded Mountains. Most species, such as the tree vipers (*Atheris* spp.), are associated with moist montane forests.

Tree frogs, as well as those species inhabiting ground litter, are well represented in moist montane forests, particularly within the tropics. One of the largest groups are the painted tree frogs (*Hyperolius* spp.), which occur widely in the tropics. A few species have wide distributions but in the mountains there are a number of localised endemics, for example *Hyperolius puncticulatus*, which only lives in the East Usambara Mountains in Tanzania. There is often a shortage of standing surface water in these forests and some species have developed specialised ways of breeding, for example the bamboo frog (*Callixalus pictus*) from the Itombwe Mountains in eastern Zaïre lays its eggs in the rain-filled hollows of broken bamboo stems. In the Cape Folded Mountains several species of rain frogs (*Breviceps* spp.) lay their eggs (few and large) in self-excavated holes in damp soil or moss, and there is sufficient food in each egg to sustain the young until metamorphosis is completed. Some frogs have adapted to living in swift-flowing mountain streams and they include the ghost frogs (*Heleophryne* spp.) and torrent frogs (*Phrynobatrachus* spp.). In the pools and streams at the top of the Drakensberg range a large aquatic frog (*Rana vertebralis*) spends all its time in the water and can withstand freezing temperatures. A number of small toads have found niches in marsh and sponge-bog in the higher montane zones, including *Capensebufo rosei* of the Cape Folded Mountains. Another tiny frog, *Rana wittei*, lives in marshes in the Ethiopian Highlands and on the northern slopes of Mount Kenya, and the males will continue to call as the temperature drops but stop as soon as freezing point is reached.

Invertebrate populations are as diverse on mountains as in any other habitat, with the greatest number of species being located in the forested and well-vegetated habitats. It is believed that only a small percentage of African invertebrates are actually known to science. Variation is at its greatest in tropical montane rain forest and at its lowest in the alpine zone. There are scorpions, spiders, mites, centipedes, millipedes, molluscs, beetles, butterflies and moths, bees, wasps, flies, ants, praying mantids, grasshoppers, termites and more. Many species are restricted to a particular mountain or range, or even a tiny area within one of the vegetation zones where a suitable niche exists. At high altitudes many invertebrates are darker in colour so they absorb short-wave ultraviolet light and in this way protect lower-lying tissues. Dark coloration also has the advantage of absorbing heat during the daylight hours.

Although insects are poorly studied on African mountains, work elsewhere has shown that many high-altitude insects rely heavily on wind-blown plant and animal detritus to supplement their diet, particularly where plants are scarce.

THE FUTURE

The highlands of Africa share the problems suffered by many low-lying regions, and all have to do with man. Montane forests within the tropics are under immense pressure from commercial logging and timber extraction, and in some cases the forests even lie within conservation areas. Compounding this is the ever-increasing demand for fuelwood and space to grow subsistence and cash crops. The mountains of volcanic origin and their surrounds come under great pressure because of the fertile nature of the soils. Forest land is cleared by cutting and burning; in the past the system of slash-and-burn cultivation was sustainable because human populations were low and subsistence farmers could plant new areas, allowing them to lie fallow and recover. As the forest is destroyed rain falls directly on the mountain slopes, causing the soil to erode and making large areas unsuitable for either natural regrowth or cultivation. In some montane areas, for example the Ethiopian Highlands, cattle and other domesticated animals graze on the high grasslands and through overgrazing and trampling further contribute to soil degradation. Even where national parks or other conservation areas have been established, such as mounts Kenya and Kilimanjaro, pressure from surrounding settlements squeezing against the boundaries is often intense. Mount Nimba is under considerable mining pressure that has resulted in the loss of most of its finest forest. The threats to the montane vegetation in the Cape Folded Mountains have been discussed in the chapter on Conservation.

Another problem that will have to confronted by the authorities is the ever-growing numbers of tourists that are visiting some of these mountain areas, notably the conservation areas in the Cape Folded Belt, the Drakensberg, and mounts Kenya and Kilimanjaro.

Above: *Jackson's francolin* Francolinus jacksoni *occurs in forest on several Kenyan mountains.*

CHAPTER 5

THE CAPE HEATHLAND

All the vegetation on our globe can be divided in six groups, which are referred to as plant kingdoms. These six are the Boreal Floral Kingdom (covering 42 per cent of the earth's land surface), the Palaeotropical (35 per cent), Neotropical (14 per cent), Australian (7 per cent), the Antarctic/Patagonian (one per cent) and the Cape Floral Kingdom (i.e. the Cape fynbos). The outstanding feature of the fynbos is that as the smallest of the six it only covers 0.04 per cent of the world's land surface but has 8 580 species of flowering plants, almost 70 per cent of these being endemic. With this diversity it is recognised as having the richest known flora. It covers an area of some 70 000 km^2 and lies in a narrow, crescent-shaped arc at the southern tip of the African continent, extending approximately 350 km to the north of Cape Town and 800 km to the east of that city, forming a fragmented belt reaching 40 km to 160 km inland from the coast. Elements of fynbos are also found on the higher mountain ranges of southern and eastern Africa where conditions allow for the continued existence of outliers of a once much more widespread vegetation type. Geologically the area covered by the Cape heathland can be portioned into three principal rock types. The lower layer, known as the Malmesbury Shales, consists of mud sediments that were deposited under the sea. Between 610 and 500 million years ago great volcanic activity caused magma to break through to the surface, covering and intruding into the Malmesbury Shales. As the magma

Background: *Typical mountain scenery in the fynbos region.* **Above left:** *The largest spider seen scuttling through the fynbos is this baboon spider,* Harpactira *sp.*

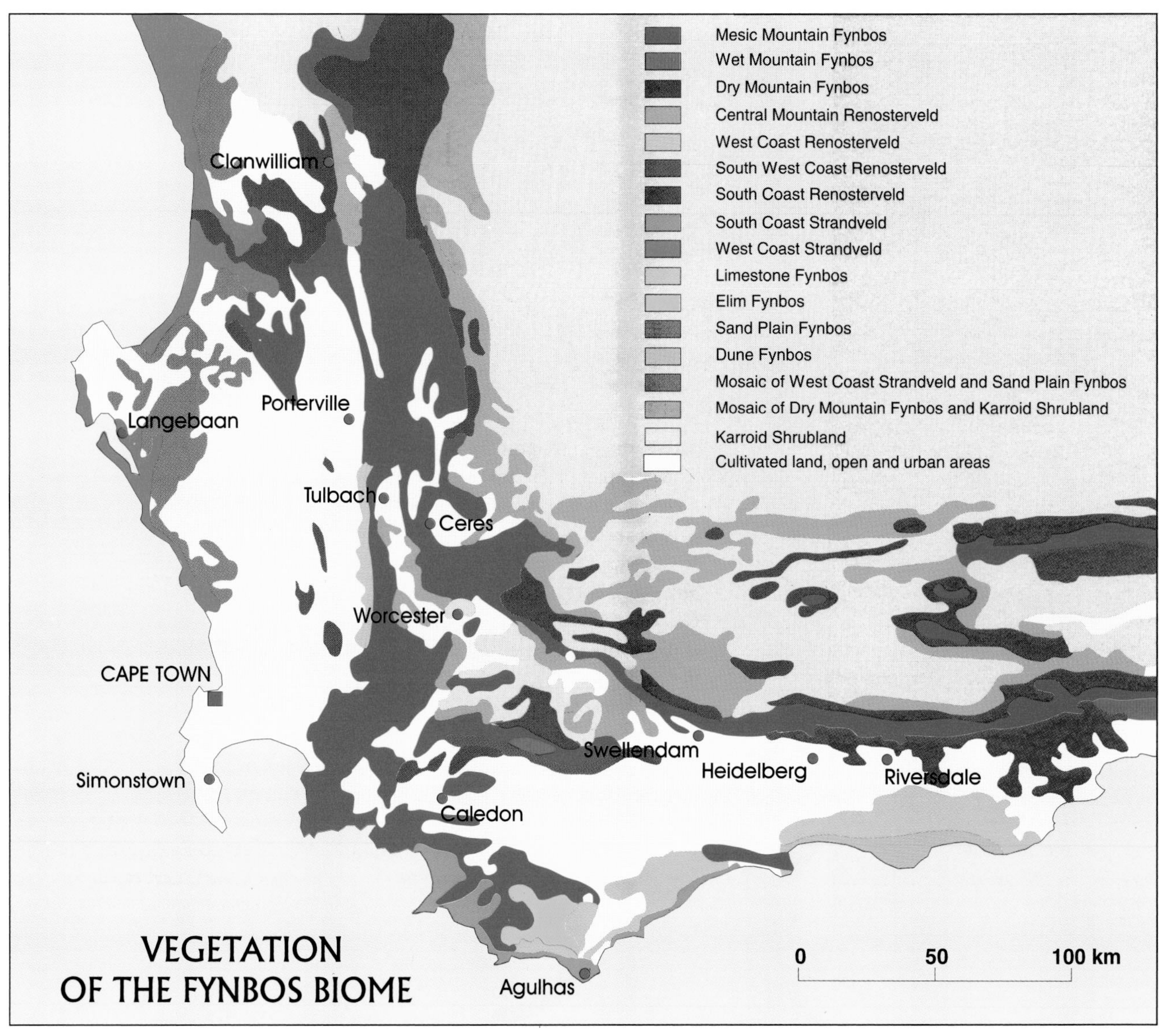

cooled and solidified the so-called Cape Granites were formed. The region then rose gradually above the surface of the sea and for 50 million years erosion and weathering created a level plain. Once again the land mass sank and was covered by a shallow sea for some 200 million years. During this time marine and land-origin sediments were laid down on top of the sunken plain, in places to great depths, to ultimately form the group collectively known as the Table Mountain Series. These sandstones consolidated to form weather-resistant rock and once again the region rose above sea level. As this process was taking place the earth's crust was subjected to massive folding and tilting and the mountain ranges we know as the Cape Folded Belt came into being. These ranges have changed little, in contrast with the coastal plain which has been influenced by sea level fluctuations and the processes that were put into play by these events. Most of the soils in the mountainous areas are highly leached and acidic, whereas those in the valleys and on the lowland plains tend to be more fertile.

Approximately 100 million years ago flowering plants appeared for the first time in large numbers. Over millions of years the great continent of Gondwanaland started to break up and the continents that we know today started to drift apart from each other, each land mass carrying with it its own elements of a once-communal flora. New ocean currents and shifting weather belts produced climatic changes that resulted in drier conditions setting in. The cold Benguela Current, which pushes its cold waters relentlessly northwards close to the west coast, has a major influence on present-day weather conditions. Fynbos vegetation once covered great swathes of southern Africa but suitable conditions decreased as the African continent drifted northwards until it came to rest against Europe. This northward drift served to reduce the conditions suited to the growth of heathland (fynbos) but favoured "invasions" by other plant species from the north and east. Then about 6 million years ago the Antarctic ice layers began to form and this resulted in a winter-rainfall pattern developing in the area and a drier climate in the adjacent interior. These conditions favoured hard-leaved (sclerophyllus) shrubs, which began to replace the other flora which was less suited to change.

Some 2.5 million years ago the South Atlantic high-pressure systems were stabilising and dry summers became a permanent climatic feature of the region. About 1.6 million years ago the temperate climate that prevailed in the south caused a rich flora to develope, whereas in the north the Arctic ice-fields spread over great areas and many plant and animal species perished.

The climate of the south-western sector of the Cape heathland is now characterised by cool, wet winters and warm, dry summers. Almost half the rain falls during May, June and July, with over 3 000 mm being deposited on some of the high mountain ranges but as little as 300 mm falling in parts of the lowlands. As one moves eastwards rainfall is more evenly spread through the year and in the most easterly segments of the Cape heathlands most precipitation is dropped during the summer months. However, as one moves away from the south-west the diversity of plant species decreases. During the summer months moisture-laden clouds frequently blanket the mountain peaks, thus providing an important source of water during this otherwise dry period.

The entire coastal belt within this region is frequently lashed by strong winds, prevailing from the south-east in the summer and north-west in the winter. It is these winds that have given the area one of its names, Cape of Storms.

Above: Protea laurifolia *may reach a height of 8 m and is common in some mountainous areas.* **Below:** *Extensive grass cover on the shale belt in the Cedarberg Mountains.*

THE VEGETATION

The early Dutch settlers referred to the vegetation of the Cape Floral Kingdom collectively as "fijnbosch", this being modified to "fynbos" in more recent times. The name means "fine bush" or "fine shrub" and refers to the many shrubs in the region that have finely branched, small-leafed forms which are adaptations to withstand dehydration during the warm, dry summer months. There are several other regions of the world with a similar climate and vegetation types but the latter are not nearly as rich in plant species as that found at Africa's southern tip. There is the *maquis* of Corsica, the *chaparral* of California, the *macchia* of Italy and the *kwongan* of western Australia. In some publications the fynbos is referred to as Cape Macchia because of these similarities. If we look at the richness of the floral populations of the Cape heathland and compare this wealth with populations in other parts of the world we find that the nearest competitor is the Amazon Basin with only one-third of the number of species. One can of course give even more startling comparisons. The Cape Peninsula, which covers about 470 km^2 and lies to the south of Cape Town has 2 256 known species of flowering plants, whereas the whole of Britain and Ireland counts only 1 443 species. In the whole of western Australia, with an area 20 times that of the area covered by Cape heathland, approximately 7 000 species are known. It is certainly a floral assemblage second to none.

The fact that more than 8 580 species are present in the region is amazing in itself, but even more important is the high level of endemism. This applies not only to species; six entire families and nearly 200 genera (out of a total of 960) are found nowhere else in the world. Britain is home to four species of heather (genus *Erica*), whereas the Cape heathland has at least 605 species. Another incredibly well-represented family is the **Iridaceae** with about 625 species, which includes such genera as *Gladiolus*, *Dierama*, *Watsonia*, *Moraea*, *Babiana* and *Sparaxis*.

Both locally and elsewhere probably the best known plants are the members of the family **Proteaceae**, many of which have large and showy blooms. This family is also well represented in Australia, with other species in South America and elsewhere in Africa. But of the 330 species of protea occurring in South Africa more than 90 per cent are restricted to the Cape heathlands. Of course this is only a small selection but it serves to emphasise the great importance of Africa's southern tip. Another important point is that new

Top: *Members of the genus* Oxalis *are found virtually throughout the fynbos region.* **Above centre:** Erica inflata *is one of more than 600 species of heath that are entirely restricted to the Cape heathland.* **Above:** *The waboom* Protea nitida *may grow to a height of five metres or more. It is usually found on rocky slopes and forms distinct belts in some areas. The wood was heavily used by the early settlers because although hard it is quite easy to work.* **Left:** *The common slug eater* Dubberia lutrix *occurs in the southern parts of the fynbos.*

species are discovered on a regular basis, mainly because of the difficulty of access to many of the rugged mountains, the tiny areas occupied by many species and the problems related to finding "a needle in a haystack". Added to these, of course, is the ongoing fragmentation of the natural vegetation by the actions of man, at its worst on the lowland plain and the fertile inter-montane valleys. Looked at in its broadest sense the Cape heathland or fynbos can be separated into the following distinctive subgroups: Mountain Fynbos, Lowland Fynbos, Coastal Strandveld, and Coastal Renosterveld. Many botanists hold the view that the strandveld and renosterveld fall outside the definition of "true" fynbos on the grounds that they have few plant species which are typical of this biome. However, as they form an integral part of the Cape Floral Kingdom they can hardly be left out. None of the types occurs in continuous, uninterrupted belts; instead they form complex mosaics.

MOUNTAIN FYNBOS

Although remnants of mountain fynbos survive on ranges outside the area covered by the Cape Floral Kingdom, such as in the Drakensberg of KwaZulu/Natal, Mount Kenya, Mount Kilimanjaro and the Ruwenzoris in East Africa, it is in the south-western Cape where diversity is at its greatest. The highest peaks are the Seweweekspoortberg (2 325 m) and Matroosberg (2 249 m) with several others topping 2 000 m. Within the mountain fynbos a number of different vegetation zones can be recognised but in general most consist of mixed shrubland, with *Ericas* (heathers) and *Restios* often occurring together in a dominant combination. The plant composition is largely influenced by rainfall and soil type. Trees are scarce but where they do occur they are usually endemic. The Clanwilliam cedar (*Widdringtonia cedarbergensis*) is found only in the Cedarberg range, where it was once abundant.

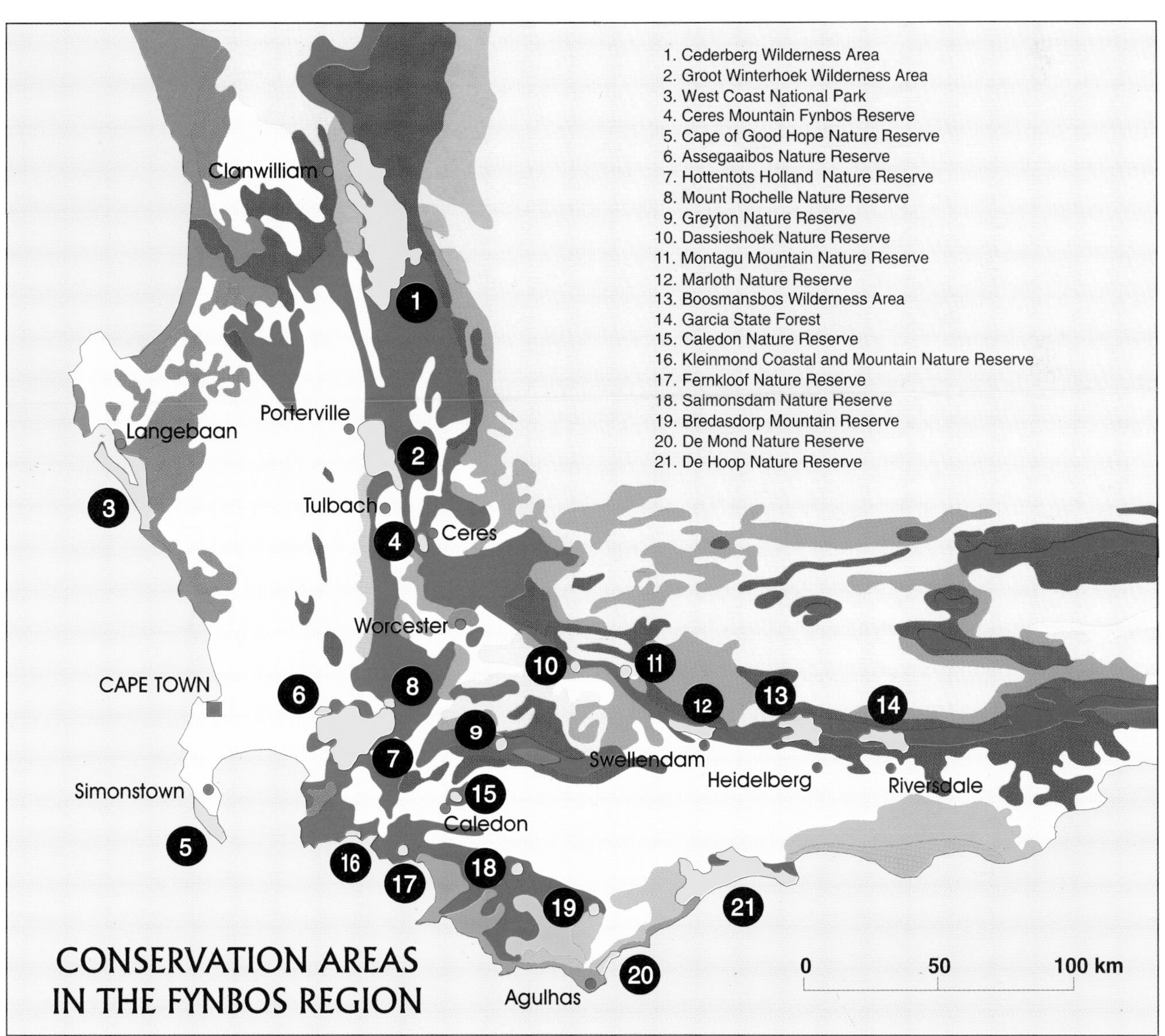

However, vast numbers were cut for use as timber for construction and the production of furniture, and in later years to provide telephone poles. It was a sad end for a hardy and noble tree. Today they are rare and old specimens are gnarled and twisted, their form having saved them from the saw and the axe. In the Baviaanskloof, at the eastern extension of the mountain fynbos, the Willowmore cedar (*Widdringtonia schwarzii*) suffered a similar fate. A few other tree species occur, such as the silver tree (*Leucadendron argenteum*), rockwood (*Heeria argentea*), red candlewood (*Pterocelastrus rostratus*) and the very widespread wild olive, *Olea europaea*, but this was never a tree-rich area.

Sadly, it is the exotic trees that dominate many of the landscapes. The mountain fynbos is the most secure of the four fynbos vegetation types, primarily because the steep, rocky slopes are not suited to cultivation. Nevertheless they have been invaded by a number of alien tree and shrub species, for example the cluster pine (*Pinus pinaster*), an import from the Mediterranean region, and several species of *Hakea* introduced from Australia. Nowadays great efforts are made to try and eradicate these invaders but only a few decades ago the authorities happily gave out seeds of these "foreigners" to hikers to scatter in the pristine mountain wilderness. No doubt at the time it was felt that the mountains would be improved by light forestation; little did people realise what a

Above: *Agriculture has destroyed much of the lowland fynbos, strandveld and renosterveld. Only the high mountain ranges have escaped severe modification.* **Right:** Charaxis *sp. butterfly photographed in mountain fynbos.*

floral "hurricane" they were unleashing! One factor contributing to the great diversity of plant species, particularly in the mountain fynbos, is the broken nature of the terrain, which has encouraged development in isolation. This can be likened to an ocean with numerous tiny islands, each developing within its own particular micro-climate, soil and associated plant species.

Lowland Fynbos

This zone extends from sea level to about 150 m above sea level, although elements are found at higher altitudes. Although variable, soils are generally made up of deep grey-coloured sands that may be either alkaline or acid. *Ericas* (heathers) are usually abundant, as are *Restios*, and in some areas such species as *Passerina* spp. and *Metalasia* spp. are dominant. In areas underlaid with limestone, primarily along the south coast, such *Leucadendron* species as *coniferum* and *meridianum* are often predominant. Trees are scarce but stands of wind-battered white milkwood (*Sideroxylon inerme*) grow close to the south coast in sheltered areas. It is said that an infusion of the bark of this tree will prevent nightmares. Lowland fynbos has been badly abused by man and the combination of alien vegetation, agriculture and unplanned burning has resulted in severe fragmentation of this fynbos type.

Renosterveld

The renosterbos (*Elytropappus rhinocerotis*), a low, fine-leaved shrub, gives its name to this, the most abused of all the fynbos plant types. Only about 9 per cent of its original area survives. Actually, renosterveld is a degraded vegetation type that is believed to have originally comprised *Themeda triandra* grassland before agriculture transformed the area. The little renosterveld which survives occurs on the undulating lowlands from sea level to about 400 m in fertile, shale soils. The degraded areas now have an abundance of *asteraceous* (daisy) species and geophytes. There are small, localised stands of wild olive (*Olea capensis/europaea*) and thicket euclea or common guarri (*Euclea undulata*), but as with the lowland fynbos the dominant trees are alien species.

Strandveld

The strandveld is located primarily along the lower parts of the western coastal plains and it is in fact a transition belt between the lowland fynbos and the more arid succulent vegetation of the north. There are a few isolated patches along the south coast. It occupies sandy plains and sand dunes, as well as low limestone and granite ridges from sea level to about 150 m. The strandveld is characterised by a lower annual rainfall (200-300 mm) than other zones within the Cape Floral Kingdom. The vegetation is very variable but includes numerous succulents, particularly in the north, elements of typical fynbos species and an abundance of annuals.

CHARACTERISTIC PLANT GROUPS

Proteaceae – the Proteas

This family includes the most showy and varied of all major fynbos vegetation groups. They take their name from the Greek sea god Proteus who according to legend could take on a bewildering array of shapes and forms. Some species develop into small trees but the majority are bush-like, with others creeping along the ground. It is one of the oldest families of flowering plants with a history extending back almost 300 million years. Of the 330 species known to occur in South Africa, some 92 per cent are found only within the Cape Floral Kingdom. In most species the leaves are tough and leathery and the small individual flowers are grouped together in often large infloresences that are usually fringed

THOSE WERE THE DAYS!

The first documented reference to elephants within this floral kingdom was made by Vasco da Gama on 1 December 1497 at Mossel Bay on the south coast.

When Jan van Riebeeck and his companions arrived at the foot of Table Mountain in 1652 elephants were found throughout the Cape heathlands, although confirmed records are lacking for the Cape Peninsula. Once Van Riebeeck had established himself in his position as Commander he started to send out expeditions to the north and east. Jan Dankaert, leading one of these forays, recorded 200 to 300 elephants feeding on the mountain slopes in the north-west and it was this sighting that resulted in the Olifants River getting its name. The Namaqua Khoikhoi soon learned that the white man viewed elephant ivory as a valuable commodity and the slaughter began.

Throughout much of the Cape heathland elephants had disappeared by 1800 but they persisted in the forest and fynbos to the east. In 1876 a forestry official, Captain Harison, estimated that between 400 and 500 elephants wandered the area between George and Tsitsikamma. By 1925 only 12 animals were known to be surviving in a section of the forest and fynbos near the coastal settlement of Knysna. In 1970 it was estimated that 10 animals remained but this has declined to four.

by colourful bracts. The first description of a protea (*Protea neriifolia*) appeared in 1605 in a book written by the Dutch botanist Carolus Clusius, and by 1810 Kew Gardens in London had succeeded in bringing 21 species to the flowering stage. Proteas are popular in the flower trade.

Ericaceae – the Ericas or Heaths

The ericas take their name from the Greek word *ereiko* which means to break, a reference to the apparent ability of a concoction brewed from their leaves to break up or dissolve gallstones. There is no scientific basis for this claim, however. It would seem that botanists cannot agree on the number of erica occurring within the Cape heathlands but there are certainly more than 600, of which the majority are endemic. If one compares this with the 14 species occurring throughout Europe and the two in northern Africa one begins to appreciate the absolute floral wealth within the region. Most species grow as small shrubs but some may reach heights exceeding 6 m. The flowers range from little more than one millimetre in length to those with "trumpet-like" blossoms reaching up to 60 mm. The flower structure of each erica species, or group of species, has evolved in such a way as to attract a specific pollinator, whether it be a moth, fly, the wind or a bird.

Restionaceae – Restios

These are reed-like, wiry plants which do not bear leaves and thrive on most soil types, including nutrient-poor soils, and take the place of grasses in the fynbos. In the latter situations they are frequently the dominant plant component. To date 310 species have been described and 290 of these are endemic to the region. The male and female flowers are carried on separate plants and frequently have the appearance of two different species – no doubt an evolutionary plot to confuse the amateur botanist. They range in height from a few centimetres to over 2.5 m.

THE ROLE OF FIRE

In 1497 the Portuguese sailor Vasco da Gama apparently observed so much smoke billowing from the hills above present-day Mossel Bay that he named the area *Terra de Fume*. It is possible that he saw the fires set by indigenous pastoralists to encourage fresh vegetation growth for their goats and sheep. There is evidence that some 125 000 years ago human hunter-gatherers deliberately burnt fynbos to increase yields of the bulbs of *Watsonia* sp. As the first settlers from Europe started to develop farms in the vicinity of Cape Town, they followed the example of burning used by the local people. However, in 1687 the authorities passed strict laws prohibiting random burning, with draconian punishments for those careless enough to ignore the new controls. A first offender was to be scoured, a somewhat brutal clearing of the digestive system, and for the second offence the death

Far left: *Coastal strandveld vegetation on the Atlantic Ocean seaboard of the south-western Cape.* **Top:** Acacia cyclops *forms dense thickets which exclude indigenous vegetation and it has become a major pest, particularly in lowland fynbos.*
Above: *Many protea species are serotinous, that is they shed only a few seeds after every flowering season, retaining the bulk in fire-resistant storage organs (usually hard, woody cones) until fire kills the parent plant and the seed store dries and splits, releasing massive quantities of seeds.*

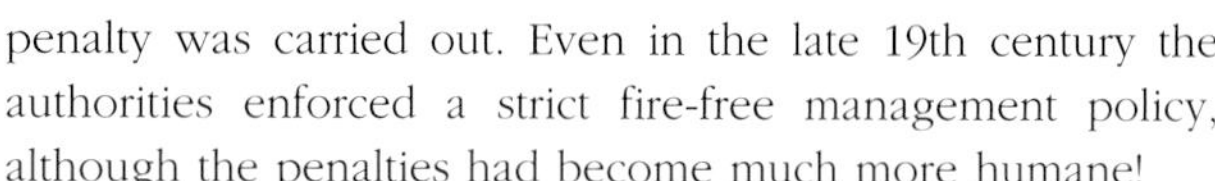

Above left: *The rameron pigeon* Columba arquatrix *may be sighted in forest pockets in the mountains as well as along the coast.* **Above:** *The lesser doublecollared sunbird* Nectarinia chalybea. **Above right:** *During winter and spring the Cape Folded Mountains are a blaze of colour.*
Right: *The redwinged starling* Onychognathus morio, *a common fynbos species.*

penalty was carried out. Even in the late 19th century the authorities enforced a strict fire-free management policy, although the penalties had become much more humane!

As this century progressed it was realised that fire was in fact an essential and healthy component of the fynbos ecology. Fire is inevitable in inflammable, often resinous vegetation. Today fire is used as a management tool, particularly in the water catchment areas and in nature reserves. Different fire zones can be recognised in the different fynbos types. Fire is rare in the strandveld because there is little ground fuel, i.e. dry plant material is scarce, and many of the plants are succulents with a high water content. Within the mountain and lowland fynbos ground fuel takes about four to six years to accumulate to levels that can promote burning and very few areas go for as long as 40 years without having fire pass through them. In the south-western Cape lightning strikes are rare and only a few fires start in this way, but sparks created by rockfalls cause about a quarter of all conflagrations. Many fires today are planned and they are usually kept within the confines of a predetermined area, although the strong winds that blow in the area occasionally result in such burns running out of control. Although it is now accepted that fire leads to healthy fynbos, there is no consensus on the ideal interval between fires. Burns within the mountain fynbos are usually carried out on a 12- to 15-year cycle. Recent studies have shown that summer fires at 20-year intervals or longer are probably ideal. If fires are too frequent it leaves many plants with insufficient time to mature and develop adequate seed stocks. Injudicious burning and lack of attention to timing has forced a number of species into decline and possible extinction.

Fynbos plants have developed four strategies to survive and thrive after fires. Many species have underground storage organs, in the form of bulbs and corms, which lie unharmed below the soil as fire sweeps across the surface. Many species produce surface growth within a few days to a few months after the passing of the fire. In fact a number of bulbous (geophytic) plant species require fire to stimulate sprouting and flowering. This enables the veld to recover quickly as synchronised post-fire flowering and seed production provides an abundance of seeds for the granivorous birds and rodents with plenty left over to produce seedlings. A number of fynbos species will flower only after a fire with the bulbs lying dormant under the soil, sometimes for several years, before the next fire strikes the area. Some woody bushes and small trees rely on thick, insulating bark to pro-

tect small, dormant buds, whereas others send out new shoots from the underground woody rootstocks. The fourth fire survival technique relies on the protection of seed in hard fireproof capsules. Fire kills the parent plant and the seed storage bodies dry and split, releasing vast quantities of seed. During non-fire seasons the plants only release small numbers of seeds, retaining the bulk in the storage organs. By the time a fire burns the area an accumulation of several years' seed stocks are available for release. More than 100 protea species have evolved this serotinous survival strategy. Unfortunately, fires do not always burn at the ideal intervals and frequent burning can destroy young plants before they have had the chance to set seed. On the other hand if intervals between fires are too long this can also impact heavily on plant survival.

Another strategy used by more than 1 200 fynbos plants is myrmecochory, the dispersal of seeds by ants. These plants produce seeds which have coats (elaiosomes) of oily, fleshy material and when they fall to the ground they give off a chemical signal to which the ants react. They scuttle around below the parent plant, collecting the seeds and carrying them into their underground colonies. Here the seed coatings are eaten by the ants but the hard seeds remain undamaged in their subterranean nursery. This ensures that the seeds escape destruction in fire and the attention of seed-eating mice and birds. The passage of fire on the surface serves to stimulate germination of the seeds in a way that as yet is

Left from top: *The* ***Cape gerbil*** Tatera afra *is endemic to the lowland fynbos and strandveld areas where it digs its burrows in deep sand. It is considered to be a pest species by farmers in the wheat-growing blocks.*
The ***Cape rock elephant shrew*** Elephantulus edwardii *can often be spotted if one sits quietly in the vicinity of rock scree or narrow cracks in the mountains.*
The ***spectacled dormouse*** Graphiurus ocularis *is not restricted to the region but does occur in the mountain ranges.*
The ***Cape spiny mouse*** Acomys subspinosus *is an inhabitant of the mountain ranges of the fynbos region.*

poorly understood. An "immigrant" species, the Argentine ant (*Iridomyrmex humilis*), has begun to upset this neat symbiotic relationship. The onslaught is on two fronts – they attack and displace indigenous ant species and they feed on the seed-coating on the ground surface, leaving the seeds to be destroyed by fire and granivorous animals.

Small rodents and insectivores within the fynbos react to fire in different ways. Few studies have been undertaken on the mammals in this rich and varied floristic mosaic so we do not attempt to generalise for the biome as a whole but offer one example. After fire plants emerge in succession and offer different types of food at different times. A study undertaken in mountain fynbos in the southern part of the region showed that Cape spiny mice (*Acomys subspinosus*) and the forest shrew (*Myosorex varius*) were present throughout all periods of plant succession. Grey climbing mice (*Dendromus melanotis*) only stayed for one to two years but Namaqua rock mice (*Aethomys namaquensis*) and spectacled dormice (*Graphiurus ocularis*) moved in two to three years after the fire and stayed for two years.

POLLINATION

The fynbos is believed to have the highest ratio of ornithophilous plant species to nectar-eating bird species recorded and after Australia it has the second richest assemblage of terrestrial mammal-pollinated plant species.

None of the small rodents and insectivores that feed on the nectar and pollen of the proteas and leucospermums are specifically adapted to nectar feeding but it is just another component of their diet. To date four mouse species and one elephant shrew have been recorded as visiting protea flowers and inadvertently transferring pollen from one flower to the next. Fynbos also has an impressive array of bee, fly and beetle species which are essential pollinators of many plants.

THE MAMMALS

Despite the unsurpassed richness of its flora, the fynbos mammal assemblage is somewhat meagre. When the first European settlers were erecting their dwellings and producing vegetables for the crews of the Dutch East India

Right: *The fynbos region is not rich in endemic mammals but the largest is the bontebok* Damaliscus d. dorcas. *This rare species is restricted to a few conservation areas and private farms.* **Above:** *The only other endemic antelope besides the bontebok is the Cape grysbok* Raphicerus melanotis. *Although fairly common it is seldom seen as it usually keeps to dense undergrowth.*

Company on their passage to the trading stations in the east, they would have been able to hear the hippos snorting in the reed-fringed marshes, the roaring of lions on the Cape Flats and the occasional unfortunate may have been charged by a disgruntled black rhinoceros disturbed while slumbering. All of these species, and more, have retreated northwards, giving way to the vineyard, the wheatfield and urban sprawl. The blue buck *(Hippotragus leucophaeus)*, once restricted to the fynbos, has the dubious distinction of being the first mammal recorded to have become extinct on the African continent in historic times. Another fynbos restricted antelope, the bontebok (*Damaliscus dorcas dorcas*), almost followed the blue buck into extinction but the action of a few farmers saved it from a similar fate. The largest herds are now located in one national park and two nature reserves, with smaller numbers held in other reserves and on private farms. Although evidence is scarce it seems likely that the animals moved between the coastal plain and uplands at the foot of the mountains, but today all are confined behind fences.

Another near fynbos endemic is the Cape grysbok *(Raphicerus melanotis)*, but unlike the bontebok it is still widespread and not uncommon in some areas. It is a small (weighing about 10 kg), skulking antelope that seldom leaves the cover of dense scrub.

Several more widespread species occur within the region, including the grey rhebok (*Pelea capreolus)*, which lives in small herds in hill country and on the lower mountain slopes, and the steenbok *(Raphicerus campestris)*, which shows a strong preference for open country with low vegetation. A predominance of browsing animals is indicative of the poor nutrient values of the natural grazing and carrying capacity is very low. Although parts of the region carry large popula-

tions of domestic livestock, these are run primarily on fertilised pastures to make up for the low levels of such elements as phosphorus, cobalt, copper and manganese.

Several rodent species are endemic or near-endemic and most of these are well distributed and abundant. They include the Cape dune molerat (*Bathyergus suillus*), the largest fossorial mammal in Africa reaching weights in excess of 750 g, the Cape spiny mouse (*Acomys subspinosus*), an inhabitant of the mountains, and the Cape gerbil (*Tatera afra*), which occupies sandy flats. Verreaux's mouse (*Mastomys verreauxii*) is a nondescript grey mouse that shows a preference for moist, well-vegetated habitats. *Micranthus junceus*, a plant growing from a corm-stock, has evolved a way of allowing itself to be partly eaten by the Cape molerat (*Georhycus capensis*). Each corm is made up of a number of segments, as with garlic, and when the mole removes the outer corm "skin" and removes one segment to feed the rest are dropped to the tunnel floor. Small cormlets attached to the stem break loose and in this way are distributed, and when conditions are right they germinate. The mole benefits from having an abundant food source and the plant does not have to use nutrients that would have otherwise gone into the production of chemical "mole repellents", a protection strategy used by many species.

THE BIRDS

About 250 species of bird have been recorded within the fynbos biome, with only six endemics. These are the Cape rockjumper (*Chaetops frenatus*), Victorin's warbler (*Bradypterus victorini*), Cape sugarbird (*Promerops cafer*), orangebreasted sunbird (*Nectarinia violacea*), Cape siskin (*Serinus tottus*) and the protea canary (*Serinus leucopterus*). In an area of such floral and habitat diversity one would normally expect

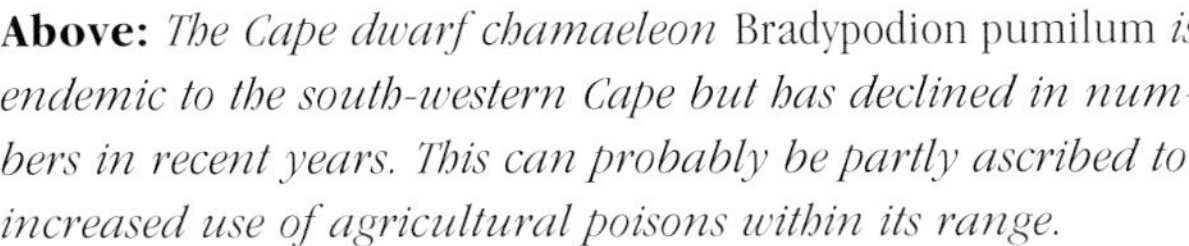

Above: *The Cape dwarf chamaeleon* Bradypodion pumilum *is endemic to the south-western Cape but has declined in numbers in recent years. This can probably be partly ascribed to increased use of agricultural poisons within its range.*
Top right: *The region covered by the Cape Floral Kingdom is relatively poor in reptile species. This is the coral snake,* Aspidelaps lubricus.
Above right: *The very widespread puff adder* Bitis arietans *is common in parts of the strandveld and lowland fynbos.*
Right: *A juvenile Cape cobra* Naja nivea.

to encounter a greater variety of bird species, as well as more endemics. A number of theories have been put forward to explain this, including the low structural diversity of the vegetation and the fact that many plants have evolved other means of dispersing their seeds and these are largely unsuitable for seed-eating birds.

THE REPTILES AND AMPHIBIANS

Several reptiles and amphibians are endemic to the biome. Most have very limited distribution ranges and several are seriously threatened. All the species facing a dim future are in the lowland areas which receive the most attention from farmers and developers. The beautifully marked geometric tortoise (*Psammobates geometricus*) is restricted to a few "pocket-handkerchief" patches – all that remains of the once extensive areas that it favours. No one knows exactly how many survive but estimates range from 2 000 to 6 000 individuals. The other tortoises in the area are able to survive in a wider range of habitats, in some cases even where disturbance is considerable. The specialists struggle whilst the generalists thrive. By far the commonest tortoise in the region is the angulate, or ploughshare, tortoise (*Chersine angulata*), which occurs in very high densities on some parts of the coastal plain. If the geometric tortoise is in trouble, a number of the frogs are teetering on the brink because of drainage, pollution, infestations of exotic plants, housing developments and general disturbance. The Cape platanna (*Xenopus gilli*) is restricted to ponds with relatively acidic waters in very few locations. Changes in the chemical composition of the water allow the more aggressive and abundant common platanna (*Xenopus laevis*) to invade, where it interbreeds with the rare species and also feeds on its tadpoles and young frogs. The interesting thumbed ghost frog (*Heleophryne rosei*), is restricted to nine localities on Table Mountain and another ghost frog (*Heleophryne purcelli*), is found in a small area of the eastern extension of the fynbos, but this species is not under any threat at this stage. The rainfrogs (*Breviceps* spp.) are well represented but their conservation status is difficult to assess because much of their time is spent in underground burrows. Two tiny species, the micro frog (*Microbatrachella capensis*) and the Cape caco (*Cacosternum capense*), inhabit shallow, vegetation-fringed pans, but most of their former habitat has been drained.

Below left: *The geometric tortoise* Psammobates geometricus *is restricted to a few isolated patches of lowland fynbos and is considered to be one of the rarest tortoises in the world.* **Below:** Cicada *species.* **Below centre:** *Several species of scorpions are found in the region.* **Bottom:** *The sand rain frog* Breviceps rosei *is one of several frog species that are endemic to the south-western region of the fynbos biome.*

THE INVERTEBRATES

A number of insect groups are well represented by endemics with some having close affinities to ancient species from other southern continents, a legacy of the super-continent of Gondwanaland. Although approximately 230 species of butterflies occur in fynbos, suprisingly few are endemics. With the great diversity of plant species one would expect a greater degree of endemism.

The cave-dwelling cricket *(Speleiacris tabulae)* has a very limited distribution on Table Mountain and the crustacean *Spelaeogryphus lepidops* is only found in one cave on the same mountain. Of the approximately 100 species of slugs and snails (Mollusca) in the region more than 60 are endemics. A number of alien species have been introduced and these are displacing several of the local species.

Many invertebrate species, particularly insects, have evolved in tandem with the unique vegetation and many species are bound to one plant species or group of species. Plant extinctions or declines result in the disappearance or reduction of their insect associates. Only a relatively small percentage of all insect species have been described and with the decline in the fortunes of the fynbos, many "unknown" species follow their hosts into extinction.

Above: *An example of weathering of Table Mountain sandstone, an important component of the geological makeup of the area. Fantastic rock formations can be seen here.*

THE FUTURE

The fynbos, or Cape heathland, occupies only one per cent of southern Africa's land surface, yet it is home to 69 per cent of all of its threatened plant species. At least 26 plant species have teetered over the brink into extinction in recent years and others may soon follow. Some plants that were thought to have gone forever have been "rediscovered", previously unknown populations of rare species are occasionally located and some reappear after fire. Overall, however, the picture is not a happy one, particularly for the vegetation on the coastal plain.

The mountain fynbos is in the healthiest state, having escaped the ravages of urban sprawl and agriculture. Much of this vegetation group is protected under the Mountain Catchment Areas Act of 1970, which is primarily aimed at ensuring that the supply of water to the impoundments located below the mountains is not diminished. The mountain fynbos has not entirely escaped change however, and it faces problems with unplanned and unseasonal fires, infestations of alien vegetation and the planting of fast-growing commercial timbers in plantations.

The worst devastation has taken place in the lowland fynbos and renosterveld where the fertile soils, derived mainly from the shales, have encouraged the planting of grains, orchards and vineyards over vast areas. Even where the natural plant mosaic survives it has been drastically modified by the actions of man. Urban sprawl has played its part but probably the greatest threat to surviving fynbos is the spreading and largely unstoppable green cancer – the alien plants. These imports, mainly from Australia, are aggressive pests and some species are so well established that there is now no hope of eradicating them. Several of the most problematic species, as with many indigenous species, benefit from fire, with the liberation of seeds and stimulation of mass germination. Species such as rooikrans *(Acacia cyclops)*, which has an annual seed fall of 10 000 per square metre, and Port Jackson (*Acacia saligna*) have formed dense, impenetrable thickets that outperform local species and result in their eventual disappearance.

In the mountains the main problems are presented by an array of Australian *Hakea* species and the cluster pine *(Pinus pinasta)*. In the 1950s the authorities in charge of the mountain catchments encouraged hikers to disperse seeds of alien trees, no doubt to add trees to a largely treeless landscape. Exotic *Acacias* and wattles were used to stabilise the shifting coastal sand dunes. They succeeded in this, but now managers have the thankless and near impossible task of ridding these areas of these "foreigners". Although physical cutting and removal has succeeded in a few situations this is proving to be grossly inadequate. These aliens are more successful when growing outside their natural ranges because they can establish themselves without the normal predators, fungi and diseases that they have to cope with in their homelands. The only hope of curbing the spread of these plants lies in biological control, that is bringing in the organisms that feed on them in the land of origin and ultimately (one can always hope) eradicate these pests.

CHAPTER 6

THE FRESH WATERS

Africa has vast tracts of desert lands but it can still boast the longest river in the world, the Nile; the river with the second largest drainage basin and water flow, the Congo (Zaïre); the second largest freshwater lake, Victoria; the second deepest lake, Tanganyika; the vast inland delta of the Okavango River and many other rivers, lakes, swamps and floodplains. Water was the original home of the earth's first living organisms and all life forms require water in order to survive. It takes two atoms of hydrogen linked with one atom of oxygen to produce a molecule of water, yet this seemingly simple structure has amazing properties which influence all life on earth. It has shaped, and continues to shape, landscapes by the process of erosion, transporting soils and often depositing them far from their origins. Water turns into a solid below 0 °C and it is the only known substance that expands when frozen. When water freezes in crevices and cracks in rocks it further contributes to erosion processes.

The sun's heat causes water to evaporate from the oceans, lakes, rivers, moist land surfaces and plants and the vapour rises into the atmosphere, where it is carried for varying distances before falling as rain or snow, replenishing water stocks and permitting the plant growth upon which all life on earth depends, either directly or indirectly. This process is referred to as the water-cycle.

Background: *The clear waters of the Okavango Delta. Photo: John Carlyon.* **Right:** *The cry of the fish eagle* (Haliaeetus vocifer) *rings out over many of Africa's rivers, lakes and estuaries but in some areas they are under threat from chemical pollution which they pick up from their piscine diet.*

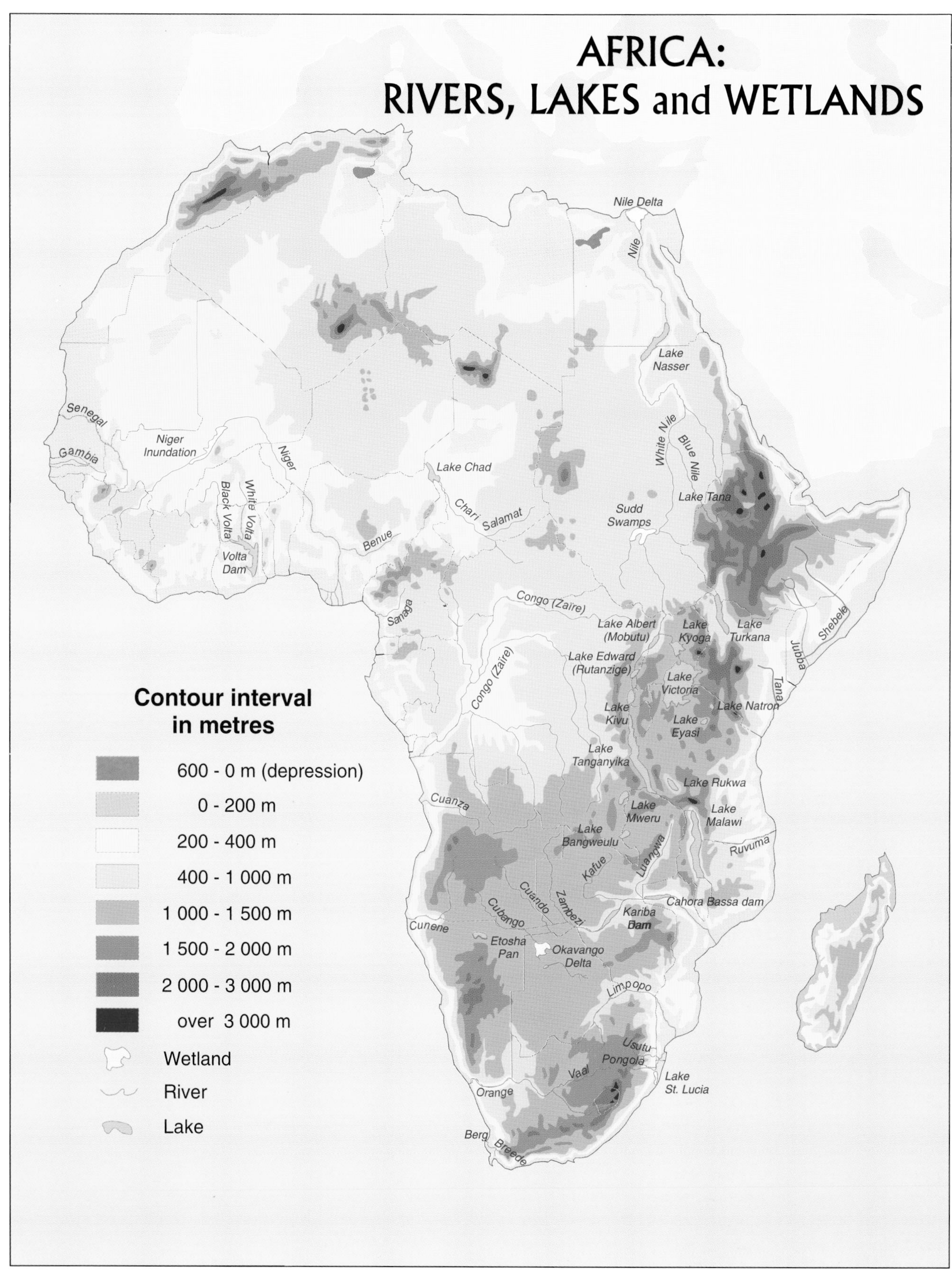
AFRICA:
RIVERS, LAKES and WETLANDS
Nile Delta
Nile
Lake Nasser
White Nile
Blue Nile
Lake Tana
Sudd Swamps
Senegal
Gambia
Niger Inundation
Niger
White Volta
Black Volta
Volta Dam
Lake Chad
Chari
Salamat
Benue
Sanaga
Congo (Zaïre)
Lake Albert (Mobutu)
Lake Kyoga
Lake Turkana
Lake Edward (Rutanzige)
Lake Victoria
Lake Kivu
Lake Natron
Lake Eyasi
Jubba
Shebele
Tana
Lake Tanganyika
Lake Rukwa
Lake Mweru
Lake Malawi
Lake Bangweulu
Ruvuma
Cuanza
Luangwa
Kafue
Cuando
Zambezi
Cubango
Cahora Bassa dam
Kariba Dam
Cunene
Etosha Pan
Okavango Delta
Limpopo
Usutu
Pongola
Vaal
Lake St. Lucia
Orange
Berg
Breede
Contour interval in metres
600 - 0 m (depression)
0 - 200 m
200 - 400 m
400 - 1 000 m
1 000 - 1 500 m
1 500 - 2 000 m
2 000 - 3 000 m
over 3 000 m
Wetland
River
Lake

Above: *Permanent pans are a feature of areas that receive a high rainfall, with rich plant and animal diversity.*

Africa has seen many fluctuations in the extent of its fresh waters, with dry periods interspersed with wetter periods. Lakes and rivers have come and gone, rivers have expanded, disappeared or been greatly modified. Some changes are ancient, others more recent. Apart from the geological influences, man has modified river flow by erecting dams across even the mightiest rivers and creating artificial lakes. Between 27 000 and 12 000 years ago Africa underwent a continent-wide dry period that resulted in the expansion of drylands and the shrinking and disappearance of lakes and rivers. Between 12 000 and 8 000 years ago conditions became more humid. During this time Lake Chad (or Mega-Chad as it is sometimes called) reached to the foot of the central Saharan Tibesti Mountains as a single water body or chain of massive lakes, covering an area of some 400 000 km². More lakes developed in other areas of the southern Sahara and large rivers flowed from the desert mountain ranges, emptying their waters into the river systems of West Africa. A vast, ancient lake once filled the Congo Basin but drained into the Atlantic Ocean when a coastal river cut a narrow gap through the lake's western rim.

There have been many fluctuations and changes to Africa's inland waters in the past and they will continue in the future. Whereas in the past these changes were totally natural processes, today man plays a major role in influencing the way the fresh waters are used and abused.

It is not possible to cover the lakes, rivers, floodplains, swamps and other water bodies as one section because of their many differences. The following short accounts deal with the formation and structure of each group separately.

THE LAKES

There are more than 200 natural lakes in Africa, varying considerably in size. With the exception of Lake Chad in western Africa, all of Africa's principal lakes are found along, or in close association with, the two branches of the Great Rift Valley. The Eastern Rift extends from the Red Sea and down the Awash Valley, cutting through the Ethiopian dome southwards to Lake Turkana (Rudolf), then it crosses the East African plateau to Lake Malawi and the Shire Valley, to peter out in Mozambique. The Western Rift runs roughly parallel to the east arm and cuts northwards from Lake Malawi to lakes Tanganyika, Kivu, Edward and Albert, and possibly includes a section of the Nile valley beyond Lake Albert. Many smaller lakes are associated with the rifts and side-arms of these great geological scars, for example Lake Rukwa. During the Pleistocene era when the Virunga volcanoes erupted, the river valley below Lake Edward was blocked and this resulted in the formation of Lake Kivu. As the river was no longer able to spill its waters northwards, the flow was forced southwards to Lake Tanganyika. Lake Tana in Ethiopia and a number of small lakes north of Kivu owe their existence to lava flows which dammed river valleys. Crater lakes are numerous in East Africa and include Naivasha and Kikorongo. Despite its great size, with a surface area of some 68 800 km², Lake Victoria was formed relatively recently (during the Pleistocene era) by downwarping of the earth's crust between the eastern and western arms of the Great Rift Valley. During this event the west flowing rivers, principally the Kagera, reversed their flow to the east and began filling the shallow basin that now forms the lake. The overflow of Lake Victoria formed Lake Kiogo and the Victoria Nile to the north. Despite its great surface area Lake Victoria averages only 70 m in depth. By contrast the much older Lake Tanganyika lying in the Great Rift reaches a depth of 1 433 m. Lake Chad lies in a relatively shallow depression fed by a number of north-flowing rivers, particularly the Logone. As it has done in the past, the lake is at present receding from its shores.

Large manmade lakes have also to be taken into account as they play an important role in human activities and impact on the environment and its biota. Some of the largest impoundments are the Kossou (Ivory Coast), Volta (Ghana), Aswan/Nasser (Egypt), Cahora Bassa (Mozambique) and Kariba (Zimbabwe/Zambia).

THE RIVERS

The vast majority of Africa's perennial rivers lie between 15 °N and 15 °S, and then down the eastern side of the continent where they drain into the Indian Ocean. The number of rivers decreases dramatically as one moves from Kenya northwards and eastwards into the Horn of Africa. The River Nile flows northwards through the Sahara in the east and short rivers rise in the Atlas Mountains. In the drylands of the south-west large perennial rivers are restricted to the northern and southern fringes.

Each major river, with its tributaries, collects the water from a given area, referred to as the drainage basin, and in most cases empties the fresh water into either the Atlantic Ocean (west coast), Indian Ocean (east coast) or in the case of the Nile the Mediterranean Sea. Some rivers empty themselves into inland deltas, such as the Okavango, whereas others pour their waters into lakes. Many of Africa's rivers have extensive floodplains that play a very important role in the lives of many organisms, including man. Floodplains are a phenomenon of periodic flooding of land adjacent to river channels as a result of seasonal rains. They produce a complex of riparian wetlands, including expansive flooded grasslands which often contain permanent lakes and swamps. A large number of these floodplains are associated with permanent swamp systems. The Sudd, lying on the Nile, is the largest of all African wetlands. During the dry season it comprises 16 300 km² of swamp but during the rainy season this area doubles as surrounding country is inundated.

Most African floodplains are associated with savanna-type vegetation but within the Zaïre (Congo) Basin and areas in Cameroon and Gabon, floodplains are located in forests.

Because of the number and diversity of African rivers it is obviously not possible to cover them all. Here we will examine a few of the principal watercourses.

The **Nile** traverses a distance of 6 695 km, which makes it the longest river on earth, and its drainage basin is about three million square kilometres in extent. It is the only major African river to drain into the Mediterranean Sea. Although the basin has been divided into five units, the most important are the White and the Blue arms of the Nile. The White Nile has its origin on the northern shore of Lake Victoria, from where it courses to the shallow Lake Kioga and after the Murchison Falls joins the flow from lakes Edward and Albert.

To the north of the town of Mongala it enters the Sudd, with the tributary Bahr el Ghazal adding its waters from the west, and the Sobat from the east where it drains the south-western Ethiopian Highlands. The White Nile then cuts its way northwards until it reaches the confluence with the Blue Nile at Khartoum. The Blue Nile drains the north-eastern

lakes and swamps of the Mweru and Bengweulu, and the Lukuga River carrying water from Lake Tanganyika. The river follows a northerly direction to the town of Kisangani, from where it follows a great westerly arc and takes the name Zaïre. Many tributaries flow into the main river from the north and the south, the two largest being the Oubangui and the Kasai. The entire central catchment of the Zaïre receives high rainfall (1 500 to 2 500 mm per annum) throughout the year, but areas away from the equator, such as near the headwaters, have distinct wet and dry seasons, thus influencing tributary flows. The central Zaïre Basin is dominated by Africa's largest stretch of tropical forest.

The **Niger River** and its network of tributaries forms the principal drainage system of West Africa. It is the third longest river in Africa and the tenth longest in the world, at 4 183 km, with a drainage basin that covers 1.125 million km^2. The Niger rises in the state of Guinea, with the Tinkisso headwater emerging from the Fouta Djalon Mountains and other feeder streams merging just before the river crosses into Mali. Much of the length of the Niger flows through the arid Sahelian belt as it sweeps north-eastwards to Timbuktu, then it turns eastwards to Gao and begins its long south-easterly swing to the Nigerian coast where it enters the Atlantic Ocean in the Gulf of Guinea. Some 460 km before the delta the Niger is joined by the Bénué River, which flows westwards for 1 400 km from the Adamaoua Massif in northern Cameroon. Few tributaries join the Niger as it passes through the states of Mali and Niger but numerous side branches contribute water in Nigeria where rainfall increases. There are a number of significant floodplains along the Niger but by far the most important is the Central Delta lying between Markala and Timbuktu. During the flood season as much as

Ethiopian Highlands where it finds its source in the shallow (up to 14 m) 3 000 km^2 Lake Tana. Of interest is that more than 60 per cent of all water discharged by the Nile has its origins in the Blue Nile, despite its much shorter course. Just 25 km below Lake Tana the Blue Nile enters the 500 km-long Abay Gorge after its waters have dropped over the Tississat Falls. From the confluence of the Blue and White Niles, the Nile cuts northwards for more than 3 000 km through the desert. The Nile valley that we observe today established itself at the end of the Miocene era, but rivers have existed here since the Eocene era.

The **Zaïre, or Congo, River** is the seventh longest river in the world and its basin drains almost four million square kilometres of land, second only to the Amazon River in South America. The massive outflow of fresh water into the Atlantic Ocean has carved a channel in the seabed extending for some 250 km and reaching a maximum depth of 2.5 km. Millions of tons of silt and other substances are carried into the ocean and the brownish tinting can be observed for more than 80 km offshore. The headwaters of the Zaïre, called the Lualaba, are fed by the Luvua River which draws from the

Above left: *Rapids above the Murchison Falls on the Victoria Nile.* **Below:** *The building of dams on many major and minor African rivers has had a detrimental effect on natural processes such as fish migrations.*

20 000 km^2 are inundated but during the dry season this decreases to some 3 900 km^2, which includes many small permanent lakes. The vegetation of the inland deltas is dominated by hardy perennial grasses but this has been greatly influenced by domestic stock and cultivation. The coastal delta covers about 30 000 km^2 and consists of numerous branch streams and small islands. For much of its length the Niger runs through areas of moist and dry savanna vegetation. It enters moist lowland forest in southern Nigeria and in the delta this gives way to a belt of mangrove. The Bénué passes through heavily vegetated country for much of its course. Nigeria has a human population of more than 100 million and riverine and associated vegetation has been greatly modified by hundreds of years of occupation.

The **Zambezi River** is the largest river flowing into the Indian Ocean and the principal system in south-central Africa, with a length of 2 524 km and a catchment area exceeding 2.7 million square kilometres. It is well served by tributaries. The Zambezi rises in the highlands of eastern Angola and north-western Zambia, close to the border with Zaïre, at an altitude of approximately 1 400 m. It then sweeps in a southerly direction passing through the Barotse Floodplain, which inundates about 9 000 km^2 of land during the wet season, continuing its journey to the Caprivi Strip (north-eastern Namibia) and northern Botswana from where it swings to the east and then pours its waters over the almost 100 m-high Victoria Falls. Some 110 km below the falls the river enters Lake Kariba and beyond this it gains inflow from the Kafue and Luangwa rivers. Where the Zambezi and Luangwa join, their waters flow into the Mozambican dam Cahora Bassa. Only one major tributary joins the Zambezi between the dam and its entry into the Indian Ocean, the Shire River carrying water from lakes Malawi and Malombe and southern Malawi. The lower reaches are dominated by a

great expanse of floodplain, vegetated by grassland but entering extensive mangrove woodland at the coast. Throughout its length the Zambezi passes through open and closed woodland of different types, which include mixed miombo and mopane (*Colophospermum mopane*) and *Brachystegia* with stretches of riparian gallery forest. The coastal plains include alluvial grassland and forest. It seems likely that the upper Zambezi once flowed through the Makgadikgadi Pans complex in Botswana and to the south joined the Limpopo River. However, during the middle of the Pleistocene era it is believed that uplifting resulted in the middle Zambezi "capturing" the flow of the upper Zambezi through the Batoka Gorge (located below the Victoria Falls). This resulted in the flow being diverted to the north-east and creating the course that we know today.

Below: *The yellowbilled duck* Anas undulata *is a very common species and is associated with a wide variety of water bodies.* **Right:** *The water hyacinth, a resident of South America, has very succesfully invaded many rivers, swamps and lakes in Africa.*

Although the above are the principal river systems of Africa and responsible for the bulk of its drainage, many other small systems are very important from a zoological point of view. In South Africa, with the exception of the Orange-Vaal and the Limpopo River systems, all rivers are short and most have their sources in the coastal mountains (Cape Folded Belt and Drakensberg) from where they cut across the narrow coastal plain to the oceans. There are also many short rivers along the eastern and western coastlines, as well as those flowing from the seaward side of the Atlas Mountains.

THE WETLANDS

There are extensive **floodplains, swamps and deltas** on the continent, with the vast majority lying within the higher rainfall areas of the tropics. These water bodies are of great zoological and botanical importance but the activities of man have drastically modified these aquatic habitats – particularly the floodplains. Many of these areas cover hundreds, and in some cases thousands, of square kilometres. The **Okavango Delta**, located in Botswana, is a vast complex (some 15 000 km^2 in extent) of channels, lagoons and floodplains which draws its waters from the western highlands of Angola. During the summer months the waters are confined within the network of channels. At this time the rains are falling in the Angolan highlands, however, so by March or April the levels begin to rise in the delta. These increased flows reach the base of the delta by June or July.

Rain falls locally from October to May and contributes about one-third of the delta's water. The waters spill over the banks and spread over the plains, isolating higher patches of ground. The Okavango River meanders between two parallel faults that create the Panhandle floodplain. Spilling over the Gomare Fault the river divides into a number of main channels and a complex of shallower watercourses. Although the flow varies according to the amount of rain that has fallen in the highlands an average flood carries in 350 billion cubic feet of water and deposits as much as 727 000 tons of sediment. Much of the flood water evaporates but some comes into contact with the Thamalakane Fault and in good years surplus flow enters the Boteti River towards the Makgadikgadi Pans in the south-east, or Lake Ngami in the south-west.

Apart from the **floodplains** already mentioned there are many others of importance, such as the Kafue Flats (fed by the river of the same name) in Zambia, and several in Tanzania, including the Usangu and Buhoro Flats, the Kilombero Valley and areas in the Uwanda Game Reserve and associated with Lake Rukwa. Tanzania also has some significant **swamps** but these are poorly known. Malagarasi in the north-west is the largest and one of the continent's most extensive wetlands. The Wembere Swamps accommodate vast colonies of water birds.

The importance of wetlands, including swamps, marshes, floodplains and swamp forest, to the health of environments is tremendous and disruption of these processes by man can result in such problems as flooding, siltation and the reduction of water quality. These wetlands are amongst the richest and most productive of natural environments on earth.

Associated with these wetlands is an incredible assemblage of plants and animals that are wholly or partially dependent on these habitats. The quantity and quality of the water in any given wetland will determine to a large extent its unique properties. Wetlands have the ability to filter sediments in suspension from the water and in this way they not only increase the quality of the water but supply essential nutrients to the plant life. The plants in turn convert the nutrients into additional vegetable matter by growth and reproduction. Through the process of death and decomposition the plants provide food for a vast spectrum of animals and a nutrient base for continued plant growth. An established wetland is a delicately balanced natural self-perpetuating "factory".

THE PLANTS

Plant life associated with fresh water ranges from single-cell algae to great forest trees, and all make important contributions to the wellbeing of each system, whether it be a small temporary pool on the savanna or one of the Great Rift Valley lakes. Some plant species float and drift freely on the water surface, such as the duckweeds (*Lemna*), but two species of free-floating plants that have been introduced to Africa by man, water hyacinth (*Eichhornia crassipes*) and the water fern (also known as Kariba weed) (*Salvinia molesta*) are a major threat to the health of many water bodies on the con-

Below: *The Nile crocodile* Crocodylus niloticus *is the most widespread of Africa's three crocodile species, the others being the African slender-snouted crocodile* Crocodylus cataphractus *and the dwarf crocodile* Osteolaemus tetraspis.

Above: *The waterbuck, of which two subspecies are recognised (the photo shows defassa waterbuck,* Kobus ellipsiprymnus defassa*), occurs patchily in southern, central and eastern Africa and occupies areas fringing water bodies, particularly in association with woodland, reedbeds and tall grass. Lake Nakuru National Park has a very high density.* **Right:** *The duckweeds are small floating plants that may be present in vast numbers in still, shallow freshwater bodies.* **Below right:** *The puku* (Kobus vardonii)*. This antelope is always associated with water fringes and floodplains but, unlike its close relative the lechwe, does not enter the water. They have been heavily persecuted in many areas and now have a patchy distribution in central Africa and the southern part of East Africa.*

tinent. They are now located in major river systems, including the Nile, Zambezi and the Zaïre, as well as many swamps, including the Sudd, and lakes such as Victoria. Why do these aquatic plants pose such a threat? Many species of plants, or animals, introduced to an alien environment arrive with no natural enemies and they can proliferate without any checks until they rapidly dominate their preferred niche, or habitat. The water hyacinth and the water fern form dense, impenetrable mats that outcompete naturally occurring aquatic plants, and they deplete the dissolved oxygen to such an extent that most animals die, including fish, thus resulting in loss of diversity. Observations in Africa have shown that the water hyacinth can double its biomass every six to 13 days; under the most favourable conditions 10 plants can multiply to 600 000 in a period of eight months. An additional problem is that the water hyacinth loses 3.5 times as much water by evapotranspiration as an equivalent area of open water. It has been estimated that a mind-blowing seven billion cubic metres, or one-tenth of the average yield of the Nile, is lost from that river each year through evapotranspiration by the water hyacinth.

A feature of many African lake fringes, permanent swamps and river banks are great beds of *Papyrus*, bulrushes (*Typha*) and "feather-head" reeds (*Phragmites*). The Sudd, on the White Nile, is dominated by *Cyperus papyrus* and *Phragmites* spp. beds and vast floating "meadows" of such grasses as *Leersia*. Some plants, such as *Nitella*, have their roots in the silt or mud and their stems and leaves remain submerged in shallow waters. The *Potamogetons* may be completely submerged, or have their stem tips on the surface but the water lilies (e.g. *Nymphaea*) have their roots attached in the mud while the leaves and flowers lie on the water surface.

It is not possible to cover all of the grasses associated with the floodplains of Africa but we will take the example of the Niger River. These plains are covered by hardy perennial grasses that follow two annual phases. With the start of the flood season a number of aquatic grasses (e.g. *Oryza barthii*, *Chrysopogon zizanoides* and *Vossia cuspidata*) show rapid growth and form an almost uniform floating mat. With the fall in water levels the grasses die back (or are burnt by humans) and are replaced by dry-season species.

Areas of extremely rich biological diversity are swamp forests which are permanently inundated and those forests and woodlands that lie on seasonally flooded river plains. Some of the best examples of swamp forest are to be found in parts of Zaïre, Cameroon and the Congo Republic.

THE MAMMALS

The mammal that has played the biggest role in modifying and influencing many of Africa's aquatic systems is the hip-

Below: *Although very rarely seen, the water mongoose* Atilax paludinosus *occurs in association with many water bodies throughout sub-Saharan Africa.* **Bottom:** *The hippo is the dominant mammal in many African aquatic systems.*

THE FLAMINGOES

One of the great wonders of Africa is the vast congregation of greater (Phoenicophterus ruber) *and lesser flamingoes* (P. minor) *on the shallow soda lakes of East Africa, such as Natron in northern Tanzania and Nakuru in Kenya. These birds are also present on many other suitable lakes and are a frequent sight on shallow coastal lagoons. They will also make use of temporary, shallow pans where food is abundant. Both species are prone to considerable local and long distance movements. Flamingoes feed with their heads hanging upside down, looking backwards between their legs. The two halves of the beak are held together, the lower mandible fitting into the upper, then the head is swung from side to side. At the same time the tongue is moved back and forth thus pumping water and silt in and out. In this way microscopic organisms are caught in platelet-like filters that lie inside the beak. The greater flamingo usually gathers food by completely submerging the head and filtering mud as well as water. They may also feed on larger organisms where these are available. The lesser flamingo usually just filters surface water.*

popotamus (*Hippopotamus amphibius*). These large animals number some 150 000 today and are found in many African rivers, lake and swamp fringes. However, they have disappeared from many areas, or their numbers have been greatly reduced, because of hunting pressure and other disturbances. The largest single population, with over 20 000 animals, is located in the Virunga National Park in eastern Zaïre. The hippos keeps river channels open by their movements, they add nutrients to the water by defecating and their grazing on land creates pastures suitable for a wide range of other herbivores. These large (up to two tons), rotund animals spend much of the day lying in water but frequently emerge to lie in the sun on sand and mud banks. At night they emerge to feed, often moving several kilometres to favoured grazing grounds. Dominant bulls are highly territorial in and close to the water but less so as the distance increases from it. The West African manatee (*Trichechus senegalensis*) occurs in many estuaries and the lower reaches of many river systems from Senegal to Angola. There are important populations of these completely aquatic mammals in Zaïre, Niger and the Gambia but they are under considerable threat throughout their range.

Several antelope species are closely tied to watery habitats, including the sitatunga (*Tragelaphus spekei*), Nile lechwe (*Kobus megaceros*), lechwe (*Kobus leche*), kob (*Kobus kob*), puku (*Kobus vardoni*), Bohor reedbuck (*Redunca redunca*), southern reedbuck (*Redunca arundinum*) and the waterbuck (*Kobus ellipsiprymnus*), but there is little competition as each has a preferred feeding and activity zone. The two most aquatic species are the sitatunga and the Nile lechwe, the former spending most of its time in dense papyrus and reed beds with water to a depth of about one metre, with the lechwe being able to spend long periods submerged with only the head and neck above water. The bulk of the Nile lechwe population is restricted to the Sudd, where it feeds mainly on the floating beds of *Leersia*. Both species have extremely long hoofs which aid them in walking on waterlogged and floating vegetation but they rest up on pads of reeds and other growth, or make use of large termite mounds and other dry ground. The lechwe takes readily to water to feed and if under threat and only rarely moves more than 3 km from permanent waters. Although the hoofs are not as elongated as those of reedbuck and waterbuck, they are well developed. The bulk of their diet is made up of semi-aquatic grasses. Puku occupy open flats adjacent to rivers, swamps and marshes but rarely occur on the floodplains utilised by lechwe. Kob occupy floodplains, adjacent grassland and hill country.

The southern reedbuck shows a marked preference for tall grass and reed beds adjacent to permanent waters, rarely feeding on open, short-grassed plains, whereas the bohor reedbuck will also utilise floodplain grasses during the dry season. Waterbuck, of which two subspecies are recognised,

DUCKS AND GEESE

Thirty-seven species of ducks and geese, and one swan, occur in Africa either as residents or as seasonal migrants. Some species have wide distributions but a few occur in limited areas, such as the Abyssinian blue-winged goose (Cyanochen cyanopterus) *which is restricted to the Ethiopian Highlands at altitudes greater than 2 400 m, and Hartlaub's duck* (Cairina hartlaubi) *which is only found in tropical rain forest and mangrove in West and north-central Africa. During the breeding seasons many resident species occur only as pairs but in the non-breeding season they may form large flocks that undertake local migrations, such as the Egyptian goose* (Alopochen aegyptiacus) *and the white-faced duck* (Dendrocygna viduata). *Most seasonal migrants enter Africa from Europe, rarely penetrating further south than the equator. Some stragglers get down to the continent's most southerly point, however.*

Above right: *A male South African shelduck,* Tadorna cana. *This species is restricted to southern Africa.* **Right:** *Red-crested pochards* (Netta rufina) *are rare non-breeding visitors to North Africa.* **Below right:** *A common species that may form large flocks when not breeding, the redbilled teal* Anas erythrorhyncha. **Left:** *The spurwinged goose,* Plectropterus gambensis, *may reach a weight of 10 kg and form flocks of several thousand birds out of the breeding season.*

Above: *Several species of antelopes live in close association with swamps, floodplains and other water bodies. The most aquatic of all is the sitatunga* (Tragelaphus spekei), *which occurs patchily through southern, central and eastern Africa, as far north as Lake Chad. Areas with dense stands of papyrus are particularly favoured. Photo: Ian Manning*

are usually found close to water and make use of reed beds, tall grasslands and woodland. They will feed on open floodplains adjacent to cover, however. Species such as elephant and buffalo will feed in most wetland situations throughout the year but particularly during the dry season, and many antelope feed on floodplains during the dry months.

As the larger herbivores move onto these plains, the larger carnivores such as lion (*Panthera leo*) and spotted hyaena (*Crocuta crocuta*) are often in attendance. In many areas these predators, as well as leopard (*Panthera pardus*), are permanent residents and only abandon areas temporarily when they become totally inundated. Lechwe, kob and puku are frequently taken by the large carnivores. The most aquatic of the carnivores are the otters, of which four species live in Africa. By far the largest are the Congo clawless otter (*Aonyx congica*) and the Cape clawless otter (*Aonyx capensis*), the latter having a very wide distribution and habitat tolerance. The widespread spotted-necked otter (*Lutra maculicollis*) spends much more time in water than the two *Aonyx* species and requires clear, relatively silt-free waters. The fourth species, the Eurasian otter (*Lutra lutra*), is restricted to the streams that rise in the Atlas Mountains in north-western Africa. All species hunt and eat fish and all take crabs, insects, mussels and small mammals to a lesser or greater extent. Although poorly known, the aquatic genet (*Osbornictis piscivora*) is restricted to part of the Zaïre Basin and is found along streams and rivers where it hunts fish and frogs. The water mongoose (*Atilax paludinosus*) is a common, though seldom seen, species that is found in association with most watery habitats where it feels with its long, naked toes in the mud and under rocks for crabs, insects, fish and mussels. They also feed on birds, rodents and frogs. Although they do most of their hunting in the shallows they will not hesitate to swim through deeper water. Another mongoose that frequents waterside vegetation is the large grey mongoose (*Herpestes ichneumon*), but it does not take so readily to water as the other species.

Many small mammals which occur in, or in association with, wetlands and other well-watered habitats, have varying degrees of adaptation. The otter-shrews (*Micropotamogale* spp. and *Potamogale velox*), of which three species are recognised, have limited distributions but all are adapted to hunting in water. The tail of the largest species (*Potamogale*) is flattened and oar-like and closely resembles those of the otters. Many species of typical shrews (Family **Soricidae**) are found in close association with wetlands and vegetation fringing other water bodies. Rodents are also well represented, with the large (3 kg to 5 kg and larger) greater cane-rat (*Thryonomys swinderianus*) being common wherever there are extensive reed beds and tall grass stands adjacent to water, in which they will swim readily. They can reach high densities and are a favoured prey of a number of carnivores, crocodiles and man. Several species of the short-tailed, stockily built *Otomys* spp. are closely associated with wetlands, as are the grooved-toothed rat (*Pelomys fallax*), the water rat (*Dasymys incomtus*), several grass-climbing mice (*Dendromus* spp.) and many others.

THE BIRDS

Lakes, rivers, floodplains, swamps, marshes and deltas attract many species and great numbers of birds, most of which are adapted to specific feeding methods or to using a particular habitat or niche. Apart from the many bird species that make direct use of the water for feeding, numerous other species are found in associated habitats and benefit indirectly from the presence of wetlands. Birds in freshwater habitats have access to a huge diversity of food, including microscopic organisms, plant parts, frogs, fish, crabs, worms, molluscs, insects and many others. Each bird, or group of birds, can be broadly classified according to the water depth, or zone, they utilise. These include those feeding on the dry fringes, wading in shallow water, wading in deeper water, swimmers, dabblers, divers and those that plunge into the water from the air. Because of this very wide range of feeding methods competition for the same resources is greatly reduced. Many birds have evolved ways of successfully utilising specific habitats, or types of food. The African jacana (*Actophilornis africanus*) has extremely long toes and claws that enable it to walk over floating vegetation, such as lily-pads, by spreading its weight over a much greater surface area. Another species with much lengthened toes is the purple gallinule (*Porphyrio porphyrio*). The ducks, geese, cormorants, anhinga and grebes have webbed toes which increase the speed with which they can propel themselves through the water. The pelicans, of which two species have wide African distributions, have large webbed feet and great pouchlike lower jaws that enable them to scoop up fish. Pelicans catch their prey close to the surface and do not dive, but birds such as the anhinga (also known as the darter and snake-bird) hunt fish under water and spear them with their beaks. The cormorants are also diving fish-hunters and can be present in large numbers where fish of suitable size are numerous.

The kingfishers hover or sit on favoured perches above water and dive to snatch fish from close to the surface. The fish eagle (*Haliaeetus vocifer*) and the osprey (*Pandion haliaetus*) snatch their fish prey from near the water surface. A nocturnal fish-eater that uses a similar method of catching its prey is Pel's fishing owl (*Scotopelia pelia*), which inhabits riparian forest. Several species of heron also include fish in their diet. The large goliath heron (*Ardea goliath*), because of its long legs, is able to fish in deeper waters than any other heron and also tends to take larger specimens. By contrast the small heron species hunt from very shallow water, or even from an elevated position such as a rock or a branch, seemingly stretching their necks to impossible lengths.

Other long-legged fish-eaters are such oddities as the shoebill (*Balaeniceps rex*) and the openbilled stork (*Anastomus lamelligerus*). The shoebill is restricted to swamps, marshes and areas of floating vegetation, primarily in areas closely associated with the Great Rift Valley. They hunt by waiting in ambush and then lunging forward and down with both feet and the large beak coming into play. Fish are the most important food component, with lungfish (*Protopterus aethiopicus*), bichirs (*Polypterus senegalus*) and tilapia being significant but they also take frogs, reptiles – including young crocodiles – small rodents and young water birds. The openbilled stork has a gap between the upper and lower mandibles of the beak that enables it to collect and hold snails and mussels.

Several other species of stork, such as the saddlebilled stork (*Ephippiorhynchus senegalensis*) and the woollynecked stork (*Ciconia episcopus*) are commonly observed in freshwater habitats where they feed on a wide range of organisms,

Above: *The beautifully coloured purple gallinule* Porphyrio porphyrio *is nearly always associated with reed beds.*

including fish, frogs and invertebrates. There are also those species with long beaks that feed on organisms buried in mud, sand or amongst decaying vegetation. They include several ibises, one of the most widespread being the sacred ibis (*Threskiornis aethiopicus*), a species that was once revered by the ancient Egyptians. Huge numbers of these birds were embalmed and placed in Egyptian tombs. Many smaller wading birds, including a number of migrant species from Europe and Asia, feed at different depths in the substrate according to the length of their beaks. The tips of the beaks are often equipped with sensitive nerve endings which allow them to identify prey items and those of some species are flexible enough to allow them to open slightly and grasp food items buried under the surface. The ducks and geese form another large group that is well represented in Africa and includes resident species and others that migrate southwards during the European winter.

Although many species are found in association with permanent water bodies, temporary wet-season lakes and shallow pans, even in some dryland areas, attract vast flocks of ducks and geese.

Wherever large numbers of birds congregate in freshwater habitats their droppings make a major contribution to the nutrient levels, both for plants and small invertebrate organisms, which in their turn provide food for many other species. Most duck species feed on plant material and small invertebrates. Their beaks are flattened to facilitate the biting off of vegetable material, and filters in the beak extract organisms from the water. A few species such as the spurwinged goose (*Plectropterus gambensis*) and the bluewinged goose (*Cyanchen cyanoptera*) are predominantly dryland grazers.

Other filter-feeding birds include the two flamingoes, the greater flamingo (*Phoenicopterus ruber*) and the lesser flamingo (*Phoenicopterus minor*).

Many non-aquatic birds, such as the warbler and weaver species, nest in reed beds and other vegetation growing from water in order to avoid land-based predators. There is also an abundance of material for nest building.

Insectivorous birds also benefit from the vast numbers of insects and other invertebrates that thrive in moist and aquat-

Right from top: *The* ***painted reed-frog*** Hyperolius marmoratus. *This small frog occurs in a wide range of colours and patterns. Reed-frogs of many species occur widely, showing a preference for marshes, pans and other water bodies with fringes of reeds. The* ***forest tree frog*** Leptopelis natalensis. *The tree frogs are characterised by the sucker-like toe tips and many species occur throughout sub-Saharan Africa in suitable habitat, such as riverine woodland and bush around other water bodies. The* ***red-backed toad*** Schismaderma carens *female. This species is widespread in the savanna water bodies of southern and eastern Africa. Mating* ***raucous toads*** Bufo rangeri. *When large numbers of this species gather for mating the calling males sound like a gathering of demented ducks.*

ic conditions. Apart from the plants, the birds are generally the most visible of the organisms inhabiting freshwater habitats and are therefore among the most studied.

THE REPTILES AND AMPHIBIANS

Whenever one thinks of reptiles in an aquatic environment in Africa, usually the first to come to mind is the crocodile. There are in fact three species, the widespread Nile crocodile (*Crocodylus niloticus*), the dwarf crocodile (*Osteolaemnus tetraspis*) and the slender-snouted crocodile (*Crocodylus cataphractus*). The last two species are largely restricted to the equatorial forest belt and are poorly known. The Nile crocodile was very heavily hunted in the past for its valuable belly skin but it is still fairly common in some regions. They occupy virtually all freshwater habitats within the tropics and spend much of their time in the water, although in areas where they are not disturbed they frequently haul out and lie on sand- and mud-banks in the sun. The bulk of their diet consists of fish, but the young feed mostly on invertebrates and frogs and adults also include birds and mammals in their diet. Adults (large specimens exceed 4 m and the record is 5.5 m) will attack and drown such species as greater kudu, blue wildebeest, impala, plains zebra and occasionally young elephant. They are in fact the principal predator of African rivers, lakes and swamps. The female Nile crocodile lays her eggs in a self-excavated hole which she covers carefully with sand or soil. She remains near the nest-hole, defending it against potential predators. However, many nests are raided by Nile (water) monitors (*Varanus niloticus*), water mongoose (*Atilax paludinosus*) and other predators when the female is not in attendance. Fifty to 80 eggs are usually laid and on hatching the young give off chirping noises to attract the female, who digs them out. Some make their own way to the water, but the female carefully carries many youngsters to the shallows in her mouth.

Freshwater turtles, or terrapins, are well represented in African fresh waters, and include soft-shelled turtles (*Trionyx* spp.), the hinge-shelled turtles (*Pelusios* spp.) and hard-shelled turtles of the genus *Pelomedusa*. One of the most successful is the widespread *Pelomedusa subrufa*, which lives in both permanent and seasonal water bodies. When the latter dry up these turtles either bury themselves in the mud until the next rains refill the depression or pan, or they may wander several kilometres across land until they find another suitable watery home.

Where food is abundant and conditions optimal freshwater turtles may congregate in large numbers. Many species are omnivorous and will feed on a wide range of animal and plant food, including the rotting carcasses of large animals killed by crocodiles. We have observed *Pelusios* sp. turtles systematically eating individuals from a large shoal of tadpoles and lunging at small birds drinking at a waterhole. They lay their eggs in self-excavated holes in sand or loose soil, but unlike the crocodiles there is no parental care of the nest or young.

The widespread Nile monitor is also a significant predator, both on land and in water, where they will take invertebrates, frogs, birds, small mammals and molluscs.

Although many species of snakes, such as the python (*Python sebae*) swim well and will cool off in fresh water or cross narrow stretches, only a few are closely associated with aquatic habitats. The *Grayia* spp. are an exception however, and the great bulk of their diet consists of fish. Several species of snakes, including members of the genus *Philothamnus*, do enter water to hunt frogs.

Frogs and toads are represented by several hundred species in African freshwater habitats, ranging from Afroalpine

Below: *The banded tilapia* Tilapia sparrmanii *(this is a juvenile) is common and widespread. It has been widely introduced into rivers, dams and pans outside its natural range, particularly in southern Africa.* **Bottom:** *Johnston's topminnow* Aplocheilichthys johnstoni. *The topminnows have a wide distribution and prefer water bodies with plenty of aquatic vegetation.*

marsh-dwellers to species which occur in vast numbers in the reed beds of marshes and swamps. In fact there is virtually no moist habitat that amphibians do not occupy on the continent. Several African frogs of the genus *Xenopus*, the so-called clawed toads or platannas, spend most or all of their time in the water, although they do undertake short-distance migrations to other water bodies during wet conditions. Amongst the great array of African frogs are several that deserve mention. They include the hairy frogs (*Astylosternus* spp.) of West Africa which take their name from the hair-like skin growths on the sides and hind legs of the males. In the rivers of the Cameroon/Gabon region dwells the largest frog species in the world, the goliath frog (*Rana goliath*), which may have an overall length (toe tip to nose tip) of almost 1 m and weigh 3 kg. A number of species, such as the ghost frogs (*Heleophryne* spp.) of southern Africa have adapted to living in mountain torrents. Some of the most colourful species belong to the diverse reed-frogs (*Hyperolius* spp. and *Afrixalus* spp.), tree frogs (*Leptopelis* spp.) and the *Cardioglossa* spp. that are associated with moist environments on the tropical forest floor. The female foam-nesting frogs (*Chiromantis* spp.) secrete a jelly-like substance which she and her male consorts beat into a foam with their hind legs and she then lays as many as 150 eggs into it. The nests with their air-dried and hardened outer surfaces are located on branches above pools of water and when the tadpoles hatch and start to develop the protective outer crust softens allowing the tadpoles to drop to the water below. Although many species of toads spend much of their time out of water, during the breeding season some species gather in huge numbers at marshes, swamps, lakes and rivers to lay their eggs. The males of the raucous toad (*Bufo rangeri*) often come together in vast numbers, calling like demented ducks to attract females.

THE FISH

The freshwater habitats of Africa are incredibly rich in fish species belonging to many families and genera, the vast majority of which are endemic. Accurate figures for the number of species in most families are difficult to establish but there are at least 300 different members of the **Cyprinidae**, more than 600 in the **Cichlidae**, over 200 species of **Mormyridae**, in the **Characoidei** more than 190 species, in the **Siluroidei** in excess of 300 species and so on. There are many "typical" fish with classic structures and form but there are also many bizarre and unusual species. The Zaïre River system has more than 700 known species, of which about 500 are endemic. This is more than any other African system even if one excludes the species-rich Lake Tanganyika, which feeds its waters via the Lukuga River into the Zaïre. It is considered likely that there are many more species that remain to be collected and identified. The Nile River system has at least 320 species but with far fewer endemics than the Zaïre. The Niger River in West Africa has at least 134 fish species, with the Volta having a known diversity of 122 species. The Great Rift Valley lakes, most notably Victoria, Tanganyika and Malawi, have a very special place in the fish world because of the vast number of species of cichlids that have evolved in these water bodies. The cichlids have more genera and species in African freshwater bodies, particularly lakes, than any other fish family. What is amazing about this colourful group of fishes, particularly in the lakes, is the fact that they managed to evolve into hundreds of different species from an ancestral stock of a few river-dwelling cichlids. They have evolved to inhabit virtually all available habitats and niches. Some feed on algal growth, some on snails and others on worms. One has enlarged "suction" lips to draw mayfly larvae from the substrate, others are specialist sponge-feeders, and there are the active predators, even one that is able to suck the eggs out of the mouth of other cichlid species. They are as diverse in appearance (particularly in the older Lake Tanganyika) as they are in their feeding methods. Many species are also underwater "chamaeleons", being able to change their colours rapidly, for example to indicate an aggressive state. This brings us to the next amazing fact about these cichlids – they are attentive parents. Many cichlids are mouth-brooders, with either the male or the female (depending on the species) taking the relatively small number of eggs into the mouth as soon as they are laid, and keeping them there until they hatch. After hatching the young spend part of the time inside the parent's mouth and part in the water. They never wander far, however. At any sign of danger they return to the adult's mouth. Most of the cichlids in lakes Victoria and Malawi are mouth-brooders, but many in Lake Tanganyika are substrate-spawners. The species which do not take the eggs into the mouth but lay them on the substrate guard them until they hatch. The young fish remain close to the parent, or parents, for about two to three weeks, after which they usually disperse.

Until recently Lake Victoria contained the second largest number of cichlid species in the world, with about 80 per cent of the fish biomass being made up by that group. Today, half of all endemic cichlids have disappeared and they make up only about two per cent of the biomass. This catastrophe has been attributed to, amongst other things, the introduction of the large, carnivorous Nile perch (*Lates niloticus*), over-fishing, rapid and extreme fluctuations in the level of the lake, eutrophication and hypoxia. This is mass extinction on a scale never before observed by scientists.

Another amazing group of small fishes, the rivulins (genera include *Nothobranchius*, *Roloffia* and *Aphyosemion*), commonly known to aquarists as killifishes, are able to make use of temporary pools by laying eggs which resist dessication. The eggs lie in the dried mud awaiting the stimulus of sustained rainfall. Development and growth is extremely rapid and many species are able to breed when only a few weeks old. Then there are the air-breathing fishes, of which many species occur in Africa, including numerous members of the families **Clariidae** (catfish/barbels) and the **Anabantidae**. The African lungfishes (*Protopterus* spp.), of which there are three species, have primitive lungs which enable them to survive in oxygen-depleted swamps and even on floodplains which dry up seasonally. If the water dries up these fish excavate burrows in the mud and then secrete a mucous cocoon that protects them from moisture loss. They breathe through a small slit at the top of the cocoon. Here they remain dormant until the onset of the rainy season when the floodplain, or lake bottom, begins to fill with water. Although this period is usually only a few months, there are records of these lungfishes surviving for more than two years.

The "elephant trunk" fish, or mormyrids (**Mormyridae**) are able to navigate and locate prey in murky waters by creating a discharge of electric impulses from special organs near the tail. These impulses are then picked up by sensory organs in the head which register any distortions in the electric field. There is also a group of small catfish (for example *Synodontis batensoda*) that swim and float upside down near the surface, making it easier for them to feed on items that fall into the water.

Large numbers of humans in Africa are partially, or totally, reliant on fish as a source of protein. At present more than 200 000 tons of fish (primarily the introduced Nile perch and Nile tilapia, *Orechromis niloticus*, and the tiny native omena *Rastrineobola argentea*) are exported from Lake Victoria. Many thousands of tons of a small shoaling fish, kapenta (*Limnothrissa miodon*), are caught commercially each year in lakes Tanganyika and Kariba, whereas an estimated yield of some 40 000 tons of fish per annum could be harvested from Lake Volta (a man-made lake of about 8 500 km^2). During periods of high water the many floodplains are extensively fished and supply many thousands of tons of fish.

THE INVERTEBRATES

Because of the vast numbers of invertebrates associated with African fresh waters we can do little more than take a glimpse at this largely hidden world. Single-celled protozoans provide the vital link in virtually all freshwater systems, where they feed on bacteria and in their turn are fed on by other organisms, and so on up to the top of the food chain. The protozoans are particularly successful because of their ability to survive the dry periods between the rainy seasons. There are vast numbers of species and under ideal conditions they reach incredibly high densities.

Nematodes and segmented worms (including leeches – Class **Hirudinae**) may also reach high densities, with most species living in mud and silt at the bottom of lakes, swamps, marshes and slow-moving rivers. One segmented worm, *Alma emini*, lives in the muddy substrate of swamps and marshes and extracts oxygen from the water with a tail extremely well supplied with blood vessels. The tail sticks out of the burrow and serves as a simple lung. Crustaceans, including crabs, also occupy many watery habitats, as do great numbers of insects and their larvae.

Many insects, such as the dragonflies and damselflies (Order **Odonata**), the mayflies (Order **Ephemeroptera**) and caddis flies (Order **Trichoptera**) spend their sometimes brief adult life out of water but their larvae live, grow and develop under water. Some species belonging to predominantly terrestrial insect orders spend their larval and adult lives in water. These include a large number of beetle species (Order **Coleoptera**) such as those in the genera *Dytiscus* and *Gyrinus*. These beetles must return to the surface of the water at regular intervals to replenish their air supply, which they hold as a bubble below the wing-cases (elytra). Freshwater molluscs, including many species of snail (**Gastropoda**) and bivalves (**Lamellibranchia**), are found in most freshwater habitats and may reach great densities.

A number of organisms that dwell in inland waters for part of their life-cycle have a serious impact on man in Africa. They include the parasites *Schistosoma mansoni* and *S. haematobium* (bilharzia), which have certain species of freshwater snail as their intermediate host, from where they are passed on to humans. The snails favour slow-moving or static water bodies – exactly those areas where man prefers to bathe and collect water. The parasites enter the body and invade the essential organs and can cause severe illness and frequently death if untreated. After malaria, schistosomiasis is the most important parasitic disease in the world. The *Plasmodium* spp. parasite that causes malaria in man is transmitted by the bite of the female *Anopheles* mosquito, and affects millions in Africa. There is a high death rate and the development of strains resistant to prevention and treatment is cause for grave concern. The larval and pupating stages of the mosquito are spent in fresh water. Black flies of the genus *Simulium* transmit the parasite *Onchocerca volvulus* to man causing onchocerciasis, commonly called "river blindness". The parasite affects the skin, lymph nodes and eyes and can lead to blindness. It is most prevalent in the vicinity of fast-flowing streams and in parts of West Africa it has forced people to move away from a number of floodplains.

Below left: *An emerging adult dragonfly. Photo: John Carlyon.* **Above:** *The Victoria Falls on the Zambezi River is one of the most impressive waterfalls on earth.* **Below right:** *One of Africa's strangest birds is the shoebill,* Balaeniceps rex, *also known as the boatbill and whalebill.*

THE FUTURE

The inland waters of Africa, as we have seen, are varied and cover extensive areas, yet they face numerous problems and these pressures will intensify as the human population continues to grow. Many of these problems are not exclusive to Africa but are shared with the rest of the world. The raising of dams, both large and small, across many rivers has resulted in the disruption of fish breeding migrations, altered the water flow on floodplains and brought about other negative changes. There have been advantages in that commercial fisheries became viable on large impoundments and regulated flow can serve to increase agricultural production downstream. However, agriculture in its turn increases the flow of poisons, such as herbicides, into the waterways, and cultivation is able to expand into previously marginal areas. Impoundments also serve to attract more people to a more secure water supply thus placing increased pressures on surrounding environments. Channelisation, and the modification of inland waters in other ways, results in a reduction of the number of habitats and species richness decreases according to the severity of the changes.

Floodplains and other inland waters are extremely important in Africa as a source of fish protein for local people and for sale to populations further away. With the ever-increasing numbers of people, demand escalates and some areas are suffering from over-exploitation. Traditional fishing methods have given way to the more efficient use of small-mesh gill nets in many areas thus increasing offtake. The extensive cutting of reeds also reduces available organic material, as does too frequent burning. Many floodplains are increasingly used for grazing herds and flocks of domestic animals, such as cattle, and cultivation during the dry seasons. This places considerable pressure on such systems. The removal and cutting of riverbank vegetation reduces the amount of organic material entering the water but increases siltation levels as nothing remains to bind the soils. Increased siltation proves unsuitable for many species and they either dwindle drastically in numbers or disappear completely from the system. Even in large conservation areas, such as the Kruger National Park (South Africa) the effects of river flow, water quality and toxins entering the systems from outside the area can scuttle even the finest environmental conservation policies. The results are often felt far from the area that has been damaged, for example siltation of coral reefs along the coastal margin.

Another serious problem is the introduction of exotic plants and animals into African inland water systems. We have already mentioned the tragic consequences of releasing the Nile perch into Lake Victoria and the green, cancerous spread of the water hyacinth through many water bodies. The introduction of carnivorous angling fish, including several species of bass and trout, to the river systems of the Western and Eastern Cape provinces in South Africa, has resulted in the near-extinction of several small endemic fish and the great reduction of several larger species because of predation on their young.

Despite these and a great many other pressures placed on African aquatic systems, many are still in an amazingly healthy state. Ever-increasing demands are unlikely to allow this situation to continue, however. An environment is only as healthy as its water resources.

CHAPTER 7

THE COASTAL ZONE

Africa has a coastline of more than 29 000 km which is shared amongst 33 different nations, with the remaining 15 countries being totally landlocked. Somalia has a coastal frontage of 3 200 km and South Africa some 3 000 km, but most of the other countries have much shorter shorelines. Only three countries have their shores lapped by two different water bodies: South Africa by the Atlantic and the Indian oceans, Egypt by the Mediterranean and Red seas and Morocco by the Atlantic and the Mediterranean. The west coast of Africa borders on the Atlantic Ocean, the east coast on the Indian Ocean, the north on the Mediterranean Sea and the north-east on the Red Sea.

The African coastline is relatively uniform, with a narrow continental shelf and few bays or prominent geomorphological features.

These include extensive stretches of exposed sandy beaches, rocky coastlines, some of the world's finest coral reefs on the east coast and extensive mangrove swamps on the east and west coasts. The coastline adjoins forest and desert, savanna and woodland, high- and low-rainfall regions, highly developed areas and wilderness regions. Along some stretches, such as parts of the Red Sea coastline, the escarpment falls steeply to the shore. There are also rugged coastal cliffs, for example along the Mediterranean shoreline, and tall sand

Background: *A wave-lashed rock reef on the African coastline.* **Above:** *The fox face* Lo vulpinus *has a wide Indo-Pacific range in coastal waters, as have many other tropical species.*

dunes which slope steeply into the sea where the Namib Desert meets the cold waters of the Atlantic Ocean.

Many areas have been sorely abused by man, such as much of the Mediterranean coastline and the shores of South and West Africa, but long stretches still remain relatively pristine. For the purposes of this book we will not look beyond the edge of the continental shelf into the open oceans.

Many different forces and actions have influenced and moulded the coastal margins that we see today. The coastal plains were frequently inundated, or exposed, as a result of the land being uplifted or lowered by crustal actions. Ocean levels fell dramatically as the great ice sheets spread towards the lower latitudes. Then when the ice sheets retreated as temperatures rose the coastal plains disappeared below the tides. The ocean levels only stabilised at their present extent in the past 5 000 to 6 000 years. Amazingly, the Mediterranean Sea has been much larger than it is today and it has also been completely dry. Today we refer to the prehistoric greater Mediterranean as the Tethys Sea, an expanse of water that pushed deep into the underbelly of Europe and far to the east. As the African Plate moved northwards towards Europe it wedged itself under the Iberian Plate and continued its thrusting, as it still does today. In fact within a few million years Africa and Europe will push together to form one continuous land mass.

As Arabia moved to join what we know today as Turkey, the Mediterranean was closed off from the east. Then northwest Africa and Iberia crashed together, sealing the Mediterranean off from the Atlantic Ocean. This now isolated sea dried up and remained in this state until about five and a half million years ago. Evidence is presented by salt layers on the sea floor up to 2 km thick and a lack of marine fossils during the dry period. It has been estimated that the Mediterranean was dry for only about 500 000 years, but no certainty exists as to how the breach between Iberia and Africa occurred. Some believe that an earthquake caused the

that our coastlines are stable and unchanging – far from it! The action of waves breaking constantly on the shore erodes even the hardest rock over time, deposits great quantities of pebbles and sand and eats away or builds up the coastline. In some areas humans have had an immense impact on these processes. For example the building of the Aswan High Dam has resulted in a dramatic decrease in silts reaching the delta of the Nile River, causing a drastic reduction in its land area. In places almost one kilometre of the delta has been reclaimed by the sea and the loss of nutrients previously carried from the African interior has reduced fish populations to the detriment of peasant fishermen in the area. Similar problems can be related to a number of other major rivers but little documentation is available.

Coastal currents carry and deposit sediments, and rivers and streams transport millions of tons of sand and mud which end up lying along the ocean margins. These vast quantities of sediments are to a large extent deposited back onto the shore. In the vicinity of many river and stream estuaries falling within the tropics, mangrove trees become established and their root systems serve to stabilise great quantities of fine sediments and organic materials. Mangroves occur on both the west and east coasts of the continent but coral reefs are only established in the waters of the Indian Ocean and Red Sea. There are, however, solitary corals along the west coast and some coral assemblages found in association with islands in the Gulf of Guinea.

The movements and nature of ocean currents have a profound influence on the climate of the coastline and the interiors of all land masses. They also determine to a great extent the diversity and biomass of marine organisms. Warm ocean currents – such as the Mozambique and Agulhas currents, which sweep down the east coast of Africa, and the Guinea Current which pushes round the West African bulge into the Gulf of Guinea – ensure that there is an impressive assem-

Above: *Many stretches of the African coastline are very rocky in nature.* **Right:** *The blue surgeon fish* Paracanthus *sp.*

breach and the great flood of Atlantic waters back into this salty wasteland. Other experts think that the level of the ocean rose, allowing its waters to pour between present-day Gibraltar at the tip of Spain and Ceuta at the northernmost tip of Morocco, eventually eroding a deep channel.

Whatever the cause, Africa was once again separated from Europe, albeit by a very narrow stretch of water. The Red Sea was formed during the triple fracturing of the great Ethiopian rock-dome, when Africa and the Arabian Peninsula were rifted apart and the resulting "canyon" filled with sea water. Huge amounts of sediments and rock debris, mainly from the highlands, have almost cut the Red Sea off from the Indian Ocean, where it links with the Gulf of Aden. Today, this long (some 3 000 km) and narrow sea is home to some of Africa's finest and richest coral reefs. This does not mean, however, blage of both animal and plant species along these shorelines. However, the number of individuals within each species is comparatively small. If one then looks at the principal cold currents – the Benguela Current sweeping northwards from the sub-Antarctic along the south-west coastline, and the Canary Current which influences the north-western shores – they are low in diversity. This is made up for in many cases, however, by very high biomass within many species, such as plankton and pelagic fish species.

The Indian Ocean shoreline of Africa is totally influenced by warm currents, whereas almost half of the Atlantic Ocean coast is coursed by cool currents. Warm currents on the western side of the continent extend from the vicinity of Senegal through to the Gulf of Guinea and extend to the Angolan coast, where the warm water is pushed out into the Atlantic by the cold waters of the Benguela Current. Because of its comparatively small size, currents in the Mediterranean Sea are strongly influenced by the seasonal weather patterns. During the summer, when evaporation is usually at its greatest, particularly in the eastern basin, salinity is high. In the winter the highly saline water cools and sinks and moves to the west to flow through the Straits of Gibraltar, whilst water with lower salinity enters above the western current from the Atlantic to maintain salt levels. Of course there is a constant interchange of water throughout the year but it is at its highest during the winter. Despite this it has been estimated that

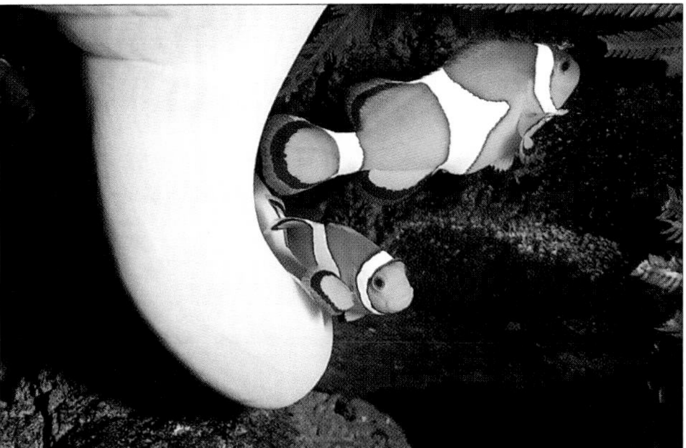

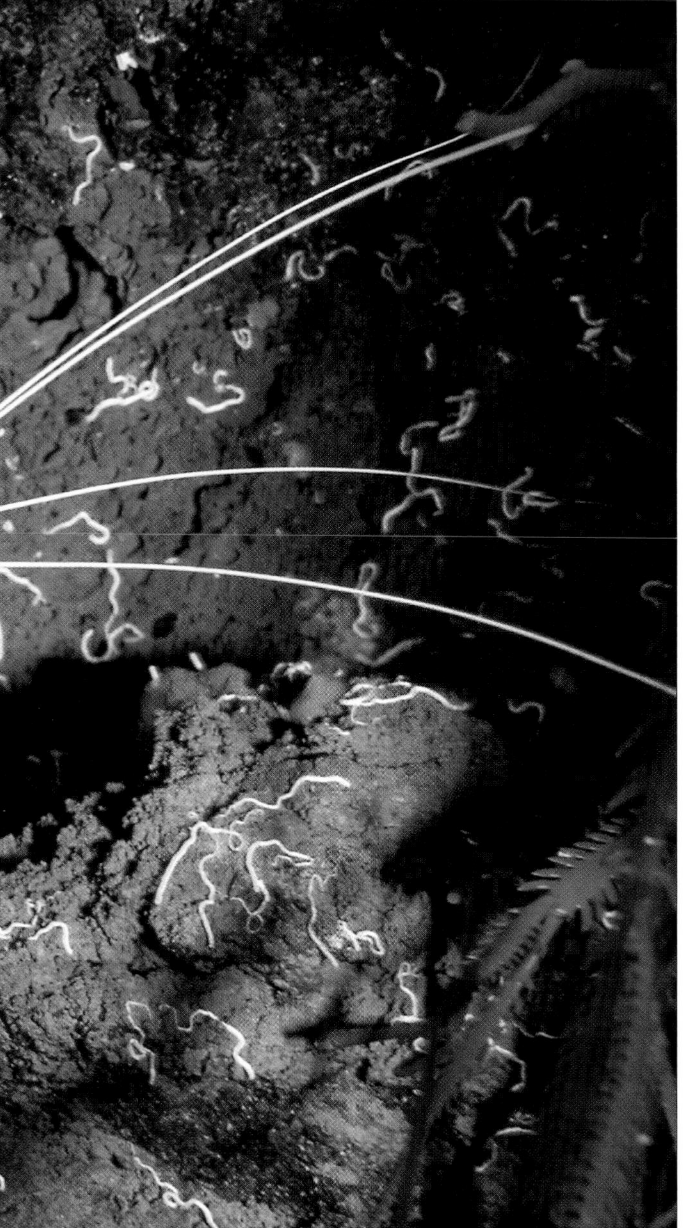

Left: *This colourful cleaner shrimp* Hippolysmata grabhami *is a relatively common resident of the Red Sea coral reefs.* **Above left:** *Marine sponges* (**Porifera**) *occur in many different colours and forms. In the littoral they are mainly associated with rocky and coral shores.* **Above right:** *An anemone fish* Amphiprion ocellaris *at the base of a giant anemone.*

it takes up to 80 years for a complete turnover of all the Mediterranean waters. In comparison with the warm Indian Ocean and Red Sea with their high species diversity, and the cooler Atlantic Ocean with its great biomass of creatures, the Mediterranean Sea is not particularly rich in either species or biomass. Because of its very limited access to the open ocean and restricted water flow, as well as the rapidly growing human population around its shores (it may be as high as 400 million by 2030), it has far higher pollution levels than any other marine body off Africa's coastline.

Because of the massive diversity of plants (phytoplankton and algae) and animals in the marine environment, particularly close to shore, we can only provide a brief summary of some of the principal habitats available to them and the biota that inhabit them.

THE CORAL REEFS

As already mentioned there are extensive coral reefs located along the shores of the Red Sea and the tropical sector of the Indian Ocean coastline as far south as southern Mozambique and the adjacent area of South Africa. However, these reefs are not continuous along the coast and the principal concentrations are found off the shores of the Red Sea countries, Kenya, Tanzania and Mozambique. Many of the western Indian Ocean islands falling within the Afrotropical Realm, such as Madagascar, the Mascarenes and the Comoros, are partly fringed by coral reefs but some are built entirely by corals that lie atop submerged rock islands.

There are three principal types of coral reef. The barrier reef is separated from the shore by a wide channel, whereas the fringing reef lies close to the shoreline and is frequently linked to the mainland at low tide. The third type of reef is

TREE SURVIVAL IN THE MANGROVE SWAMPS

Trees of the mangrove swamps, sometimes referred to as tidal forest or more confusingly as coastal woodland, all have one thing in common – their adaptations to survive in salty water for varying periods of time. Mangrove trees only grow in the zone that lies between the high-water mark of the spring tides and just above the average sea level. At the highest level flooding only takes place twice during each lunar month but at the lowest levels the tides inundate the mud flats twice a day. These forests are very poor in tree diversity, with only six species in this habitat on the west coast of Africa and nine species on the east coast. No tree species occur along both coastlines. All mangroves are restricted to the narrow intertidal belt, nearly always in sheltered situations where they are not subjected to aggressive wave action and with their roots in fine silt or mud. All mangrove trees are halophytes, that is they are salt-resistant plants that have evolved special adaptations to survive in what would otherwise be an inhospitable environment. Some species are able to tolerate greater levels of salinity and inundation, and in large, long-established swamps zonation is clearly visible. Despite this high salt tolerance the trees need a constant supply of fresh water in the form of river-flow or in some cases regular and heavy rainfall. This is why nearly all African mangrove swamps are found in association with river deltas and stream estuaries.

Mangrove trees are evergreen, with thick and leathery leaves. Many species have viviparous seeds which start to develop on the parent plant; when shed they "spear" into the mud where root development is rapid. They are also characterised by surface roots which allow the root system to respire in the anaerobic silt. These breathing roots can be divided into three groups, "pencil roots" or pneumatophores, "knee roots" and "prop" or "stilt" roots. These specialised roots allow the gaseous exchange of oxygen and carbon dioxide to take place through small openings known as lenticels, at low tide. This tangle of surface roots can greatly hinder movement through such a swamp but without them these highly adapted trees would be unable to survive. Each species has also evolved ways of ridding itself of excessive salt loads. The white mangrove (Avicennia marina) *gets rid of salt by excreting salt-laden fluid through specialised glands which are located on the leaf surfaces, particularly on the underside.*

Below: *Black and white mangrove trees growing along a permanent channel.*

the atoll, but these coral-structured islands are only found far to the east of the African mainland.

There are many different species of coral, including such beauties as brain corals, staghorn, fungus corals and soft corals. They are divided into the forms that are reef builders and those that are solitary, or live in loose groupings. Despite the plant-like appearance of many coral species, they are in fact colonies of vast numbers of tiny carnivorous animals, referred to as coral polyps. These polyps are tiny and resemble miniature sea anemones, differing from them in their ability to produce a skeleton. The latter may take the form of a hard, rigid structure, a horny skeleton or a scattering of hard particles that are embedded in the coral polyp. Although there are many species of solitary corals, it is the colonial reef-forming corals that are the most easily observed. Each colonial coral structure is a veritable mega-city of individuals, living polyps on the outer surfaces building upon the skeletons of dead polyps. Many of these coral reefs are thousands of years old and in the case of the oceanic atolls on sinking islands may be hundreds of metres thick. Reef-forming corals thrive in tropical waters over 21 °C, and under these conditions they provide one of the richest habitats on earth. Not only are the corals diverse in species, colour and form but they provide a cornucopia of habitats and niches for a bewildering array of other animals and algae. Many of the organisms found on and around the African coral reefs have a wide Indo-Pacific distribution, with only a small percentage of species being endemic.

Why are the corals so prolific and so successful? The reef-building coral polyps have unicellular algae known as zooxanthellae living within their tissues and this symbiotic relationship is of great benefit to plant and animal alike. The algae benefit from the protective environment and they utilise the nitrogenous wastes produced by the polyps; whereas the polyps benefit by having a live-in waste-disposal service and being able to utilise organic substances that pass out of the algal cells.

Africa's coral reefs face a number of threats including dynamiting for fish, siltation from streams and rivers, the removal of edible organisms such as fish and molluscs, and collection of coral and molluscs for the tourist and export trade.

THE MANGROVE SWAMPS

This is one of the most interesting but also the least hospitable of the African coastal habitats. Mangrove swamps are present within the tropics on both the Atlantic and Indian Ocean coastlines. Virtually all are found in association with riverine estuaries and deltas, as well as sheltered bays with rivers or streams feeding into them. In areas receiving heavy rainfall, mangrove communities can survive with this type of freshwater flushing. Some of Africa's most extensive mangrove, or saline swamp, forests are located along the West African Gulf of Guinea coast and the Indian Ocean shores of Kenya, Tanzania and Mozambique. The West African mangroves are closely allied to those of the American Atlantic coast, and those of eastern Africa belong to the Indo-Pacific group. Despite the fact that large areas of mangrove have been cleared significant blocks remain, such as the approximately 300 000 ha on the Cameroon coast, some 500 000 ha in association with the delta of the Niger River, almost 300 000 ha along the shores of Guinea and 100 000 ha fringing the coastline of Guinea-Bissau. Gabon also has extensive but largely unsurveyed mangroves.

In general very little research has been undertaken on this fascinating habitat in Africa. Mangroves are absent from the arid coastline of southern Angola and Namibia, and most of the South African shoreline. Extensive mangrove systems are

Top: *The flowers of the black mangrove. An intricate mechanism explosively exposes the stamens when they are visited by an insect, or other potential pollinator, and the unsuspecting visitor is showered with pollen.* **Above:** *Pneumatophores of the white mangrove* (Avicennia marina).

located in and around several major river estuaries on the east coast, including those of the Zambezi, Rovuma, Rufiji and the Tana. It has been estimated that Tanzania has about 200 000 ha of mangrove woodland, with at least 100 000 ha in Mozambique. As with the mangroves of West Africa, those of the east coast are under pressure, primarily from wood cutting. The timber is used for building and also for the production of high-quality charcoal.

Mangrove tree diversity is very low around the African coastline, with six species on the Atlantic shores and nine species on the east coast. Interestingly, no species is shared between the two oceans and the trees on the west coast most closely resemble those growing on the east coast of South and Central America. All the trees growing within the mangrove environment are highly adapted to coping with regular inundation of their root systems by sea water. In large, well-established swamps it is usually easy to see clear stratification of the different tree species. Apart from the true mangrove tree species, very few plants can tolerate setting their roots in this harsh saline environment.

Although at first glance the muddy substrate appears to be largely devoid of life, it is in fact inhabited by an array of strange creatures including fiddler crabs, sesarmid burrowing crabs, tree-climbing whelks and mudskipper fish which are as at home on land as in the water. As with the mangrove trees, the different animal species have preferred areas, or zones, which they occupy. The mangrove-inhabiting animals occupy three principal zones: those that dwell on, or under, the mud, the species that live in the tree canopy and creatures that are restricted to the permanently flooded channels.

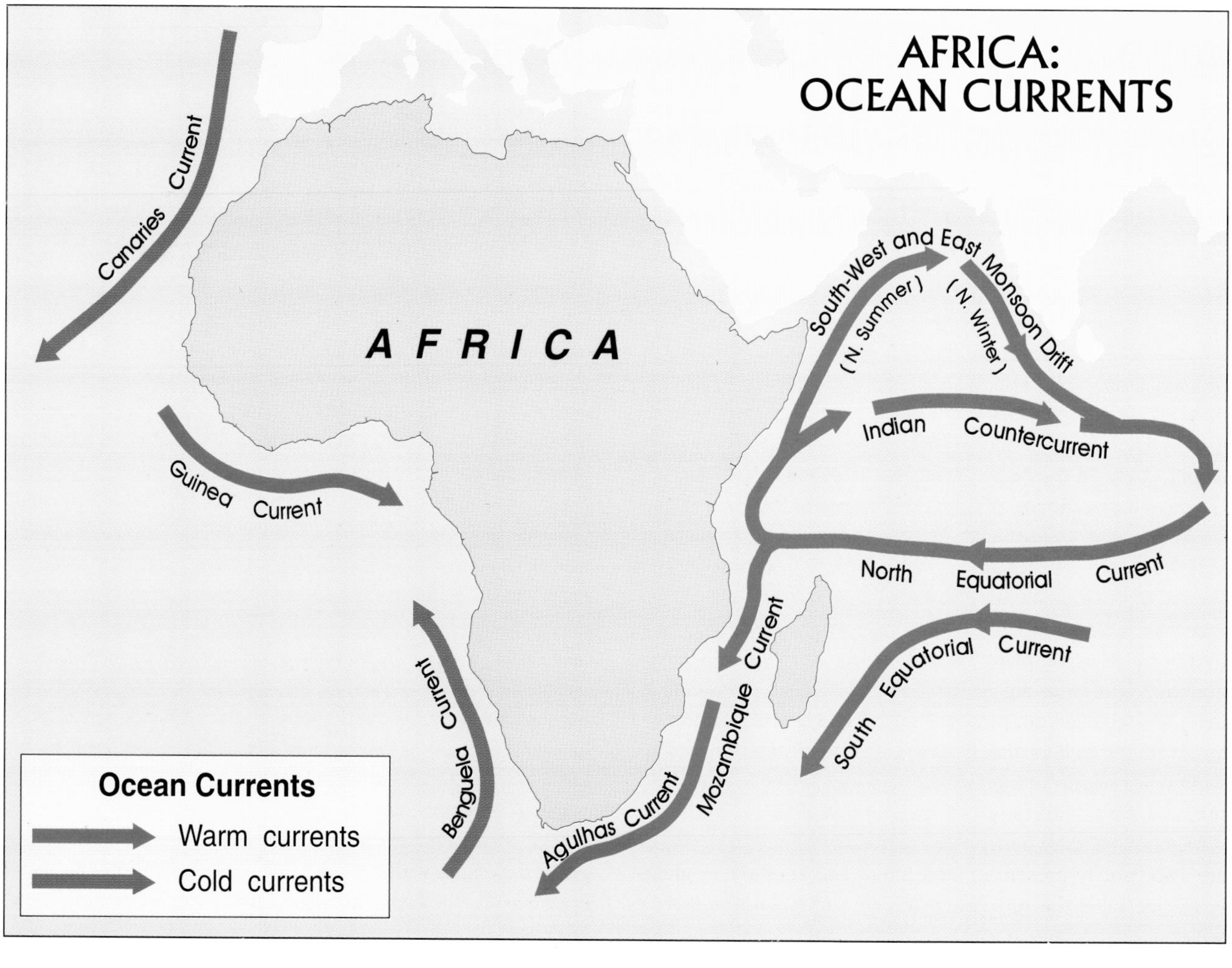

AFRICA:
OCEAN CURRENTS

AFRICA

Canaries Current
Guinea Current
Benguela Current
Agulhas Current
Mozambique Current
South Equatorial Current
North Equatorial Current
Indian Countercurrent
South-West and East Monsoon Drift
(N. Summer)
(N. Winter)

Ocean Currents
Warm currents
Cold currents

Above left: *The mudskipper* (Periophthalmus *sp.*) *is a fish but is atypical in that it is amphibious, spending much of its time out of water.* **Above:** *A sandy beach with rock outcroppings.*

Diversity is not particularly high but population densities can reach impressive levels. Let us look at a few of the creatures that call the mangrove swamps home. The mud-dwelling animals are the most numerous and the most noticeable are the crabs. Although they are small, it is usually the fiddler crabs (Family **Ocypodidae**), particularly the males, that first attract attention to themselves. Most species are brightly coloured and the males have one very large chela, or pincer, which is used to attract the attention of females, as well as to warn off and fight rival males. The second pincer is minute and it is used for feeding on plankton stranded on the mud by retreating tides, as well as algae. The females have an advantage in that they can use both pincers for feeding. As with most mangrove mud-dwellers the fiddler crabs excavate burrows to which they retreat at high tide, partly to avoid predators. The burrows are also in frequent use at low tide.

Members of crab genera such as *Sesarma* and *Ilyograpsus* are also usually present in large numbers. They range greatly in size from the red mangrove crab (*Sesarma meinerti*), which may reach a carapace width of 70 mm, to *Ilyograpsus rhizophorae*, which is less than 10 mm in size. At low tide huge numbers emerge from their permanent burrows to collect tree leaves and other plant debris which they carry to the safety of their burrows to eat. The larger species also scrape surface bark from the mangrove trees.

Another interesting denizen of this seemingly hostile environment is the mudskipper, of which there are several different species. The mudskippers, also known as skipping gobies, are fish with a difference; the adults are amphibious. They have eyes located at the top of the head, the pectoral fins resemble seal-like flippers that enable them to "walk" around on the mud, and the gills are specially evolved to allow these fish to spend long periods out of water. As the tide rises they retreat ahead of it, frequently clambering into the mangrove trees. During the breeding season they also make use of burrows excavated by the males. The female lays her eggs on the burrow wall and for a short period after hatching the young fish remain in its shelter and then move into open water as they are entirely aquatic.

Many other marine fish species utilise the rich feeding grounds to be found in the permanent channels. The mangrove waters, as with estuaries, are extremely important nursery areas for the eggs and young fish of many commercially exploited species.

ROCKY SHORES AND BEACHES

Apart from the coral assemblages and the mangrove swamps there are also vast stretches of rocky shoreline ranging from sheer sea cliffs to gently sloping shelves which may be exposed for several hundred metres seawards at low tide. After the coral reefs the rocky coastlines are the richest in both algal and animal species. Because of the extent of the African coastline and its considerable range of water temperatures and nutrient levels we can do little more than give a brief overview of the zonation of life on these rocky shores. Many intertidal organisms have wide oceanic distributions but some species are restricted to limited stretches of coastline. Not all species are jumbled at random in the intertidal zone – each is adapted to a particular area. Some organisms are only exposed twice a month with the spring tides, whereas others are exposed for a limited period twice a day. Those species at the upper limits of the high tide are only briefly exposed to the tides. On gently sloping shores zonation is usually clearer, whereas on steep slopes this zonation may be hardly visible. Many of the animals inhabiting these shores have evolved adaptations to help them survive the twice-daily battering by waves, exposure to the dessicating effects of the sun at low tide, and differences in light intensity, temperature and salinity that exist at low and high tides.

Many intertidal creatures seek shelter in permanently inundated rock pools, or they crawl into crevices which remain moist and cool during low tide. There is considerable competition between the animals for these most favoured microhabitats. However, many species, such as the limpets, barnacles and periwinkles, are able to withstand exposure by "sealing" themselves into their shells and in this way retaining moisture as well as avoiding direct contact with the air. The limpets, of which there are many species, are particularly interesting. During high tide they move about, feeding on algal growth, but before the tide begins its retreat they return to their home base where the shell edge and the rock form a tight fit. Inhabitants of this littoral, or intertidal, zone include numerous sponges, sea anemones, sea urchins, starfish, a bewildering array of molluscs, crustaceans, segmented and unsegmented worms, sea squirts, barnacles, fish and many types of algae.

At first glance the long stretches of African beaches seem to be largely devoid of life, but this is not so as many invertebrate organisms call this environment home. Living in sand presents its own difficulties, not least of which is the need to avoid being constantly pounded by waves. This is usually accomplished by burrowing below the surface. Burrowing under the sand is relatively easy, but as sand tends to collapse many organisms have had to evolve ways of preventing suffocation. Some groups of species, such as the polychaete worms, construct tubes which provide access to the surface.

Others, including numerous lamellibranch molluscs (bivalves) have long siphon-tubes which allow the animals to live well below the surface and in safety. On shores where large quantities of algae wash up after storms, such as the south-western African coast, vast numbers of herbivorous crustaceans (for example isopods and copepods) are concentrated along the high-water mark.

On the beaches located within the tropics one of the most frequently observed inhabitants is the ghost crab, of which

there are several species (Family **Ocypodidae**). All construct distinct burrows, usually close to the level reached by the high tides. Most are active at night and it is an unforgettable sight to watch these long-legged crabs scuttling around in their thousands on moonlit evenings.

Other species of crabs live along the sandy shores but, unlike the ghost crab, most do not construct burrows and simply shuffle their way below the surface.

Below far left: *The white pelican* Pelecanus onocrotalus *is at home on inland, as well as coastal, waters.* **Above left:** *The beautiful but poisonous devil fish* (Pterois *sp.*) *is associated with rocky coastlines and coral reefs. Photo: Antwerp Zoo.* **Below left:** *A sandy beach with rock intrusions.* **Above:** *The Cape clawless otter* Aonyx capensis *is most frequently associated with freshwater habitats but it is a coastal resident in some areas.*

THE MAMMALS

Apart from the vast array of invertebrate organisms associated with the African coastline there is also an important assemblage of reptiles, birds and mammals. The mammals can be divided into two distinct groups, those which are wholly aquatic and those which come to shore mainly to rest and breed. Whenever one refers to marine mammals it is usually the cetaceans, or whales, dolphins and porpoises that come to mind. Many species have wide global distributions, particularly the giants such as the humpback whale (*Megaptera novaeangliae*), the blue whale (*Balaenoptera musculus*) and the right whale (*Balaena glacialis*). Populations of the humpback move from their Antarctic feeding grounds to breed close inshore to the south of the Bight of Biafra on the African west coast and on the east coast off Somalia and Kenya. The right whale also moves from its colder feeding grounds to breed in sheltered bays off the southern African coast. However, most of the larger whale species only rarely occur close inshore. Several dolphin species can be observed close inshore, but probably most common are the Atlantic (*Tursiops truncatus*) and the Indian Ocean (*Tursiops aduncus*) bottle-nosed dolphins, which may form large schools that can be seen from the shore. The humpback dolphin (*Sousa teuszii*), which occurs close inshore from Mauritania to Angola, and *Sousa plumbea*, which is found along the eastern African seaboard, feeds and breeds in shallow coastal waters. One of the smallest cetaceans is Heaviside's dolphin (*Cephalorhynchus heavisidii*), weighing about 40 kg and restricted to the cold inshore waters of the Benguela Current along the south-west coast of Africa. This species is not usually seen from shore. Another small species is the common, or harbour, porpoise (*Phocoena phocoena*), usually observed off the Mediterranean coastline.

Apart from the cetaceans which are observed moving and feeding close to the coast there are also fairly regular strandings of deeper ocean species, such as the false killer whale (*Pseudorca crassidens*). These may number a few to many

hundreds of whales and although many theories have been put forward there is still little understanding of why these mass "suicides" take place.

Two other entirely aquatic mammals occur in African waters, namely the manatee (*Trichechus senegalensis*), which lives along sheltered coastlines and in bays and lagoons, as well as penetrating larger rivers from Senegal to northern Angola. Along the Indian Ocean and Red Sea coasts a similar species, the dugong (*Dugong dugon*), occurs patchily in sheltered waters. These harmless aquatic grazers are heavily hunted as a source of meat and they have disappeared, or have been greatly reduced in numbers, in many areas.

Only one species of fur-seal (*Arctocephalus pusillus*) and one "true" seal, the Mediterranean monk seal (*Monachus monachus*) are resident along African shores. The Cape fur-seal is restricted to southern African waters, primarily on the Atlantic coast, where they form rookeries on offshore islands as well as on the mainland. It is a common species with well over one million individuals. In contrast the monk seal is in danger of becoming extinct, with only a few hundred individuals occurring along the coast of north-west Africa and into the Mediterranean. This seal is threatened by hunting and pollution. Several other species, such as the southern elephant seal (*Mirounga leonina*), crabeater seal (*Lobodon carcinophagus*) and leopard seal (*Hyrurga leptonyx*) are occasional vagrants to southern African waters.

Apart from those mammals that are entirely reliant on the sea, there are a number which utilise the coastal environment. The water mongoose (*Atilax paludinosus*) is a versatile small carnivore that occupies both freshwater and coastal fringes. Along the coast it forages in rock pools, along sandy beaches and in mangrove swamps for crabs, molluscs and

Above: *A double-banded anemone fish* Amphiprion bicinctus *seeking shelter in a large anemone. These fish are immune to the toxins of the anemone's stinging cells and can thus use them as sanctuaries from predators.* **Right:** *A tropical sea-horse,* Hippocampus *sp., of which there are several species. Photo: Antwerp Zoo*

sea urchins. It will also scavenge from animals cast onto the shore. The Cape clawless otter (*Aonyx capensis*) is a well known coastal hunter at the extreme south of the continent but this habit may also extend to other areas. Certain other mammal species that are not usually associated with the marine environment should also be mentioned. Although generally believed to be strictly a freshwater inhabitant the hippopotamus (*Hippopotamus amphibius*) has taken to the coastal environment in some areas. Probably the best known are the "marine hippos" which spend the daylight hours in the waters around the Bijagos Archipelago off Guinea-Bissau in West Africa. Hippo also occur in a number of estuaries.

Lions (*Panthera leo*) are recorded as coastal scavengers and seal-hunters along the northern Namibian coast and both the brown hyaena (*Hyaena brunnea*) and the black-backed jackal (*Canis mesomelas*) rely to a large extent on marine food along the entire Namibian coastline. Elephants (*Loxodonta africana*) have been recorded as bathing in the sea.

THE BIRDS

Birdlife along the coastline of Africa is both varied and abundant. Many species, such as the albatrosses, shearwaters, petrels, storm petrels, skuas and prions, are birds of the open ocean and are only rarely seen close inshore but the gannets (two species), cormorants, gulls, terns and the jackass penguin (*Spheniscus demersus*) are inshore birds that do not forage more than a few kilometres from the coastline and breed either on the mainland or on offshore islands. The jackass penguin, the only member of this family occurring in Africa, is restricted to the fish-rich waters of the south-western coastline. A number of species, including the frigate birds, tropicbirds and the boobies, breed on oceanic islands and are only occasional visitors to the mainland.

While there are many coastal and marine birds with wide distributions and a few localised ones, the number of African endemics are few. Kenya has the largest roseate tern (*Sterna dougallii*) breeding colony in the world on the Kiunga Islands and internationally important breeding populations of royal terns (*Sterna maxima*) and slenderbilled gulls (*Larus genei*) breed in Senegal, particularly in the delta of the Senegal River. Large breeding colonies of Cape gannets (*Sula capensis*) and Cape cormorants (*Phalacrocorax capensis*) are restricted to the cold waters of South Africa and Namibia, although young birds may disperse further afield.

Africa has many important over-wintering grounds for a great diversity of Palearctic waders, most of which are found in river deltas, estuaries, lagoons and mud flats associated with mangrove swamps. There are many sites along the coastlines of Senegal and Sierra Leone, with concentrations of up to 2.5 million waders and other waterbirds in the Banc d'Arguin National Park on the Mauritanian coast. Another site of international importance is the Bijagos Archipelago in Guinea-Bissau. In Namibia, Walvis Bay and Sandwich Harbour have many thousands of migrants, as does the estuary of the Orange River and Langebaan Lagoon on the South African west coast. A number of species are primarily freshwater inhabitants

Top: *The avocet* Recurvirostra avosetta *is commonly seen in flocks in estuaries. Photo: John Carlyon.* **Above:** *The white-tailed tropicbird* Phaethon lepturus *is an offshore species that occasionally visits the African coastline. Photo: John Carlyon*

but also make use of the coastal environment. Several heron species can be observed feeding on rocky shores and coral reefs, as well as on mud banks and estuaries, with both species of flamingo filter-feeding in shallow waters of sheltered lagoons. One of Africa's most famous birds of prey, the fish eagle (*Haliaeetus vocifer*), is frequently seen hunting over estuaries and lagoons in some coastal regions, as is the osprey (*Pandion Haliaetus*). A much smaller raptor, Eleonora's falcon (*Falco eleonorae*), has its breeding grounds around the fringes of the Mediterranean and several associated islands. Several kingfisher species, such as the very widespread pied kingfisher (*Ceryle rudis*), are as at home hunting in sheltered coastal waters as they are in lakes and rivers.

REPTILES AND FISH

The reptiles that occur in the coastal waters around Africa are restricted to the marine turtles, the Nile crocodile (*Crocodylus niloticus*) and a small number of sea snake species. The Nile crocodile is present in many sub-Saharan coastal estuaries, permanent channels in mangrove swamps and river deltas. It also makes occasional forays into the open sea, particularly where there are inshore islands. However, hunting pressure has drastically reduced crocodile numbers in many parts of its range. The sea turtles are not entirely aquatic as the females must haul up on sandy beaches to dig holes into which they lay their eggs. All species are under serious threat as both the eggs and the turtles themselves are hunted by people for food. The largest species of all is the leatherback (*Dermochelys coriacea*), which frequently exceeds 1.5 m in length and more than half a ton in weight. This magnificent reptile can be expected anywhere around the African coastline but only breeds at a few sites, the most southerly being just south of the Mozambique/South Africa border. Adult leatherbacks feed exclusively on jellyfish.

Other turtle species which occur on the African fringes are the green turtle (*Chelonia mydas*), hawksbill turtle (*Eretmochelys imbricata*), the smallest of the sea turtles the olive ridley (*Lepidochelys olivacea*) and the loggerhead turtle (*Caretta caretta*). Apart from the heavy toll inflicted on the turtles by man, the eggs and newly hatched young are eagerly sought out by a range of predators including the water mongoose, large crabs and birds such as the larger gulls. Those that survive this deadly gauntlet are further decimated by marine predators which start adding to the toll as soon as the baby turtles enter the water. Although breeding populations of these turtles are found along the shores of many African countries falling within the bounds of the sub-tropics and the tropics, numbers are generally low and in many cases still declining.

Sea snakes (sub-family **Hydrophiinae**) are in most cases restricted to an aquatic environment and in Africa they are only found along the shores lapped by the waters of the Indian Ocean and the Red Sea. However, these snakes are uncommon off Africa and their greatest centres of species diversity and density are located in the eastern Indian Ocean and the Pacific Ocean.

Of course the most diverse and numerous vertebrate group in the oceans and seas are the fish, which come in a bewildering array of shapes, forms, colours and patterns, and in sizes ranging from a few millimetres to several metres. There are species that are restricted to specific habitats, such as the mudskippers of the mangrove swamps, and others that are generalists and forage and hunt over a wide range of habitats. There are many commercially exploited fish species which spend most of their lives in the open sea but enter estuaries, mangrove swamps and sheltered lagoons to breed. In the warm waters of the Indian Ocean and Red Sea, as well

THE BENGUELA BONANZA

The great ocean current known as the West Wind Drift sweeps from west to east in the cold Southern Ocean and "gives birth" to the cool Benguela Current which peels away and heads northwards along the south-western coast of Africa. As it thrusts its way northwards it causes deep-lying cold water to be pushed into the shallower coastal zone in a process known as upwelling. As this nutrient-rich water enters the light zone near the surface it serves to support vast populations of minute organisms known collectively as phytoplankton, which in their turn provide bountiful grazing grounds for zooplankton. This combination of minerals such as phosphorus and energy-producing sunlight support the planktonic pastures and herbivores which in their turn support great shoals of pelagic fish (pelagic species occur in the upper layers of the open sea) which are an essential source of food for huge flocks of marine birds such as the Cape gannet (Morus capensis), *Cape cormorant* (Phalacrocorax capensis) *and the jackass, or blackfooted, penguin* (Spheniscus demersus). *There are of course many other predatory and herbivorous species, including the Cape fur-seal* (Arctocephalus pusillus), *cetaceans (whales and dolphins) and non-pelagic fish.*

The Benguela Current is a vast storehouse of life and the unbroken chain, if left to its natural course, is self-sustaining. Unfortunately, man has overfished the pelagic stocks, harvested the bird-produced guano for use as fertiliser, persecuted those predators of fish that he perceives as competing with him for a diminishing resource and polluted the coastal waters with oil and chemicals. Despite this reckless exploitation the Atlantic Ocean off the south-western coast of Africa remains one of the world's richest fishing grounds.

The most important pelagic fish-eating birds, such as the gannets, cormorants and jackass penguins found along the south-western coast of Africa, breed primarily on small offshore islands. The vast bulk of the Cape gannet population breeds on only six islands from where they make forays to feed on the shoals of pilchards, horse mackerel, mackerel and anchovies, each bird eating about 300 g each day. The cormorants feed on much the same species as the gannets but the penguins show a preference for anchovies, pelagic gobies and squid. Cape fur-seals, of which there are more than one million, breed on offshore islands and at a few sites on the Namibian coast.

Below: *The Cape cormorant is abundant and hunts pelagic fish in the Benguela Current.* **Below centre:** *The Cape gannet. This is a common species in southern African coastal waters.* **Bottom:** *Only two seals are resident on African shores, the endangered Mediterranean monk seal of northern Africa and the abundant Cape fur-seal illustrated here.*

as on the west coast in the vicinity of the Gulf of Guinea, fish diversity reaches its highest levels but in the cold Benguela and Canary currents diversity is comparatively low. Great shoals of pelagic fish sustain internationally important fisheries in this area, however. Apart from commercial fisheries many African people living around the extensive coastline rely to a large extent on marine organisms, particularly fish, as a source of food. Probably the richest fish fauna is found in and around those underwater "tropical forests" the coral reefs. By far the greatest number of fish species are littoral dwellers, that is they live in the coastal margin most influenced by the tides. Although several thousand species of fish are found in African waters and around associated oceanic islands the inventory is far from complete, with long stretches of shore having been poorly explored by scientists.

THE FUTURE

The sea is critically important as a provider of resources for man. There are internationally important commercial fisheries, particularly along the Atlantic coastline, which provide not only food but also revenue and many jobs. South Africa and Namibia are home to two of Africa's largest commercial

Above left: *Sesarmid crabs feeding on detritus taken from the mud surface.* **Left:** *Ghost crabs are a common feature of Africa's tropical beaches.* **Bottom left:** *The large mangrove crab* Sesarma meinerti *will collect fallen mangrove leaves and feed on them in the safety of its burrow.* **Below:** *Commercial fishing has depleted pelagic fish stocks in the south-west.*

fleets but boats from many other countries exploit this oceanic bounty, both legally and illegally. Apart from the pelagic fish, rock lobsters (for example *Jasus lalandii*), various molluscs including oysters, mussels, *Haliotis*, reef fish and various seaweeds are also entering the local and export markets. For centuries man has looked upon the oceans as providers of infinite resources, but in recent decades there has been a growing realisation that this is in fact not the case. The pelagic fisheries have declined and quotas have to be constantly adjusted, usually downwards; in fact this applies to nearly all exploited marine organisms.

There are also many indirect causes of species loss and decline. The mangrove swamps are assaulted for the timber they provide, as well as the fish that live in the channels; they are further threatened by decreases in silt flow in rivers as a result of dam construction in their higher reaches. This decrease in silt flow has also had serious implications for several river deltas, such as that of the Nile, as without the constant replenishment of sediments wave action erodes the seaward edges. Conversely, coral reefs are threatened by increased levels of silt carried down to the sea by rivers that flow through degraded and eroding land. The silt smothers the coral polyps and other organisms, causing them to die. In some areas, for example Tanzania, coral reefs have been seriously damaged by dynamiting in order to catch fish. The reef-building efforts of millions upon millions of coral polyps can be destroyed in seconds by each explosion. Some of the more accessible reefs are stripped of attractive molluscs and corals to be sold to unwitting tourists. Other threats are posed by toxic materials that are washed into the oceans by rivers from agricultural and industrial regions, and substances such as crude oil which leaks, or is deliberately flushed by ships into coastal waters when in passage. A more recent and extremely troubling trend is the "dumping" of toxic wastes by industrialised countries in some of the poor nations of Africa in exchange for small amounts of desperately needed foreign exchange. Reports indicate that virtually all of these wastes are deposited in sensitive coastal environments.

Uncontrolled tourism in some countries, such as Morocco, Senegal, Ivory Coast, Namibia, South Africa and Kenya, has resulted in considerable pressures being placed on coastal resources, with little or no attempt to limit these impacts.

CHAPTER 8

CONSERVATION
ENSURING OUR FUTURE

Contrary to popular opinion, humans have been influencing the environments and biota of Africa for many thousands of years. Even during the Pleistocene era, which was dominated by the Neolithic hunter-gatherers, evidence shows that bands of people were widely dispersed through the continent. Although overall numbers of people were probably low it is possible to correlate the extinctions of a number of large mammals, including several species of elephants, the giant giraffe-like *Libytherium*, as well as several antelopes and large pigs, to the appearance of these human hunters on the fossil record. These extinctions do not coincide with any record of major climatic or geological occurrences that could have caused their disappearance. We can therefore safely assume that early man was the cause of their demise, as was the case with numerous large mammal species in North America and Europe. Leading up to, and during, the Iron Age agriculture and the keeping of livestock was being developed. With the advent of crop cultivation and the keeping of domestic animals, groups of people were able to establish permanent settlements. Most of these settlements were located on, or near, fertile river floodplains, around

Background: *The spectacular Kerio Valley and its steep sided walls form a portion of the Great Rift Valley system in west-central Kenya.*
Right: *One of the "blue" monkeys,* Cercopithecus mitis kolbi, *a denizen of forests.*

lake shores and close to the coast. These settlements became, in many cases, the core areas of kingdoms with the rulers vying for political, military and trading power. Under these relatively stable conditions the human population began to grow and expand into previously unoccupied areas. This expansion resulted in considerable modification of the non-tropical forest habitats and much of the "pristine and untouched" Africa referred to by the early European colonists was in fact much altered from its original state by centuries of settlement and hunting.

With the invasions of Arabs and Europeans came considerable disruption, warfare, disease, famine and the beginning of the infamous slave trade. Although accurate records of the numbers of slaves traded are difficult to obtain, at least 15 million were shipped to the Americas and countless millions were traded in North Africa, Arabia and Asia. Although this trade in human cargo was to meet the demand for labour in plantations and mines and as servants, most of the slaves were captured during wars and raiding forays by African kings, chiefs and merchants and then sold to European and Arab slave traders. Apart from the huge numbers of slaves shipped out of Africa, unknown millions died on the way to the coast of disease and starvation. Large areas were depopulated and it is believed that the number of humans in Africa dropped to its lowest level in probably 2 000 years. With the exception of elephants, which were extensively hunted for their ivory, most wildlife populations were able to increase and in some cases expand their ranges. Cattle were decimated by such diseases as rinderpest.

With the "scramble for Africa" reaching fever pitch at the end of the nineteenth century, and the colonial era extending to the 1960s, there was a frenzy in the corridors of power in Europe to carve up the last unexploited continent. Political stability was largely achieved by wielding both administrative and military power and this resulted in an increase in the human population as warfare and inter-tribal conflicts came under control. At the same time the colonial powers introduced disease control measures for both humans and livestock, and they implemented controls over the random killing of game species. However, by the 1930s new areas were being opened up for settlement and development and conflicts with wildlife started to increase. Elephants and buffalo do not mix with wheat and maize cultivation! Areas were set aside, often in marginal agricultural and pastoral land, to conserve game populations. As the emphasis was on the protection, in many cases, of the herding species there was a bias towards setting aside areas of savanna.

What are the problems facing Africa and its biota today? It is important to stress again that the "untouched" Africa encountered by Europeans at the beginning of this century was in fact already degraded. Civil strife and political instability are rife throughout the continent and one of the most detrimental results is the world's largest movement of

Below: *Although commercial cattle farming is undertaken in parts of Africa, the vast majority of cattle are kept as an indication of wealth and for ritual and ceremonial purposes. The impact of these great herds on the vegetation is considerable.*

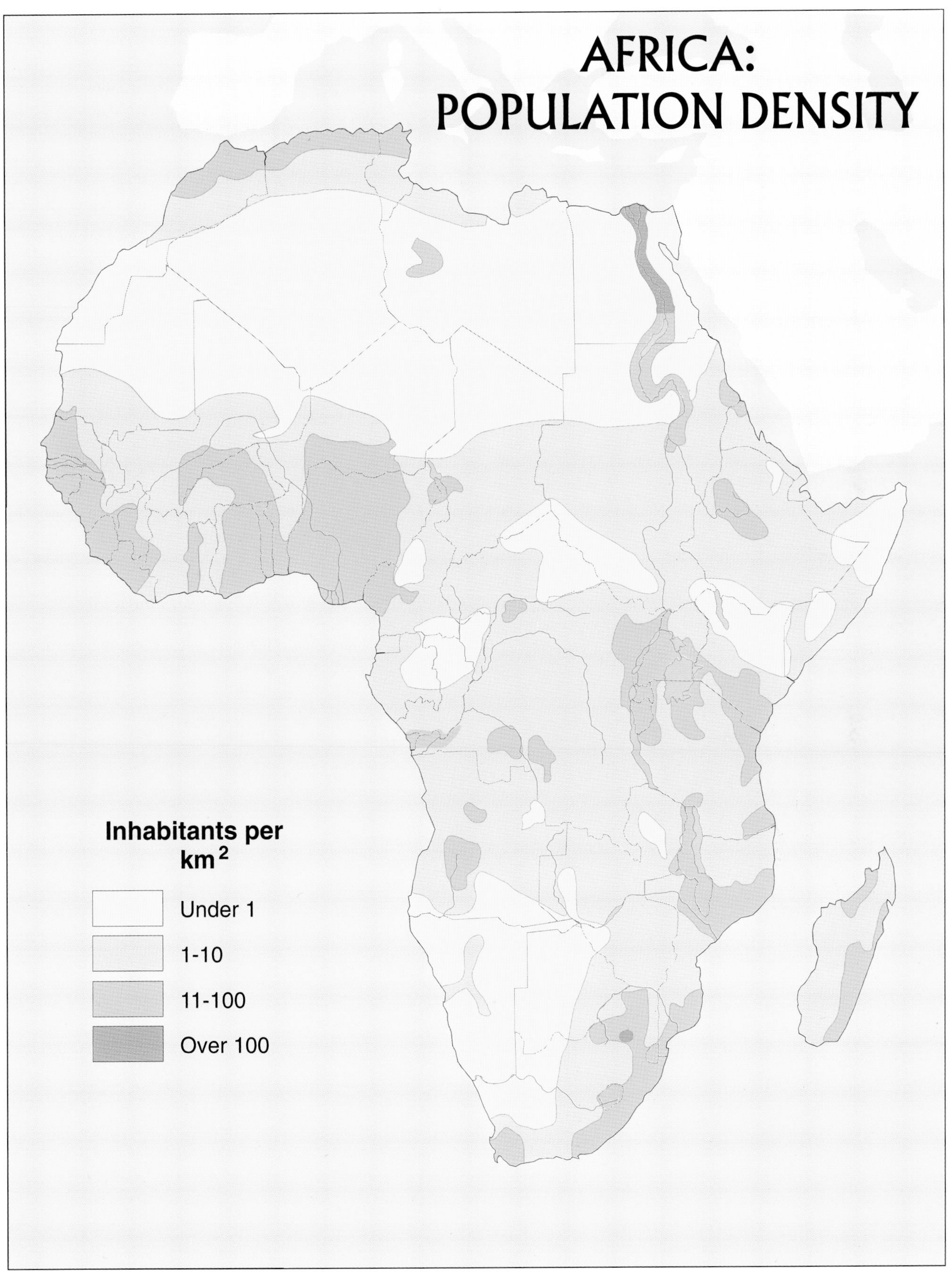
AFRICA:
POPULATION DENSITY
Inhabitants per km²
Under 1
1-10
11-100
Over 100

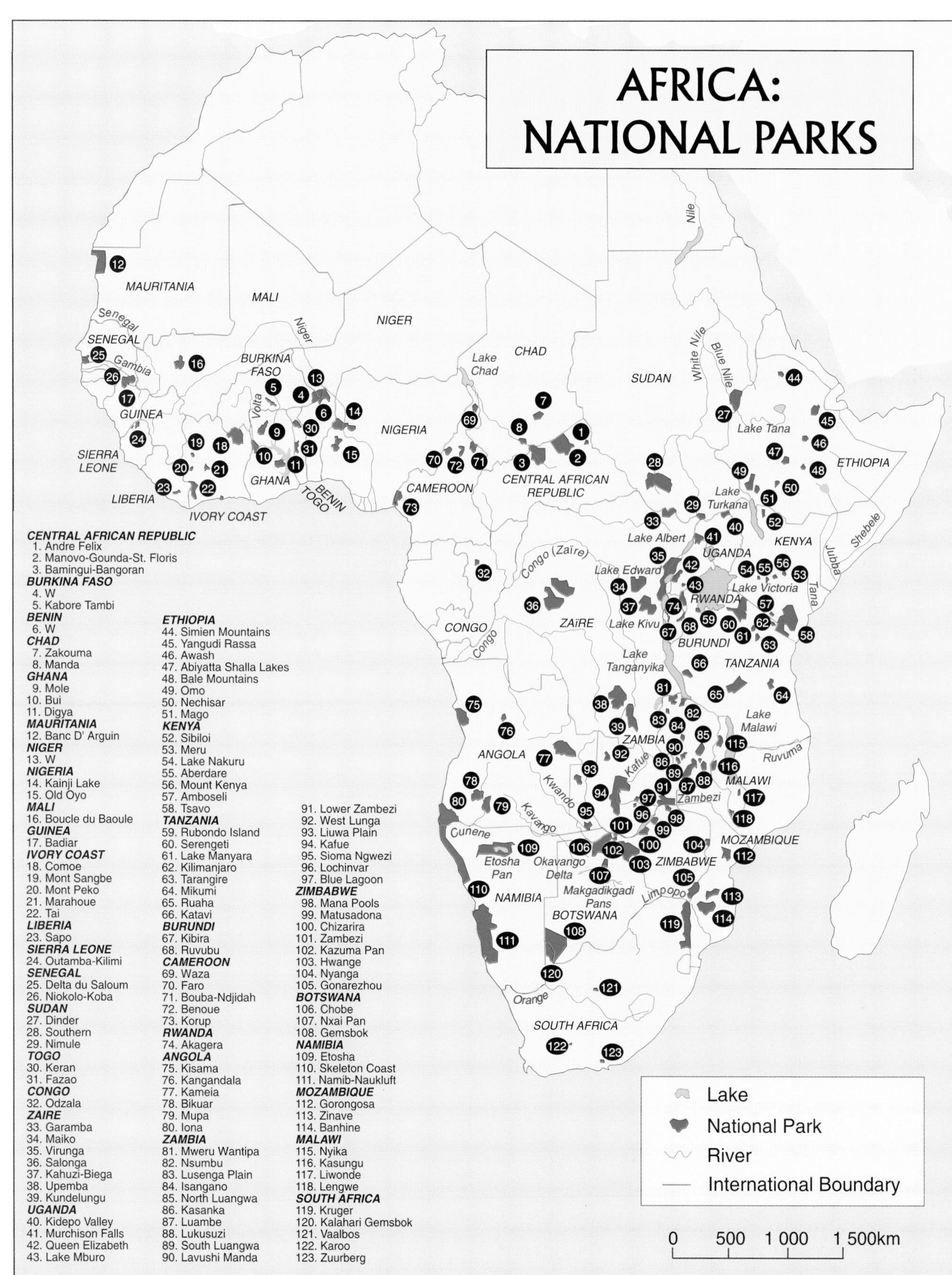
AFRICA:
NATIONAL PARKS
CENTRAL AFRICAN REPUBLIC
1. Andre Felix
2. Manovo-Gounda-St. Floris
3. Bamingui-Bangoran
BURKINA FASO
4. W
5. Kabore Tambi
BENIN
6. W
CHAD
7. Zakouma
8. Manda
GHANA
9. Mole
10. Bui
11. Digya
MAURITANIA
12. Banc D' Arguin
NIGER
13. W
NIGERIA
14. Kainji Lake
15. Old Oyo
MALI
16. Boucle du Baoule
GUINEA
17. Badiar
IVORY COAST
18. Comoe
19. Mont Sangbe
20. Mont Peko
21. Marahoue
22. Tai
LIBERIA
23. Sapo
SIERRA LEONE
24. Outamba-Kilimi
SENEGAL
25. Delta du Saloum
26. Niokolo-Koba
SUDAN
27. Dinder
28. Southern
29. Nimule
TOGO
30. Keran
31. Fazao
CONGO
32. Odzala
ZAIRE
33. Garamba
34. Maiko
35. Virunga
36. Salonga
37. Kahuzi-Biega
38. Upemba
39. Kundelungu
UGANDA
40. Kidepo Valley
41. Murchison Falls
42. Queen Elizabeth
43. Lake Mburo
ETHIOPIA
44. Simien Mountains
45. Yangudi Rassa
46. Awash
47. Abiyatta Shalla Lakes
48. Bale Mountains
49. Omo
50. Nechisar
51. Mago
KENYA
52. Sibiloi
53. Meru
54. Lake Nakuru
55. Aberdare
56. Mount Kenya
57. Amboseli
58. Tsavo
TANZANIA
59. Rubondo Island
60. Serengeti
61. Lake Manyara
62. Kilimanjaro
63. Tarangire
64. Mikumi
65. Ruaha
66. Katavi
BURUNDI
67. Kibira
68. Ruvubu
CAMEROON
69. Waza
70. Faro
71. Bouba-Ndjidah
72. Benoue
73. Korup
RWANDA
74. Akagera
ANGOLA
75. Kisama
76. Kangandala
77. Kameia
78. Bikuar
79. Mupa
80. Iona
ZAMBIA
81. Mweru Wantipa
82. Nsumbu
83. Lusenga Plain
84. Isangano
85. North Luangwa
86. Kasanka
87. Luambe
88. Lukusuzi
89. South Luangwa
90. Lavushi Manda
91. Lower Zambezi
92. West Lunga
93. Liuwa Plain
94. Kafue
95. Sioma Ngwezi
96. Lochinvar
97. Blue Lagoon
ZIMBABWE
98. Mana Pools
99. Matusadona
100. Chizarira
101. Zambezi
102. Kazuma Pan
103. Hwange
104. Nyanga
105. Gonarezhou
BOTSWANA
106. Chobe
107. Nxai Pan
108. Gemsbok
NAMIBIA
109. Etosha
110. Skeleton Coast
111. Namib-Naukluft
MOZAMBIQUE
112. Gorongosa
113. Zinave
114. Banhine
MALAWI
115. Nyika
116. Kasungu
117. Liwonde
118. Lengwe
SOUTH AFRICA
119. Kruger
120. Kalahari Gemsbok
121. Vaalbos
122. Karoo
123. Zuurberg
Lake
National Park
River
International Boundary
0 500 1 000 1 500km

refugees. These refugees move into "safe areas" and neighbouring states, placing enormous pressures on the occupied environments. This includes the cutting of firewood, soil degradation and erosion, pollution of rivers and other water bodies and depletion of wildlife and food plants.

Largely uncontrolled human population growth is a problem in all African countries, despite high infant mortality rates and low life expectancy in many areas, and rising death rates from such diseases as malaria, measles and Aids. Sub-Saharan Africa has a human population of more than 550 million people and this is projected to increase to almost three billion by the year 2050. That population level lies only 56 years away! During the course of this century the introduction of greatly improved health care has dramatically increased survival; as the populations grew (and continue to grow) there was obviously a greater need to increase food production, the flow of goods and so on.

The importance of natural products to the peoples of Africa becomes abundantly clear when one considers some facts of utilisation. Wood and dried animal dung supply as much as 90 per cent of the total domestic energy needs in Malawi and Tanzania. This figure is generally higher in most Sahelian countries. In Botswana over 50 species of wild animals provide an average of 90 kg of protein per person each year; in Ghana approximately 75 per cent of the population relies almost entirely on wild sources of protein in their diet and in Zaïre game animals provide three-quarters of all protein consumed. In fact "bush meat" is of critical importance in most West and Central African countries. If these resources were destroyed or over-utilised, mass starvation would result as no alternatives are available.

Traditional slash-and-burn cultivation in areas with low human population density is usually sustainable but in areas of high density the land rarely gets the chance to recover as the people are no longer able to rotate around uninhabited areas. With this method of cultivation small patches of natural vegetation are cleared and burnt, crops planted for one or more seasons until the nutrient levels are depleted, then the patches are abandoned for new patches.

Improved control of the tsetse fly (*Glossina* spp.), the carrier of *nagana* which is deadly to cattle, has allowed pastoralists to penetrate areas previously closed to them and their domestic animals. Livestock numbers have greatly increased but slaughtering levels have not kept pace. This is largely a result of the traditional view that cattle are wealth but only on the hoof and not if they enter the commercial meat market. It has been frequently stated that the tsetse fly is Africa's greatest conservationist and not without reason. Initial attempts at controlling this fly involved shooting hundreds of thousands of game animals as it was believed that without them as hosts these insect blood-feeders would die out and the land could be occupied. For example, up to 1960 in Southern Rhodesia (now Zimbabwe) some three-quarters of a million animals were killed. This drastic measure had only limited success and then the second front was put into action, using millions of litres of pesticides. As far as fly control was concerned it was by and large a success but the toxins also killed vast numbers of harmless insects, many species of mammals, birds and reptiles. More than 300 000 km^2 of formerly tsetse fly occupied country has been cleared by the use of poison and spraying programmes continue in at least six countries.

DESERTIFICATION

Desertification is one of Africa's more pressing worries and much of the blame can be laid at man's door. Probably the desertification scenario best known to the outside world is the tragedy of the Sahel, the dryland belt that runs along the southern fringe of the Sahara Desert from the Atlantic Ocean in the west to northern Kenya and Somalia in the east. In the south along much of its length it borders on higher rainfall zones that were once largely covered by forest and woodland. There is much controversy as to what has caused the

Below: *Wood provides more than 90 per cent of fuel needs in many African countries and over-utilisation is denuding vast tracts of land of their trees.*

increasing aridity of the Sahel but sound arguments have been presented to show that a combination of massive harvesting of wood for timber, firewood and charcoal production, large-scale commercial crop production (primarily groundnuts), large numbers of domestic stock and increasing settlement of nomads have played a pivotal role.

The nomads were first prevented from entering their southern dry-season grazing grounds by commercial farming and in order to encourage them to settle (largely for reasons of political expediency) boreholes were sunk. As the nomads ceased or scaled down their wanderings, areas became denuded of vegetation and large-scale erosion resulted. Well-meaning donor nations outside Africa provided money for commercial cropping and the sinking of boreholes, and the area was flooded with food aid and battalions of "experts" who prescribed more aid and schemes that proved ill-suited to the prevailing situation.

In fact foreign aid and loans from such international organisations as the World Bank are the albatross around the neck of Africa. These institutions have financed many projects that have been poorly planned and have often merely served the interests of the donors. There are also several instances where aid has been taken "in care" by a dictator, president or general but the nation concerned has been left to carry the debt repayment burden. There is also no shortage of cases involving conservation issues. For example, millions of dollars have been pumped into efforts to conserve the black rhinoceros, but despite this largesse the rhino has continued its precipitous decline both in range and numbers. Money alone is not enough to solve conservation issues and other problems facing Africa.

Desertification is also a problem in parts of northern, eastern and southern Africa. In many cases the problem arises because of too many people, too many domestic animals, insatiable exploitation of firewood and climatic fluctuations. However, this does not fully explain the phenomenon in the stretches of commercial farmland in the south. Many of these farms are located on marginal land and in order to obtain a return they are frequently overstocked and therefore overgrazed. In a number of cases farmers have only been kept on the land by subsidies. This does not make good economic sense and it is no good for the land and its associated life forms. In order to reverse the trend of desertification, or at least bring it under control, drastic measures are called for. However, one cannot help wonder whether the governments and the people of Africa have the will to implement them. Areas would have to be largely depopulated, people would have to be educated in new rural economies, domestic herds and flocks would have to be drastically culled, new agricultural and pastoral systems would have to be developed to

work with the environment and not against it. But without meaningful efforts to implement family planning and reduction in human population growth all these measures would come to nought. Too many people, too little time!

THE TOLL ON GAME

Although subsistence hunting has been part of the African scene since man's ancestors first descended from the trees it was only in the nineteenth century that large-scale commercial hunting took place. The Romans and ancient Egyptians, among others, valued ivory as an item of trade and this had a significant impact on the elephant populations of North Africa and the lower Nile valley. The Arab traders also traded keenly in this white gold and many tribal rulers valued tusks as a measure of their wealth as well as trade items. However, the elephant population only came under major hunting pressure during the 19th and early 20th centuries. The slaughter accelerated in the 1970s and 1980s, when the herds were reduced from an estimated 1.3 million to about 600 000 animals. This massive increase in poaching and slaughter was a result of a combination of factors, including political indifference and corruption, a breakdown in discipline and law and order, easy availability of firearms and ammunition, and the downward spiral into poverty.

Other species have suffered even more than the elephant – most notably the two rhinoceros species. The once abundant and widespread hook-lipped (or black) rhinoceros has been brought to the brink of extinction, and the square-lipped (white) rhinoceros survives only in some southern African countries and in the Garamba National Park in north-east Zaïre, where there are about 30 animals. All this slaughter was carried out simply for the pair of horns that each animal carries. The horn is shipped to several countries in the Far East where people use it in medicines in powdered or ground form. There is no sound evidence that it has any medicinal benefit whatsoever. One of the largest consumers, North Yemen, uses the horn to carve into dagger handles.

At first glance many countries in sub-Saharan Africa have a commendable portion of their surface areas under formal conservation protection but with a few exceptions many of these parks and reserves are under threat by peasant settlers, illegal gathering of natural products including commercial timbers, firewood and meat. Some 4.4 per cent of the African land mass and its associated oceanic islands has been designated as protected, with about another one per cent having been proposed for protection. It is highly unlikely that additional areas will be set aside in view of the more immediate demands being made on available land. Because of this it is essential that conservation thinking should lean increasingly towards the management of animal and plant resources outside formally protected blocks of land. Even large reserves are proving inadequate to protect many species, particularly as the areas themselves are fenced, or human settlement

Above: *Although fire is a natural process, in many areas wood- and grassland are burned too frequently, causing plant composition to change and exposing soil to erosion, both by wind and water.* **Below left:** *The slopes of many African mountain and hill ranges are heavily cultivated, particularly those with rich volcanic soils. These are tea and maize "patches" in the Aberdares of Kenya.*

causes disruption of migration routes. Large numbers of blue wildebeest and other game species leave the Nairobi National Park (Kenya) in July each year to feed on the Athi Plains to the south. However, more and more fences are erected each year by farmers, and this could eventually result in a much-reduced wildebeest population being restricted entirely to the park. The great blue wildebeest herds of the Ngorongoro/Serengeti/Mara which migrate through the system must pass through corridors and belts belonging to the Maasai pastoralists, and the survival of this wonder of the natural world lies almost entirely in their hands. Although there are several large parks in the Sahelian belt they are totally inadequate to contain the largely remnant populations of the once-great migratory herds, of such species as hartebeest and addax, that followed the rains in search of fresh grazing.

CONSERVATION MEASURES

The idea of setting aside tracts of land for the conservation of game was not introduced by the European colonists, as royal hunting preserves had previously been reserved for the exclusive use of the rulers, or particular tribal groups. In many cases there was a realisation that over-exploitation would result in the loss of a valuable resource. Penalties for hunting without the ruler's permission were usually severe and the perpetrator was often put to death. This penalty has been reinstated in the "shoot to kill" orders given by game

Above: *There is an urgent need to control the numbers of tourists entering a number of African conservation areas, particularly those on the East African tourist route.*
Below right: *Effective monitoring of wildlife populations in conservation areas is essential, with particular attention devoted to the control of commercial poaching.*

departments in several countries against rhino and elephant poachers. The Shilluk people live on the White Nile in southern Sudan where they have preserved Fanyikyang Island as a hunting reserve for the Nile lechwe for hundreds of years. Each year a hunt takes place when a percentage of the lechwe are culled but never to the point that threatens their continued survival. This is an excellent example of the wise utilisation of a natural resource. There are also other reasons for protecting natural biota, usually involving religious taboos or the fact that a particular species may be the totem (emblem or symbol) of a particular clan, group or tribe.

The setting aside of formal, or proclaimed, conservation areas was an innovation of the European colonists. In most cases these settlers earmarked land for game conservation without taking the needs or desires of the local tribespeople into consideration. These actions have resulted in a feeling amongst populations living around many of the parks and reserves that they have been set aside as "playgrounds" for well-heeled tourists. The local people are often bitterly opposed to such areas because they do not benefit from the income generated and the natural resources such as meat, thatching reeds or grass and firewood. A few authorities and landowners are trying to overcome this animosity by involving local people in the reserves, by giving them jobs, money to erect schools, clinics and other amenities, cheap meat from culling and access to other harvestable products on a controlled basis. However, at this stage such measures are the exception rather than the rule. In reserves where controls are limited or nonexistent, peasants simply move in and help themselves to resources, plant crops, graze domestic stock, set fires and so on.

The first conservation areas proclaimed in Africa were the Umfolozi, Hluhluwe and St Lucia game reserves in KwaZulu/Natal (South Africa) in 1897. They remain Africa's oldest surviving formal conservation areas. President Paul Kruger of the then Zuid-Afrikaansche Republiek (Transvaal) was instrumental in establishing the Sabie Game Reserve in 1898, the forerunner of the expanded area now known as the Kruger National Park. The famous parks and reserves of East Africa were only to be proclaimed well into the 20th century. For example the Murchison Falls and Queen Elizabeth National Parks of Uganda were only proclaimed in 1952 and the Ruaha National Park in Tanzania in 1964. The Serengeti, arguably Africa's most famous reserve, was established in 1951. Mount Kenya National Park was formally protected in 1949, Aberdare National Park in 1950 and the Maasai-Mara National Reserve, then known as the Mara Game Reserve, in 1961. Although many of Africa's reserves were established during the colonial era, a number of countries proclaimed many conservation areas in the years following their independence. With a few exceptions the best-managed reserves and other conservation areas are located in some southern and east African countries.

Many African parks and reserves have been established and proclaimed in order to conserve great herds and spectacular species and only a relatively small percentage of the conservation areas protect less spectacular biota. In many cases the authorities have laid emphasis on reserves that attract tourists. This of course is acceptable but the need for protecting areas that are less appealing cannot be overlooked. Although the following overview concentrates on formally protected areas, it must be emphasised again that these "islands" lying in an ocean of humanity cannot stand alone in the long term. Great efforts will have to be made to improve the conservation of biota outside reserves on a sustainable utilisation basis with the people's interests and needs in mind. Fancy ideas and schemes developed in Europe and North America, unless suited to African conditions, should be turned back at the door.

Problems in managing conservation areas are complex and numerous. They include lack of funding for vehicles, radios, firearms, research and monitoring equipment, poorly trained, motivated and underpaid staff, poor or nonexistent management programmes, no attempt to involve local people in the running of the reserve. Where local people are involved in running reserves, such as the Maasai and Samburu in Kenya, little in the way of benefits may filter through to the peasants because of the tribal hierarchy, thus building up resentment. There is also the problem of allowing too many visitors into reserves and not enforcing regulations, such as driving off roads and collecting firewood. Reserves, particularly in West Africa and the Sahel, face influxes of peasant farmers, livestock, and in the forest zones illegal timber harvesting.

A number of reserves have been so badly abused that their value is greatly diminished. There is also the problem of fencing and the lack of it. Fences have the benefit of clearly defining reserve boundaries and controlling the movement of certain species but they also cut off traditional migration routes, isolate many biota from the surrounding areas, and in some cases force the authorities to control certain populations by culling. The issue of culling is highly emotive, particularly where it involves elephants as in the Kruger and Hwange national parks. In the former park buffalo have also to be culled but the public and animal rights/welfare groups say nothing about this, as this ungulate is seen only as a wild cow. Although recent attempts to capture family groups of elephants and transfer them to small reserves and private ranches were seen as a victory for "good conservation", they hold absolutely no value in conserving the elephant as a species. These areas can only accommodate small populations and one cannot help but wonder what will be done about surplus animals in the future.

Each reserve has its own unique set of conditions and problems and the above list is a very skimpy summary of the difficulties facing managers and field staff.

Eight different categories of protected areas are currently recognised: *scientific reserve/strict nature reserve, national park, natural monument/natural landmark, nature conservation reserve/managed nature reserve/game reserve, protected landscape or seascape, resource reserve, natural biotic area/anthropological reserve, multiple use management area/managed resource area.* Although there are representative examples of all of the above in Africa, the majority of protected areas fall within national park, nature reserve/game reserve and multiple use management area categories. Of the three it is the national park that receives (or should receive) the highest level of protection, with the management area receiving the lowest level of protection but with the goal of utilising resources on a sustainable basis. With a few exceptions the latter goal has been elusive but it promises many benefits if properly implemented. It will allow local people access to resources in the management area, but at the same time it will act as a buffer area for nearby national parks and reserves. Although their management leaves a great deal to be desired, Zambia has the most extensive network of such areas.

GEOGRAPHICAL OVERVIEW

We will now go on a brief tour of Africa's conservation areas, following the chapter sequence used in this book.

It is in the vast **savanna** regions of the continent where many of the largest, best known and most frequented national parks and game reserves are located. There are several reserves in the savanna country of West Africa but most are poorly managed and access is limited because of a badly deteriorated infrastructure. The largest and most accessible is the Comoe National Park in Ivory Coast, with some of the largest remaining game populations in this part of the continent. There are a few significant savanna reserves in southern Sudan but these are not accessible due to the longstanding civil war between the Islamic government and the rebel Christian and animist militia. It is not known whether significant game populations have survived the turmoil. The Garamba National Park in north-eastern Zaïre is important for the last surviving population of northern white rhinoceros (about 30) as well as significant populations of other game species, the last herds of any importance in the north of that country. Kenya, Tanzania and the southern African countries manage the most important savanna reserves, many of which have national parks status. Most are well managed and frequented by large numbers of tourists, and therefore represent important sources of revenue both for conservation and the state coffers. For example, the Kruger National Park plays host to well over half a million visitors each year, with Serengeti/Maasai-Mara, Tsavo, South Luangwa, Hwange, Chobe and Etosha attracting streams of big-spending tourists. It is worth mentioning that most of these reserves would cease to exist without this income flow.

Although the reserves in each major habitat grouping, such as savanna, have certain things in common, each is unique in many different ways. Africa's largest reserve is the Selous Game Reserve in eastern Tanzania with a total surface area well over 51 200 km² in extent, with a number of others exceeding 10 000 km², such as Serengeti (14 760 km²) and

Ruaha (10 200 km²). Serengeti is actually part of a larger protected area which incorporates the Ngorongoro Conservation Area of 8 380 km², Maswa Game Reserve (2 180 km²) and in Kenya the Maasai-Mara National Reserve at 1 510 km². Therefore the complex totals some 26 830 km², although levels of management differ. Other large savanna reserves include the Kruger National Park (over 20 000 km²), Hwange National Park (14 650 km²) in Zimbabwe, Kafue National Park (22 400 km²) in Zambia and Namibia's Etosha National Park (22 270 km²). These are but a few of the savanna protected areas and, at least on paper, it is one of the most adequately covered of all biomes on the continent. Some are dominated by great, open tracts of grassland, others with a mosaic of grassland and woodland. Some conserve the largest surviving migratory and non-migratory game herds in Africa and also a large percentage of the non-forest elephant holdings. Small savanna reserves have only limited viability in the long term, particularly if corridors linking them with other suitable and similar areas are cut off by human activity.

Left: *Timber is cut for firewood, charcoal production, building material and for commercial trade. Increasing demand for wood is placing considerable pressure on this natural resource.* **Above:** *Clean water is at a premium in most parts of Africa, and many streams such as this are infested by the snails that carry the bilharzia parasite.*

The **drylands**, including the deserts, semi-deserts and other low-rainfall areas, are not particularly well represented in the conservation area inventory although there are a few notable exceptions. By far the largest is the Saharan Aïr and Ténéré National Nature Reserve (77 360 km²) in Niger. Unfortunately its size has not saved it from illegal hunting pressure which has reduced most ungulate populations to low levels. This reserve does however, have the largest surviving population of Barbary sheep and a remnant population of perhaps as many as 200 cheetah. Given the correct inputs and management this reserve could prove to be a major drawcard for tourists in the future. Botswana has two large reserves located in the Kalahari Desert – the Central Kalahari Game Reserve (52 800 km²) and the Gemsbok National Park (24 800 km²) which adjoins the 9 591 km² Kalahari Gemsbok National Park in South Africa. These two reserves are managed as a single unit, primarily because of the migratory antelope species that move freely between the two. Namibia also has some extensive dryland reserves, the Namib-Naukluft Park of some 49 768 km² and the Skeleton Coast Park – a relatively

Top: *Once land is turned to commercial agriculture most natural vegetation and animal life disappears. There are also negative impacts when herbicides, insecticides and fertilisers find their way into water bodies.* **Above:** *Subsistence agriculture is still dominant in most parts of Africa.*

narrow belt extending along the entire northern coastline and covering 16 390 km². Although the number of protected desert areas is small this remains one of the least threatened biomes.

The **forests** have had mixed fortunes. Some have been totally destroyed while others remain relatively pristine. Reserve coverage is not good, although the large tropical forest block of the Congo Basin is largely untouched as the human population is very low, access is extremely difficult and the area is not particularly suitable for human habitation. The largest conservation area here is the Salonga National Park with an area of 36 560 km², followed by the Maiko National Park (10 830 km²) and a number of reserves that are partly covered by lowland forest. Reserve management is virtually nonexistent because of the political situation in Zaïre and there seems to be little hope for improvement in the future. Although there are a number of proclaimed conservation areas in the Guinean forest block, with a few exceptions their management leaves much to be desired. The Tai National Park (3 400 km²) and the contiguous N'Zo Faunal Reserve protect the largest area of undisturbed lowland rain forest in West Africa. Despite its important status, particularly in view of the massive forest destruction elsewhere in the region, illegal timber extraction, poaching and the influx of refugees from the conflict in neighbouring Liberia hold serious consequences for its integrity. The conservation of the few remaining intact forest blocks in West Africa is critical but sadly no action is likely to be taken in this regard.

Some 4.5 per cent of African **montane** land is formally protected but several conservation areas, particularly those that include forest, are severely degraded and protection is minimal. Mountains and mountain ranges serve as important water catchment areas, as well as having a great variety and often unique biota. East Africa's principal peaks, mounts Kenya, Kilimanjaro and Meru, as well as the Zaïrean and Ugandan portions of the Ruwenzoris are protected, as are many of the South African coastal chains. The few montane reserves in West Africa, particularly Mount Nimba, are under severe threat and the conservation future of reserves in the Ethiopian Highlands is uncertain at this stage.

The tiny area covered by the **Cape Floral Kingdom** at the south-western tip of Africa is divided into two distinct types, namely lowland and highland. The highland component is well conserved although there are some threats but the lowland areas are massively degraded. There is a network of tiny "pocket handkerchief" reserves but the fact that they are ringed by agricultural, urban and industrial development does not bode well for their long-term survival.

Freshwater systems of numerous types are incorporated into many reserves but particularly in the case of major rivers much of their lengths lie outside conservation areas, subjecting them to such problems as siltation, over-utilisation, pollution and infestation by exotic vegetation. Most of Africa's principal wetlands fall outside reserves, primarily because of their importance in supplying resources to people. Small parts of such large lakes as Malawi, Tanganyika, Victoria and Turkana, deltas such as the Okavango and marshes in several countries are conserved. It is unlikely that large systems will ever be completely confined within formally protected areas.

Despite the great extent of Africa's **coastline**, few coastal areas are actually conserved. The reasons for this are much the same as were given for the freshwater environments: man values the coastal and ocean resources for commercial as well as recreational purposes. The most extensive marine reserves are located in South Africa, in part to protect specific commercially exploited species such as shellfish, crustaceans and fish. Only limited areas conserve all marine organisms. Kenya has established marine reserves, primarily aimed at conserving coral reefs and their related organisms, but their effectiveness appears to be limited. Otherwise the few coastal reserves that exist, or include coastline within their real estate, usually do not extend their jurisdiction below the high-water mark.

Despite the many problems that beset the African continent, its incredibly rich diversity of habitats, flora and fauna deserve greater efforts aimed at their conservation.

SELECTED BIBLIOGRAPHY

Berjak, P *et al. In the Mangroves of Southern Africa.* Natal Branch of the Wildlife Society of Southern Africa, 1977.

Branch, B. *Field Guide to the Snakes and other Reptiles of Southern Africa.* Struik Publishers, Cape Town, 1988.

Branch, G & Branch, M. *The Living Shores of Southern Africa.* Struik Publishers, Cape Town, 1981.

Broadley, D G. *FitzSimon's Snakes of Southern Africa.* Delta Books, Johannesburg, 1983.

Cott, H B & Pooley, A C. "Crocodiles: the Status of Crocodiles in Africa". IUCN Publications, New Series, Supp. Paper no. 33, 1972.

Day, J H. *A Guide to Marine Life on South African Shores.* A A Balkema, Cape Town, 1969.

Dorst, J & Dandelot, P. *A Field Guide to the Larger Mammals of Africa.* Collins, London, 1983.

Douglas-Hamilton, I & Douglas-Hamilton, O. *Among the Elephants.* Collins & Harvill, London, 1975.

Halliday, T & Adler, K (Eds). *The Encyclopaedia of Reptiles and Amphibians.* George Allen & Unwin, London, 1986.

Haltenorth, T & Diller, H. *A Field Guide to the Mammals of Africa including Madagascar.* Collins, London, 1984.

Heydorn, A E F & Tinley, K L. "Estuaries of the Cape, Part 1: Synopsis of the Cape Coast". CSIR Research Report 380, 1980.

IUCN. *The IUCN Sahel Report.* IUCN, Gland, Switzerland, 1986.

Kingdon, J. *East African Mammals, an Atlas of Evolution in Africa.* (Vols 1-3). Academic Press, London, 1971-1982.

MacDonald, D W. *The Encyclopedia of Mammals.* Vols 1&2. George Allen & Unwin, London, 1984.

MacKinnon, J & MacKinnon, K. *Review of the Protected Areas System in the Afrotropical Realm.* IUCN Commission on National Parks and Protected Areas, Gland, Switzerland, 1986.

Maclean, G L. *Roberts' Birds of Southern Africa.* John Voelcker Bird Book Fund, Cape Town, 1985.

Mepham, R & Mepham, S. *Directory of African Wetlands.* IUCN, Gland, Switzerland, 1990.

Palgrave, K C. *Trees of Southern Africa.* Struik Publishers, Cape Town, 1977.

Ross, C A (Ed). *Crocodiles and Alligators.* Merehurst Press, London, 1990.

Schaller, G B. *The Serengeti Lion: A Study of Predator-Prey Relations.* University Press, Chicago, 1972.

Skaife, S H. *African Insect Life* (second edition revised by J Ledger). Struik Publishers, Cape Town, 1979.

Skinner, J & Smithers, R H N. *The Mammals of the Southern African Subregion.* University of Pretoria, Pretoria, 1990.

Stuart, C & Stuart, T. *Field Guide to the Mammals of Southern Africa.* Struik/New Holland, Cape Town and London, 1993.

Stuart, C & Stuart, T. *Guide to Southern African Game and Nature Reserves* (third edition). Struik/New Holland, Cape Town/London, 1993.

Stuart, S N & Adams, R J. "Biodiversity in Sub-Saharan Africa and its Islands". Occasional Papers of the IUCN Species Survival Commission No. 6, Gland, Switzerland, 1990.

Walker, E P. *Mammals of the World.* Johns Hopkins University Press, Baltimore, 1975.

White, F. *The Vegetation of Africa: A Descriptive Memoir to Accompany the UNESCO/AETFAT/UNSO Vegetation Map of Africa.* UNESCO, Paris, 1983.

Williams, J G. *A Field Guide to the National Parks of East Africa.* Collins, London, 1991.

INDEX

ADAPTIVE HETEROTHERMY	: To allow body temperature to fluctuate in response to environmental pressures. "Temperature of the brain is kept at a lower and more constant level than that of the rest of the body. A network of blood vessels lies below the brain and as the animal pants blood in the nasal sinuses is cooled. An exchange of heat takes place between the veins and arteries so that blood entering the brain is several degrees cooler than in the rest of the body".
POIKILOTHERMIC	: Body temperature is controlled by their surroundings and not by their internal body mechanisms.
DIOECIOUS	: With male & female organs on seperate plants
FOLIOSE	: Bearing numerous leaves or leaflets.
CAULIFLOROUS	: Flowers & fruits growing directly on or from the branches and trunk of a tree.
PISCIVOROUS	: Feeding on fish / fish eating.
OSSARIES	: Favoured sites formed by vulture behaviour by the act of dropping bones from a great height onto rocks therby shattering the bones which may accumulate as large numbers of bone fragments.
HERPETOFAUNA	: The FAUNA category consisting of reptiles and amphibians.
INFLORESCENCE	: A characteristic arrangementof flowers on a single main stem
SEROTINOUS	: That is they shed only a few seeds after every flowering season : retaining the bulk in fire-resistant storage organs(usually hard woody cones) until fire kills the parent plant and the seed store dries and splits, releasing massive quantities os seeds.
MYRMECOCHORY	: The dispersal of seeds by ants.
FOSSORIAL	: Adapted for or used in burrowing or digging.
EVAPOTRANSPIRATION	: To secrete water vapour by the process of transpiring especially through the stomata of plant tissue regulated by heat.
EUTROPHICATION	: Designating a body of water in which the increase of mineral and organic nutrients has reduced the dissolved oxygen, producing an environment that favours plant life over animal life.
HYPOXIA	: Deficiency in the amount of oxygen reaching bodily tissues.

PNEUMATOPHORE	:	A specialised root in certain aquatic plants,such as the mangrove, that grows upwards and through which exchange of respiratory gases occurs.
HALOPHYTE	:	A plant that grows in saline soil such as that of a marsh.
VIVIPAROUS	:	Germinating or producing seeds that germinate before becoming detached from the parent plant.
ANAEROBIC	:	Of or designating a process, such as respiration, that does not require free oxygen.
LENTICEL	:	Any of the small pores on the surface of the stems of woody plants, allowing the passage of gases to and from the interior tissue.
LITTORAL	:	Of or existing on a shore. A shore or coastal region, especially the zone betweenthe high-andlow-tide marks of spring tides.

RIPARIAN : PERTAINING TO A BANK OF A RIVER.

BIOME : A COMMUNITY OF LIVING ORGANISMS OF A SINGLE MAJOR ECOLOGICAL REGION.

BIOTA : ANIMAL AND PLANT LIFE OF A PARTICULAR REGION CONSIDERED AS A TOTAL ECOLOGICAL UNIT.

1 Photographs are replaced by the STAMP PORTRAITS.
2 Compilation of factual detail extracted & transferred from books or written material.
3 Combination effected to combat the inability to partake in travel Worldwide but to enjoy each countries Natural History through the "PHILATELIC NATURAL"
4 Each stamp issue invites RESEARCH to discover how the species fits into its "niche" building into an overview of the natural world.

5 THE 28 VOLUME SG STOCKBOOKS are the collecting medium to assemble the collection awaiting transfer into the A4 SG CONTRY STOCKBOOK where the issue is developed and admitted within the PRIME COLLECTION.